BERKLEE PRESS

HOW TO

GET A JOB IN THE MUSIC INDUSTRY

by Keith Hatschek

edited by Jonathan Feist

2nd Edition Includes
New Career Resources, Workshops, & Interviews

Berklee Press
Vice President: David Kusek
Dean of Continuing Education: Debbie Cavalier
Managing Editor: Jonathan Feist
Director of Business Affairs: Robert F. Green
Senior Designer: Robert Heath

ISBN-13: 978-0-87639-072-6
ISBN-10: 0-87639-072-6

1140 Boylston Street
Boston, MA 02215-3693 USA
(617) 747-2146

Visit Berklee Press Online at
www.berkleepress.com

DISTRIBUTED BY

HAL•LEONARD®
CORPORATION
7777 W. BLUEMOUND RD. P.O. BOX 13819
MILWAUKEE, WISCONSIN 53213

Visit Hal Leonard Online at
www.halleonard.com

Contents

Foreword

By Tony Brown,
President of Universal South Records

Universal South Records President Tony Brown has left an indelible mark on the modern country sound. Throughout his career, he has worked with an incredible range of artists, including Emmylou Harris, Vince Gill, Jimmy Buffet, Elvis Presley, Wynonna, Lyle Lovett, George Strait, Alabama, Shirley Caesar, Rosanne Cash, Rodney Crowell, the Mavericks, Reba McEntire, and Trisha Yearwood. He joined MCA Records in 1984, and guided the company to its position as the number 1 label in Nashville in the 1990s. In 2002, eager for a new challenge, he founded Universal South in partnership with former Arista Nashville head, Tim DuBois.

Tony Brown has been awarded Billboard *magazine's coveted Top Country Producer honor seven times, while album projects he has produced have exceeded 100 million units in sales. His track record with singles is equally impressive, garnering more than one hundred number 1 singles. Through it all, he has retained his reverence for great performers, a wonder for the "magic" in melody, and the simple joy of making music.*

When I started playing piano professionally, more than thirty-five years ago with the Stamps Quartet, if a person had come up to me after a performance and predicted that I'd be the president of a record company one day, I would have replied, "Not in a million years!"

At the age of 13, I got my first glimpse of the life I wanted when gospel groups like the Statesmen and the Blackwood Brothers mesmerized me. The performers wore flashy clothes and drew huge audiences that they left cheering for more at the end of the night. To me, they were just like movie stars. It was then that I decided that I wanted a career in entertainment.

I started to play piano with a number of local gospel groups and began meeting the people who have helped me build my career. Meeting J.D. Sumner of the Blackwood Brothers forged one of the first links in my "chain" of the people and the relationships that have opened doors for me. J.D. introduced me to a number of important people and eventually helped me land a gig as a piano player for Elvis Presley in 1974.

As I worked with Elvis, that relationship led me from playing gospel music to country music. When Elvis died three years later, his previous piano player was leaving Emmylou Harris's band and recommended me as his replacement. Soon my chain grew to include Emmylou, Ricky Skaggs, Vince Gill, Rodney Crowell, and Rosanne Cash, each of whom influenced my career tremendously. Constantly striving to meet and work with people more talented than me helped me learn and grow. I believe that I learned so much because my eyes and ears were wide open, and I was soaking up every bit of knowledge I could.

However, today, I've noticed that many young people aspiring to a career in the music business tend to remain in small circles of friends, and as a result, their world becomes very limited. From my point of view, the only way to succeed and enjoy this business is to enjoy all of it. You've got to constantly work to expand your universe.

Another important attribute to develop is self-assurance: learn to trust your vision and instincts. When Jimmy Bowen invited me to join him at MCA in 1984, he asked me if I had a vision that I wanted to achieve. I told him that, yes, I wanted to bring the amazing talent of instrumentalists like Mark O'Connor, Edgar Meyer, and John Jarvis to the public. These were session players I hung out with and played with every day, but they were completely unknown outside of Nashville.

I put a proposal together, and soon, MCA's Master Series was born. The Master Series allowed me the opportunity to collaborate with a tremendous range of jazz, classical, and pop artists with whom I might have never worked. And it proved so successful that eventually MCA merged it with a larger jazz label, GRP. The impact of the Master Series on the artists involved has been long lasting. I was thrilled when Edgar Meyer performed for an audience of millions with cellist Yo-Yo Ma on the 2000 Grammy telecast.

To bring the Master Series from a dream to a reality, I had to trust myself to know the difference between something that's really good versus something that's mediocre. There were times when I felt that I was in way over my head, but I realized I just had to keep my ears open and keep asking questions.

As I've made transitions from musician to producer to record company executive, a number of other skills have helped me to succeed. Being aware of what's happening around you, always remembering to follow up, developing the skill to really listen to people, and working to keep up with the trends and technologies shaping the music business are all critical skills that have to be practiced constantly.

You should take advantage of the people around you who can teach and help you expand your world. Keep your vision focused on what you want to do and make the most of every opportunity. Take the information in this book and combine it with your own creative abilities, and you've got the makings for a great career in the music business.

Tony Brown
Nashville, Tennessee

Acknowledgments

The impetus to share my ideas on what it takes to launch a successful career in the music industry came more than twenty years ago. I found myself fielding a regular stream of calls from colleagues and acquaintances asking me to speak with a relative or friend who "wanted to get into the business." A few years later, my friend, entertainment attorney Marc Greenberg, and I were talking about what things we would still like to accomplish in our careers and I mentioned teaching. Shortly thereafter, he introduced me to the program director of the San Francisco State University Music and Recording Industry program, Mary Pieratt, where I enjoyed lecturing for seven years. Josh Hecht and John Altmann, who also teach recording arts, generously answered my numerous questions as I learned to become an effective teacher at SFSU. When I decided to make teaching my first priority in 2001, moving to University of the Pacific, I undertook a substantial challenge: to help students build the necessary portfolio of skills and knowledge to succeed in the music industry. After six years, I still enjoy getting up for work each day and interacting with tomorrow's industry leaders. My students stimulate and challenge me by asking difficult questions. They continually surprise me with their resourcefulness. At Pacific, I've been surrounded by supportive colleagues including Steve Anderson, David Chase, Dave Duggan, Carolyn Eads, Bob Coburn, Ray Sylvester, Mark Plovnick, Margaret Roberts, Rhonelle Runner, John Carvana, Joanna Royce-Davis, Deb Crane, Chris Haruta, and many other faculty and staff.

Since the day in 1965 when my first guitar—a red Orpheus with a chrome pick guard, three pickups, and a whammy bar—captivated me, I've had the good fortune to travel an always-evolving road in the music industry. My journey has been one of enlightenment and friendship shared with so many colleagues that it would be impossible to name each one. But I wish to especially thank David Porter for believing in me early in my career and for teaching me a great deal about what it takes to succeed in any business, Bruce Merley for sharing his balanced outlook on life and business when it has been most needed and for offering constructive criticism to an early draft of the first edition of this book, Carson Taylor and Jim Treulich for instilling in me the need to aim high, and Roger Wiersema for helping provide "training wheels" and friendship to a journeyman engineer.

I am indebted to Richard A. Payne and his excellent volume, *How to Get a Better Job Quicker* [Taplinger, 1987]. Mr. Payne's book has provided me with an excellent guide in my own career development. The volume provides any job seeker with a very complete and highly detailed presentation on successful résumé development, salary negotiations, interviewing, and many other aspects of career development. It represents an excellent investment for any job seeker, regardless of their field of interest.

As my career grew, I was fortunate enough to become acquainted with a number of recording studio sages through the Society of Professional Audio Recording Services (SPARS): Murray Allen, Tom Kobayashi, Chris Stone, Nick Colleran, Guy Costa, and Shirley Kaye. Thank you for sharing so many of your insights. This same crew also taught me that when one has friends in the industry, access to a wealth of knowledge and experience capable of solving almost any problem is only a phone call away.

When I shifted gears and launched my music-technology marketing agency in 1995, I was fortunate to tap the wisdom and wit of outstanding mentors Peter Weiglin, Marc Greenberg, and Al Rose. I hope I retain a fraction of the knowledge you have shared with me over our years of friendship.

My colleagues and friends in the NAMM Affiliated Music Business Institutions (NAMBI) have been a tremendous resource, assisting me in refining my teaching and curriculum. Likewise, the Music and Entertainment Industry Educators Association (MEIEA) has provided me with access to a diverse group of thinkers and educators with whom I share the common goal of furthering our student's readiness for a successful career in the industry.

Hats off to my publishing team at Berklee Press, headed by David Kusek. Thanks to Kristen Schilo and Sue Gedutis-Lindsay for outstanding editing that shaped the words that worked so well in a lecture hall into a cohesive manuscript that formed the first edition. Thanks to Jonathan Feist for his early advice and belief in the workshops and other key elements that have expanded and improved this work. He has also thoughtfully edited this second edition. Special thanks to Debbie Cavalier for her enthusiasm from the very beginning. Debbie's energy, insights, and candor are a wonderful aid to any author fortunate enough to collaborate with her. My research assistant, Jenna Stehney, contributed data management, research, fact checking, and many of the necessary tasks to bring this updated version together.

To the ten professionals who kindly agreed to be interviewed for this book and shared so much of their experience, I salute you. I don't know of a better way to learn practical career advice than to be speaking with and listening to those who have gone before us.

Without the patience, encouragement, and support of my family: Laura, Elyse, and Megan, this book would still be just an idea simmering on the back burner of my brain. And thanks to my parents, Helene and Hans Hatschek, who taught me the power of communication and the importance of love.

Keith Hatschek
University of the Pacific
Stockton, California
Spring, 2007

Introduction

You are likely reading this book to find out what kinds of jobs exist in the music industry. Or you've already made a decision and know that working in one of the fields relating to "the business" is for you. But where do you start to prepare for your career planning and job search?

When I am lecturing about music industry careers, students usually ask me two questions: "Are there jobs in the music industry?" and "How do I go about locating and landing those jobs?" This book will answer those questions and also provide you with an introduction to the career development tools, workshop exercises, and job search strategies that will increase your chances of success in this highly competitive field.

What kinds of opportunities are out there? What kind of research skills will you need to uncover those opportunities? And how do you get plugged into specific job opportunities and develop a network where you can find out about job leads as they come up?

In the following chapters, we'll take an in-depth look at the music industry, often using the recording studio business as a case study for my examples. That's the business that I've been involved in for more than twenty-five years, and it is like a microcosm of the entertainment industry as a whole. Certain rules and regulations apply, career-wise, and most apply to other career paths, be they at record labels, management companies, music publishers, Internet music startups, booking agencies, tour companies, or many others.

Workshops throughout the book will help you assemble and organize information related to your current job search and your ongoing career development. Additional support materials for these workshops are available at www.berkleemusic.com in the Jobs and Gigs section. Appendices B and C provide additional resources.

In the chapters and workshops, you'll find out how to develop a marketable skill set and skills inventory. Only by identifying what makes you special or valuable to an employer, when you send in a résumé or go for an interview, will you be able to communicate a clear message that positions you to win that job.

This book will help teach you to differentiate yourself in the job market so that a person hiring will see that you are a person who has something special to offer them.

You will learn about internships, and then we'll get into what it takes to conduct a job search. Some of you may be actively looking for a job now. Others may be just beginning to think about what kind of career opportunities exist. Either way, you will have a much better perspective on how to succeed after you read and work through the text and workshops in this book.

Discover what kind of tools you need for your job search. It may surprise you that most people already have a majority of them. We're going to talk about goal setting for career development. Your goal is to get a job, but that sometimes seems like a distant objective. So we'll break that down into smaller tasks, so you can make the first milestone on your journey towards finding and keeping your dream job. Small steps will lead to your eventual goal, which is landing a great job.

Then we'll tackle the oft-dreaded résumé. This is the task that creates the most hangdog looks from students I teach and many job seekers. I have often heard, "I don't know how to write a résumé. Why do I have to have one? I just want to push faders, play my axe, and listen to great music all night."

Well, I'm here to give you the news: You must have a strong résumé. I keep my résumé current today and have for the last two decades. It's a critical tool you will need throughout your career, whatever field you're in.

You probably are wondering: how do you get your résumé into the preferred pile of contenders and not the rejection pile? You will learn how to build a résumé that clearly communicates your special skills and worth to future employers, thereby separating yourself from other job seekers.

In addition to a well-crafted résumé, you will need to do some research on the jobs that interest you. How do you get started on your job search? Have you established some short-term goals, and are your long-term goals in mind?

Soon, you will be ready to go out and start working. How do you get there? What's the first step? Do you pick up a phone? Can you find your dream job by surfing the Internet? Do you contact an employment agency? Do you purchase a subscription to *Billboard* magazine? This book provides a step-by-step approach to succeeding in your job search, and it will increase the odds dramatically of landing the position of your dreams in the music industry. It won't be easy, but you will develop career development skills that will be worth their weight in gold throughout your working life.

We will look at many types of careers. A host of opportunities exist in a number of rapidly expanding fields, such as the computer gaming industry, the Internet, the recession-proof music products industry, new forms of broadcasting, and other affiliated fields where sound is becoming increasingly important. Many of these jobs pay significantly higher salaries than an entry-level position in a recording studio or record label.

Finally, we'll look at the view from the top as we talk with ten professionals who share their experiences on making it in this competitive business. What led to their first break? What skills and attributes do they identify as crucial for someone starting a new career? What's the best strategy to get a foot in the door today? Read on, and prepare yourself for a career in one of the most exciting industries.

PART ONE

Chapters and Workshops

CHAPTER 1 Today's Job Market: The Big Picture

People looking to get into the music industry share a common buzzword: passion. They talk about their love of music and how much it means to them. However, no matter how great your passion for music, an accurate understanding of the job realities is necessary before you plunge into developing a career in this field.

JOB SUPPLY AND DEMAND

Like all industries, the music industry adheres to the law of job supply and demand—a basic rule of all economic systems. When it comes to jobs and opportunities, the supply of industry jobs falls well below the demand of those wishing to enter the industry. This makes every job precious—even those internships that don't pay one cent. It also means that in order to better your chances for success, you have to take advantage of every single ethical opportunity to better your skills and status in the industry.

When I was managing a recording studio, we would receive an average of four to five résumés a week. Half of those job seekers would follow up with a phone call. Some would say, "I'd love to just stop by, meet you, see the room, see the studio." Others would boldly state, "I'll do anything to get started, from scrubbing the bathroom to running for lunches."

When there are more people willing to work for no pay, it makes it harder to get paid. That's the first reality you'll discover about entry-level positions in the industry.

The second reality is that when it comes to succeeding as a recording artist, the vast majority of recordings fail to break even for their record label. A well-known manager and label president shared a staggering statistic quoted in *Billboard* in the late 1990s: Of the approximately 32,000 records released each year, only 189 sell at least 250,000 copies, which is considered the break-even point for major labels.

Making a hit record is a bit like winning the lottery. Only about half of 1 percent of people break even. The other 99.5 percent fail to do so. Don't be discouraged by this statistic.

Instead, understand that although it can be done, it's a long shot to hit it big, as a recording artist. That's why I encourage you to look at careers not only as a recording artist or record producer, but at the cornucopia of other jobs in the music industry. Don't lock yourself into one career path too early in the game. The very same skills and passion you've developed for your music can be a tremendous asset in the business side of the industry.

PLAYING FOR A TEAM

Talent, perseverance, and people skills are givens to making it in the business. A colleague who worked as a tech at George Lucas's renowned Skywalker Sound once said, "Fifty-one percent of my job is getting along with my coworkers, and 49 percent of my job is knowing how to keep all of our technology running." Her statement has stayed with me over the years as one of the most important pieces of information I could share with you.

> *"Fifty-one percent of my job is getting along with my coworkers, and 49 percent of my job is knowing how to keep all of our technology running."*

To make it in the music industry, you've got to be able to work in a group environment. If you feel compelled to work alone, be your own boss, compose on your own, perform on your own, then perhaps you shouldn't be working in a studio, or for a record label, or at a management company. Why? Because you've got to be able to get along with people around you. Don't panic now if "people skills" don't appear to be among your strongest talents; you can develop them. Basically, it's just a matter of wanting to play on a winning team.

CLIMBING TO THE TOP

Perseverance is obviously a big asset. Depending on the opportunity, there may be from 25 to 2,500 or more people knocking on the door for an industry job opening. You've got to be willing to persevere. Otherwise, you're going to run out of gas in your quest.

Just about everybody starts out at the bottom in this business, even today's top dogs. I encourage you to read one of the books penned by a top record-label executive. One such book is *Follow the Music* by Jac Holzman, the founder of Elektra Records. Another is Ian Copeland's entertaining bio, *Wild Thing*. (All books referenced can be found in "Selected Resources" at the back of this book.) Seeing that just about every top executive started out as a mail clerk, gofer, or assistant will help you strengthen your resolve to climb the mountain ahead with respect to your music industry career.

The benefit of starting out at the bottom of the company's organizational chart is that you meet a lot of people on the way up, you see how a company works, and you learn about every function in an organization. It's very helpful to learn about what parts work efficiently as well as what parts may not run smoothly, and more importantly, the reason why.

Competition is central to the industry. There's always new blood coming in—new bands, new songwriters, new musicians, and new Artist & Repertoire (A&R) staffers. It's the nature of the game. You've got to have a bit of a competitive streak in you to make it in this business.

Radio and television both use a formal rating system. That's the way the entertainment industry works. The statement that recording artists are "only as good as the sales of their last record" is true in an economic sense. Competition is always going to be there, so you have to have the drive—the "fire in the belly"—to stick with your dream and push yourself to make it. Few, if any, things will come easy to you as you journey along your career path in the industry. You will be earning your stripes every step of the way.

HOBBY OR CAREER?

Are you pursuing a hobby or a career? Why is it important to know the difference? This is an issue that sometimes trips people up, as they look to make a career in the music industry. Many come to the industry because of their love of music. But the reality is, you've got to have bankable skills to deliver, or you're not going to be gainfully employed or grow your career. Many people have sacrificed years of their life because they felt they wanted to be "near the music."

A hobby is the pursuit of a field for personal enjoyment. I'm a hobby guitar player today, and I play my guitar once or twice a month. I used to be a professional guitarist, and I was paid well for my skills.

A career is your vocation—the daily occupation in which you must excel. Either a hobby or a career can be rewarding; however, you have to decide which one of these roads you're on.

If you plan to make a career in the industry, you've got to be serious about developing your job-search strategies, building your skill set, and researching what competition you'll face in specific entry-level job areas. Discover what your earning prospects are.

It's okay to switch from hobby to career. But make sure you have the required commitment, as the road will be challenging and you will need to stay focused on achieving your goals.

WORKSHOP 1. CREATE YOUR CAREER BINDER

Start by purchasing a sturdy three-ring binder. I recommend a 2 ½- or 3-inch model. In front of the first tab divider, you should include two one-year calendars: one for this current year and a second for the following year. You can find these online at http://Timeanddate.com. They will come in handy to mark important events, deadlines, and tasks for which you have set a target completion date.

Then create the following sections in your Career Binder using sheet dividers with ID tabs.

Jobs. Compile job descriptions, open-job listings, references to specific positions, or internship opportunities.

Target Companies. Any time you hear or read about a new company that interests you, start a new page with the company's name and URL on it. Fill in more information as you discover it.

Clippings. Every time you come across an article that interests you, especially those that identify specific companies, photocopy it or clip it and add it to your Career Binder.

Correspondence. Keep letters to and from the various people and companies you will encounter in your career development.

Events. Record information on industry conferences, conventions, charity events, or any other type of function that may provide you with the chance to meet and learn from others.

Reference. Include notes, handouts, and other classroom or lecture materials that relate to your industry career journey.

My Résumé. The evolution of your résumé and your skills at résumé development will go in here.

My Journal. You are embarking on a process of career development that includes a component of self-discovery and personal evaluation. Workshop 2 will give you a start on developing the material for this section. Use this section of your Career Binder for notes to yourself, wish lists, reflections on key events such as interviews, workshops, mentoring opportunities, and the like.

As you journey down your own unique career path, feel free to add new sections as you need them. Perhaps you'll start a section to record details of the job and informational interviews you have and what you learned from them. Keep some blank sheets of lined paper in the front so that you can quickly jot down notes or details of a conversation, a reference book, or a company's contact information.

The importance of your Career Binder will become clear as the variety and amount of information that you uncover widens. Don't be concerned at first if you have little to include in each of the sections. By the time you finish reading this book, completing the workshops, expanding your network, and becoming a detective in your industry areas of interest, you will have plenty to add.

Keeping your Career Binder up-to-date and at hand gives you instant access to the information you develop. This can be an important time-saver when you or a colleague are hunting for a specific piece of data.

USING YOUR CAREER BINDER

Your Career Binder will be a visible investment of your time and brainpower to get your journey started properly! It will help you build a dossier or backlog of resource information that you can continually reference. A number of my former students have come back, called, or written—often three or four years after our interaction—and said things like, "I'm so glad I kept my Career Binder going. I sent that guest lecturer an e-mail, and she sent me back a tip on a company, where I just landed an interview!"

The whole music and entertainment business is interconnected, and it's important to remember where to find things and where to look for people. Your Career Binder should have sections on careers that interest you today, clippings on companies that are expanding, notes from meetings, articles on new technology, or magazine interviews with people in the business you admire. If you are interested in a career in recording, list the studios in your region, as well as facilities in New York, Los Angeles, and Nashville. Go through their Web sites, print out any pages that tell you what kind of work they do, and add those to your Career Binder.

A Career Binder becomes a reference work to help you determine which career paths interest you and will be a good fit for you. You'll find that over the years, it will become a valued resource—a shortcut to get you closer from where you are today to where you want to be tomorrow. Keep that information at your fingertips. And when the first binder is full, begin another one.

VISUALIZATION

Another very important step for your career is to visualize yourself in your target career. For instance, if your career goal is to become a professional songwriter, you have to cross that bridge and say, "I am a songwriter. Okay, now that I'm a songwriter, how do I get to be a better songwriter?" That's a critical career step.

Once you see yourself developing in this new career, it doesn't matter if you're going to work by day as a paralegal, a waitress, a grocery clerk, or a data-entry "droid." In your heart, you know that you are working on developing your career and that you're a songwriter. If becoming a songwriter is your industry career goal, rename your Career Binder, "Songwriter Career Binder." Your Career Binder is a key resource you construct over time to help you reach your career destination.

MAKING CONNECTIONS TO GROW YOUR CAREER

The music industry is forever evolving, and currently it is morphing itself via the Internet. In the six years since this book's first edition was published, the means that artists use to promote themselves, to sell records (CDs or downloads), and appear live has been irrevocably changed by the explosion of the information revolution. To keep up with the changes, you've got to commit yourself to continuous learning. It's interesting, because in the years that I've been teaching an entertainment industry career class, the primary group of students in the eighteen to twenty-five-year-old age group have been joined by a second smaller twenty-five to forty-nine age group who have decided to shift gears mid career. No matter what age you may be, the skills and talents necessary for a successful industry career are the same.

If you find ways to meet people that are doing what you want to do and ask them intelligent questions, you will most likely discover your path to get into the business. That is the surest way to be aware of the changing trends that affect our business.

It is vitally important that you become well-read on the industry and that you talk to people who are working in the business. If you find ways to meet people that are doing what you want to do and ask them intelligent questions, you will most likely discover your path to get into the business. That is the surest way to be aware of the changing trends that affect our business.

As an example, in the Northern California region, there's a songwriting organization—West Coast Songwriters, with 1,200 active members—which hosts fifteen events each month. They host an outstanding annual fall symposium. You should attend the symposium if you live in the region and want to make it as a songwriter. You should be networking with other songwriters. You've got to be talking to those publishers who are in attendance at their fall symposium. That's your Super Bowl. You have to be there. You've got to commit yourself to lifelong learning and getting involved with others doing what you aspire to do.

Here's another example, for those aspiring to be record producers. At the Audio Engineering Society (AES) Convention in the fall, and the International Music Products Association (NAMM) conventions in winter and summer, there are producer's forums that are open to the public (for a small admission fee) co-hosted by the Recording Academy. You can listen to some of the most successful producers in the business talk about what it takes to make it as a producer. Top producers talk for two hours about what they do, how they got their breaks, and what they recommend for up-and-coming producers of the future. How can you miss that if you want to be the next Kanye West or Tony Brown? You've got to find opportunities to learn and network such as these.

If you can't get to an event, find out if there is a tape or transcript, or whether it was broadcast on the Internet. This information is out there. The people who have presented and appeared at the event are usually happy to talk to you in the right setting, and share the information and ideas and experience that they have. You've got to always be looking for opportunities to soak up more information. Become an information sponge. Fill your Career Binder with clippings, notes, and information on careers and companies that pique your interest and spark your imagination.

Obviously, you've got to learn and practice your craft too. You've got to keep engineering or writing songs, you've got to keep booking bands—whatever avocation you aspire to. But focus part of your energy on getting near people that are doing what you want to do at the highest level possible. That's the fastest way to learn about the dos and don'ts and the ins and outs of our business. There is no substitute for exposure to working professionals.

CHAPTER 2 Why Geography Matters

This is your music industry geography lesson. On the map below are the most important cities in the United States for the combined music and entertainment industries: New York, Nashville, and Los Angeles.

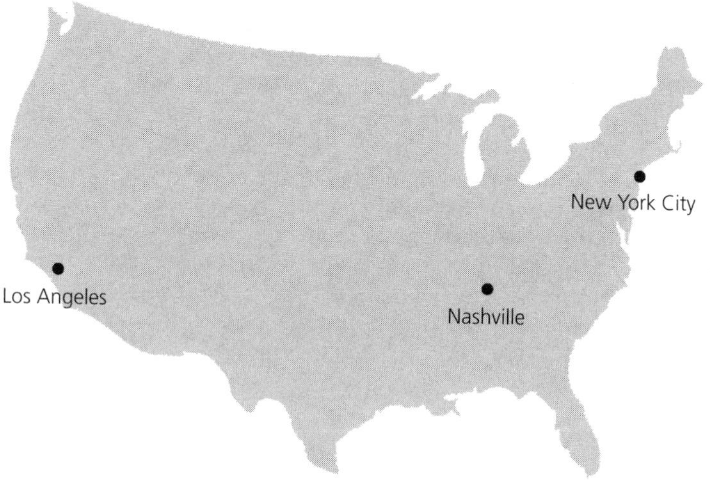

Certainly, for the record business in North America, these cities represent the top of the mountain. If you aspire to make it to the top, at some point you're going to go to one of these three cities. That's where it happens for the record business. So if you're recording, if you're a songwriter, if you're an engineer/producer, or if you're going to work with a label, sooner or later you will be living or working in one of these three regions.

Don't despair if you aren't living now in one of the major cities. If you live in or near Seattle, Chicago, San Francisco, Atlanta, Miami, Boston, Austin, St. Louis, Denver, Memphis, Houston, New Orleans, Philadelphia, or another good-sized metropolitan area, you can develop an excellent skill set and put it to use in the regional music industry. For instance, you might work at an indie label, or with a radio station, or learn how to make a great-sounding recording at a studio, and then build up your skills without having to be in such a big shark tank where there is such intense competition that you need a fully developed skill set along with buckets of ambition and drive to succeed.

Rather than jumping feetfirst into one of the top three music markets, it's an excellent strategy to work in a smaller market to really learn the basics of how the industry works.

Rather than jumping feetfirst into one of the top three music markets, it's an excellent strategy to work in a smaller market to really learn the basics of how the industry works. It may be helpful to work with a concert promoter, a booking agency, or other related firm in your area of interest. One day, you will feel that you may have outgrown your situation and that you're ready to take the next step in your career development.

When my former students tell me they are ready to make their move to the big markets, I suggest they visit first. I encourage them to take two weeks off from their current job, travel to one of the major markets, and rent a room or stay with a friend to do some networking and some interviewing. You need to make sure that you're ready to go on to the next level. Moving to one of the top markets is expensive, and it's emotionally intense. Check it out before you pull up your stakes and jump in. You have to have your eyes open before you take the plunge. Prepare yourself to succeed when you make your move to one of these three regions. Those are the practicalities of music industry geography.

WORKSHOP 2. LANDING IN AN ENTERTAINMENT CAPITAL

Pick one of the three major entertainment capitals and research the following information.

1. Identify three firms in your chosen city that have business operations in the area of the industry that most interests you. For instance, if you are planning to work in entertainment marketing, you might identify the marketing department at a record label, concert promoter, and a radio or TV network.
2. Using a localized resource such as Craig's List, look up the cost to rent an apartment or a room in a house or apartment.
3. Next, make a short list of your current living expenses. Replace your current rent or housing costs with what you've researched on the major market.
4. Finally, think about whom you currently know that might provide an introduction to a working professional in the city you've chosen to research. Finding a "local expert" is an important step toward learning about the actual working situation, job market, and cost of living in one of the major markets.

CHAPTER 3 What Kind of Jobs Are Out There?

In my career development classes for the music industry, my students ask, "What jobs are there, in addition to songwriter, musician, or recording engineer?" Look carefully anywhere that music or sound is needed, and you'll discover dozens of jobs to investigate. The list at the end of this chapter reveals just a smattering of the hundreds of jobs in our industry. Affiliated music and sound careers abound in the film, theater, and educational arenas. Education is an often-overlooked career path, but it's essential, because if no one is learning how to make or appreciate music, there won't be any music—and certainly many less savvy music consumers.

Television and radio, computer hardware and software, videogames, and theme parks. At Disney, rather than calling their audio staff "engineers," they call them "imagineers." I like that terminology. Think of all the sounds there are at a theme park such as a Disney or Universal Studios location. Imagineers not only create the sounds, but they also design the playback systems and keep the sound running around the clock.

Mobile audio, recording equipment, the latest concert sound equipment, recorders, compressors, reverbs, amplifiers, mixing boards, and microphones. Someone has to imagine, design, and build them all. Perhaps you're interested in music publishing or journalism? Or what about working at a record company, as it will have all the positions of any other going business, from mail clerk to president. You will soon read about careers in recording studios in much greater detail.

Do you know what a "Foley artist" does? A Foley artist recreates the background sounds in feature movies, such as an Indiana Jones epic. When the actors are running through the jungle, the sound of the actors running wasn't recorded while they were filming. All of those sounds you hear of the hyenas, the tropical birds, the footsteps, and the waterfall were all created afterward in a sound studio. Foley artists create all the human-generated sounds, such as footsteps, body hits, punches, doors being opened and closed, and even the sounds of bedclothes or curtains rustling in a breeze. It's a fascinating field, and the artists who do the work are in great demand.

If you go see a low-budget movie, then perhaps most of the Foley and sound effects are coming out of a sampling keyboard or computer that plays back sounds from a digital sound-effects library. But when you see a movie by Peter Jackson, George Lucas, Stephen Spielberg, James Cameron, or other mainstream Hollywood directors, Foley artists have added the Foley work the old-fashioned way. If you listen very carefully to both types of films, you will hear that the old-fashioned way sounds most realistic.

For the sound of the T-Rex in the film *Jurassic Park*, a team of sound designers at Skywalker Sound spent days developing that one growl to make it believable. After all, who really knows what a T-Rex growl sounds like? But the sound they imagined, and then created, has a strong impact.

Music editor, sound editor, singer, songwriter, personal manager, publicist, music video director, record producer, and videogame project manager. For example, a project manager plays a huge role for a software company like Electronic Arts or Sony. These firms have twenty, thirty, or more project managers on staff, managing teams and developing new games. On each team, there are programmers, writers, consultants, digital artists, cinematographers, sound editors, composers, sound designers, and budget analysts. A complex interactive videogame has to come together in a precise manner. The project manager is the person responsible for making sure it's all rolling forward and will make the target dates.

Music educator, music librarian, orchestrator, and copyist. What do copyists do? They copy music notation. Computers, using notation software, generate more and more music scores. But copyists can also arrange music used by bands, symphonies, or orchestras for films, television commercials, music dates, and the like.

Newcomers to the music industry have often been attracted to the field by the glamour of a particular job or artistic pursuit. There are thousands of successful recording artists, and there are at least fifty support people behind each one, many in high-paying, exciting careers. They may not share the spotlight on stage, but they have very rewarding careers in the music industry.

In the resource section at the end of the book is a listing for two books that provide snapshots of many different jobs that relate to our industry: *Career Opportunities in the Music Industry* by Shelly Field and *100 Careers in the Music Industry* by Tanja Crouch. Field's book details job descriptions, salary ranges, and necessary skills. Crouch's book is much more intimate, using first-person interviews with many leading professionals to profile exactly what they do in their work and how they got their start in the industry. Each book complements the other. I recommend you find a copy of each and keep them handy to see the diversity of music industry jobs. Many libraries may also have a copy of these books. Also, if you are enrolled in a college or vocational program, your school may have a career day where local professionals visit and talk about what they do every day in their jobs.

Getting to know about the variety of jobs and what kinds of skills and aptitude are required for each is one of the most important activities you can undertake. How can you find out if you are well suited for a job if you don't know what it takes to do it well?

How can you find out if you are well suited for a job if you don't know what it takes to do it well?

After reviewing some of the general fields listed below, as well as a few specific jobs, start your own list of the jobs that most intrigue you. Keep your list handy in your Career Binder. (You *have* started your Career Binder, haven't you?)

Hopefully, the list below will get you thinking about the dozens of jobs that you may never have known about in our industry.

On the right-hand side of the chart are career fields, and on the left-hand side, selected job titles. You could add another dozen if you thought about it and started reading up on what's happening today in the music and recording biz.

MUSIC INDUSTRY JOBS

Selected job titles		General fields relying on sound and music skills
Recording Studio Manager	Business Manager	Record Companies *(all functions)*
Recording Studio Scheduler	Music Attorney	Recording Studio
Sales or Marketing Department	Publicist	Film Music/Soundtracks
Maintenance Engineer *(repair)*	Instrumentalist *(live or studio)*	Theater Music
Foley Artist	Arranger	Music Education
ADR Mixer	Copyist	Television Production
Sound Designer	Music Librarian	Radio
Composer	Recording Engineer	Computer Hardware *(sound)*
Disc Jockey	Producer/Project Manager	Computer Software *(music and sound)*
Location Recordist	Production Assistant	Videogames
Sound Editor	Program Director	Theme Parks
Software Designer	Research and Development Engineer	Mobile Audio
Compressionist	Editor/Writer *(journalism and publishing)*	Digital Distribution of Media
Music Editor	Music Educator	Recording Equipment
Music Supervisor	Sales Executive (in all aspects of the entertainment industry)	Live Sound Reinforcement
Singer		Music Journalism
Songwriter		Music Publishing

WORKSHOP 3. MAGIC LAMP

Imagine you've just found the proverbial "magic lamp" in the attic of your family home. You have three wishes, but a note attached to the handle says that the wishes can only be used to discover the perfect career for you.

Although such a lamp didn't come with this book, this workshop will allow you to identify the three jobs that most interest you. What jobs do you wish for?

A. ____________________

B. ____________________

C. ____________________

Now, using an Internet search engine, find an interview with a working professional for each of the three dream jobs you've identified. Print the articles, and after reading them over carefully, ask yourself if your interest remains high for each job. What is it about that person's job or career that excites you? Do they mention how they got to where they are in the industry today? Will you be willing to go through a similar learning process to reach a similar position?

Write down the answers to these or any other questions or observations that come to mind after reading the articles.

Finally, add the articles to your Career Binder clippings section.

These are only a handful of jobs and fields that need talented newcomers to jump in and help make a difference. In fact, as the baby boomers (who in large part operate the entertainment industry today) come to grips with the impact of the Internet and other new technologies such as mobile content delivery, they will only continue to be successful by utilizing the skills, talents, and adaptability that today's younger generation has with regard to such technology. By the time you are reading this, there will be many new job titles created as our industry continues to evolve and change in the face of new technologies. Don't limit your view to one or two career paths. Do some serious investigation before you settle on any one route.

CHAPTER 4 Gizmos, People, and Gender

It's a fact. Most people prefer to work with either technology or people. Now is an appropriate time for you to ascertain whether you are primarily a "people person" or what I call a "gizmologist"—a gizmo and technology person.

How can you do that? Consider this hypothetical question. Suppose you're working as an intern at a record label in L.A. You have the opportunity to help a label producer set up the new demo studio or to give the tour to a group of businessmen to show them how the label is structured. Which do you prefer?

The answer to that question may lead you to evaluate, do I prefer working with technology or with people? It's important to know your preference. You've got to be able to do both today, to some degree. You've got to be familiar with computers and the Internet. You really can't start a career in the entertainment industry today without knowledge in these areas. Regardless of your proclivity for technology or working with people, your career in the music industry will require you to become proficient at interpersonal skills, listening, talking, and networking. Even the most hard-core programmer will need to have a network of colleagues who know him and support his career development. Don't fall into the trap of believing that your technology chops alone will get you to the top. Without a reasonable complement of interpersonal and networking skills, tech skills alone won't lead anywhere in the music industry.

If you wake up at night thinking about ways to wire your home-studio patch bay or just installed your new car stereo player, you're likely a gizmo person. If so, you have good career opportunities ahead, because it's essential that there be gizmologists to keep the music world wired and working. Technology is a core component of recording, producing, and now, merchandising music via the Internet. Computer tech and network skills are also prized in the entertainment industry as more and more reliance on computing permeates our industry.

Visualize a singer with a guitar playing a song to a roomful of people, with no microphone, no sound system, and no electronics. The minute that singer has to perform for a larger audience, you need technology. You've got to have mics, cables, amps, TV monitors, and a person to run them.

The people side of the business is equally important. Companies must set goals and objectives, and develop the means to accomplish those goals. They must manage team building, finance, sales, promotion, and human resources, and tackle long-term planning. These tasks are people-related. Hence, business types provide the structure needed to make a record label, recording studio, management firm, or other music-related business a success.

That's why you should consider which you prefer, people or gizmos, so that you can focus your career research in an area that suits you. Interestingly, the people who make it to the very top of the industry are generalists, meaning that they have experience in both areas. They may be stronger in one or the other, but they are conversant in both.

So, you'll find that the top people in most big organizations are adept at delegating and managing, and good judges of people. They have the ability to say, "Here's a person, and this is what motivates her, and how she could contribute to our company's effort." These kinds of leaders usually have a good grasp of technology—not only of where things are today, but where they're headed in the future. Lastly, top leaders share one other common trait: an unquenchable desire to succeed.

WORKSHOP 4. SELF-ASSESSMENT QUIZ

Rate yourself using the following questions.

Part 1

1. I am comfortable learning and using new technologies such as computer programs.

   Yes No

2. I read about and investigate the latest music and entertainment technologies.

   Yes No

3. My friends ask me to help them install or use new audio or video gadgets or software.

   Yes No

4. I'm interested in how music-making devices work.

   Yes No

5. I enjoy pushing the envelope with the music technologies that I have access to.

   Yes No

Part 2

6. I am able to function in situations where I meet and talk with new people.

   Yes No

7. If a conflict arises, I am able to maintain composure and work to settle the conflict.

   Yes No

8. I have succeeded in situations where I helped lead a team of my peers.

   Yes No

9. I have a genuine interest in listening to and learning from many different people.

   Yes No

10. I have the ability to communicate with people who others say are difficult.

    Yes No

Score your test. If you answered yes to four or more questions in part 1, chances are you are well on your way to a career in music technology. Conversely, if you answered yes to four or more questions in part 2, you will likely find the greatest career success by participating in the business and management side of the industry. If you scored high in both areas, surprise! You may be CEO material!

EQUAL OPPORTUNITY FOR ALL?

Males have traditionally dominated the music industry. Historically, 90 percent of the people working in recording studios, concert production, and most technical roles were male, and few women were found behind the mixing console. That has been changing, over the last twenty-five years. In terms of the recording industry, there are now opportunities for women to work as engineers, producers, A&R execs, technicians, label presidents, and any position that men have traditionally held. Although the number of women working at record labels has been high historically, it's only recently that women are common in the top ranks. In Hollywood, women head up some of the largest studios.

A lot of ancillary fields, such as live sound, concert production, staging, cartage, and rigging, are still dominated by men. A woman aspiring to a career in the music industry must be aware that there are a lot of people who have been in the industry for many years who possess extremely chauvinistic attitudes. A woman should be mentally prepared for that. She has to have faith in herself, and know what strengths she has and how she can utilize them. She has to conscientiously work to say and act upon what she believes in. The fix is to have the skills and ambition to do the job well, and you will move ahead on your career path. Women such as Madonna, Sylvia Rhone, Sarah McLachlan, Queen Latifah, Sheryl Crow, Melissa Etheridge, Reba McEntire, Alanis Morissette, Ani DiFranco, and many others are influencing our industry, and you can do it too. And men, remember if you are in a position to hire a person to help your company prosper, be sure to hire the best available candidate, regardless of gender.

CHAPTER 5 Career Ladders: Technical Track

In the next two chapters, we'll examine two case studies in detail. I chose these two because they are typical of the music industry. By studying them in detail, you will gain insight into what happens in any segment of the industry, what promotions occur as you build a career, and what type of earning potential there is at each step of the way. Without this depth of knowledge, you will likely be groping in the dark to find out what is involved in any music industry career.

First, we will dive into the staff structure of a world-class recording studio for an in-depth look at each rung of the music recording career ladder. Similar career ladders exist in the record company, management, booking and tour agencies, performing rights societies, and other career paths. If you are interested in becoming a recording engineer, producer, studio owner, manager, or scheduler, here's the scoop on those jobs.

We talked earlier about the "music business." There's the *music*, and then there's the *business*. In the recording studio business, there is the art and craft of recording—that is, what goes on in the actual recording session, plus the management of the studio business. Thus, there are two career tracks. Page 29 shows the technical career track in the recording studio.

As a point of reference, the charts and data in this chapter are indicative of a multiroom commercial recording facility in a major market circa 2007. The first three rungs on the ladder may have different names and duties, depending on the nature of the work being done at a particular studio. The one common aspect of all three, however, is that they are learning stops on the path to a successful career in the recording-studio business.

Let's look at the first job on the technical track, and find out just what a **gofer** does. Gofers (also known as *studio assistants*) absorb everything that goes on at a studio and learn how important all the little details are in making a studio operation run smoothly. They "go for" coffee, cigarettes, lunches, tequila . . . whatever the studio or artist needs at that moment. What if the bass player gets a flat tire in the parking lot? A gofer helps change the flat. Go for this, go for that, help with this, deal with that. Gofers get to see just about every side of the daily operation of a recording studio and the front lines of the business.

The job title **assistant engineer** perfectly describes the job function. Assistants (or *seconds*, as they are also known) set up the recording studio for a session, handle the cables, place microphones (once they have learned how to do that task), and assist the *first* engineer throughout the session. An assistant engineer accelerates his or her learning process after a successful stint as a gofer by assisting and observing the senior engineering staff during recording sessions every day. They are also likely to handle myriad other support tasks around the studio—everything from repairing mic cables, to uploading rough mixes to the producer or band's FTP site for private review by the label's A&R staff. Gradually, they will be put into situations where they have to analyze circumstances and make decisions that have an impact on a project or task. In this way, their responsibility and confidence can begin to grow.

Another important function an assistant performs is session documentation. A colleague of mine was working with members of the group Earth, Wind & Fire. He said, when they were recording tracks for a new album, "We've already recorded 100 rolls of 2-inch, 24-track analog tape of new material." All those tapes had to be fully documented and logged. Each master reel's contents had to be written up, then put into a computer. That's one of the assistant's critically important responsibilities. If it's not done properly, how will the producer, engineer, or artist locate the material they need among the hundreds of takes and thousands of tracks when they continue the project?

As an assistant engineer, you're going to use a computer daily. Get comfortable with computers, because it is an essential tool for documenting and managing information in the recording studio.

When you're working as an assistant engineer, you are exposed to clients more fully than a gofer would be. You also work with the senior technical staff to develop a better understanding of how an engineer functions productively in a commercial studio, and in the process, you will help to generate revenue and profits.

Occasionally, a technically adept assistant engineer may consider moving into studio maintenance after a stint as an assistant engineer. Today's **studio maintenance engineer** is truly a jack-of-all-trades. Fifteen years ago, the emphasis in maintenance was on electrical and mechanical aptitude. Digital recording still meant that magnetic tape was rolling. Today, a maintenance engineer must be as equally comfortable eliminating a software glitch as he is in tweaking a vintage analog 2-track tape recorder or a Fairchild tube limiter. Talented maintenance engineers are seldom out of work for very long. After all, if you were a studio owner with a multimillion-dollar investment, and your revenue earning was based on fully functioning studios, wouldn't you keep the best maintenance personnel available on staff?

If you prove to have good technical aptitude as an assistant engineer and your boss finds out that you know how to "fix things," you may be groomed for a tech or maintenance gig. Perhaps as a kid growing up, you built radio-controlled model cars, or you learned how to repair your own car or motorcycle. If the studio manager finds out about those skills, you could be in for a promotion before you know it. Studio maintenance is an area that offers financial security like few other jobs in the recording industry. A competent studio maintenance engineer knows how to keep everything running in a modern studio, keep maintenance logs, work with management, and develop a basic maintenance budget. With these skills, you'll seldom experience unemployment. You will be able to go to New York, Los Angeles, or Nashville, and start at $50,000 or more a year. It'll go up from there if you are adept at keeping the studio equipment running well.

Of course, today's maintenance engineer also has to know a good deal about computers. They must understand tapes and tape transports, both analog and digital. A solid knowledge of digital audio and Society of Motion Picture and Television Engineers (SMPTE) time code is required. You take the skills you've developed in these areas and use them. Studio maintenance people may begin their career development as assistant maintenance engineers or night maintenance engineers for a few years to hone their skills. Then they may move to another studio and be top dog in maintenance. Such a career can be very rewarding—not only financially, but also in knowing that you are responsible for keeping the studio and its clients "on the air."

Most engineers don't take the maintenance path because frankly, to many, it's not as appealing as making the move from assistant to first engineer. Becoming a **first engineer** usually happens when something special occurs, such as working with a hit artist. That may be what it takes to break out. Or a staff first engineer may leave to go independent, and you are the next logical person to assume the role of staff first engineer.

Or, if you've stuck around long enough, you've earned the respect of senior staff so that the first engineers are thinking, "I don't want to do that session tonight. It doesn't start until nine o'clock. Laura could handle it." And just like that, you are "firsting" a paying session on your own and putting the skills to work that you have developed since you started as a gofer some time back.

One day, after I "graduated" from Bayshore Studios (an 8-track studio) to Music Annex (a multiroom, 24-track facility), a popular first engineer got double booked. So he said, "Keith, go do that session in Studio A." My hesitant reply was, "I've n-n-n-never worked in Studio A with a 24-track machine and Neve board before." His response was, "Ah, it's no problem, you can do it."

The session was with a well-known gospel artist, and she brought a three-year-old girl for a duet with no advance notice! So I set up a Neumann U-67 microphone, and this little girl was in the room seated at the grand piano with the artist. I could barely hear the toddler when she was singing along, because her voice output in the room was so low. My debut as a "first engineer" quickly turned into a nightmare session.

Somehow, I barely got the performance on tape. How was my debut as a first engineer? A disaster, and the track was unusable.

But the next session I helmed, I was ready. I was empowered, totally prepared, everything was set up ahead of time, and the session went very well. It became fun. I really learned from being thrown into the fire on the previous date. I also learned that it is okay to quickly point out if something is not going well at the outset of the session. The artist or producer may be a bit miffed, but not as angry as if a great performance in the studio was lost because you, in your role as first engineer, didn't identify a problem early in the session.

The first engineer's role is basically to get the performance on tape, whatever that takes. They have to interface with the artist. They're part shrink, part den mother, and sometimes part slave driver. They must know when to say to the artist, "That's still not right. You can get that more in tune." A first engineer has to walk a fine line between technology and psychology to get the best performance possible on tape, without pushing the artist too far. Sometimes, that second take really was the best one. By going for the perfect take over and over, sometimes you may actually be regressing and not improving the track. The first engineer has technical as well as a bit of artistic responsibility to ensure that the session is flowing smoothly and that the artist's performance is being faithfully captured.

As a "first," your opinion now will count in every aspect of the studio's business. You'll be asked to review and recommend equipment for purchase, take junior members of the staff under your wing for guidance and shaping, assist in selling key artists and producers on using your studio for projects, and have a voice in the long-term planning and direction of the studio at which you work.

You'll also be exposed to a wide range of artists, producers, and talented individuals, all of who will broaden your palette of experience and engineering expertise. Your voice and your opinion will be critical to the success of the recording projects you work on as you build confidence, respect, and camaraderie with the staff and clients.

Eventually, if you're a really outstanding engineer, you may have the opportunity to evolve into an **elite engineer/producer**. Examples include Brendan O'Brien, Bob Clearmountain, Elliot Scheiner, Glen Ballard, Al Schmitt, Butch Vig, Sylvia Massy, Trevor Horn, Jimmy Jam and Terry Lewis, Phil Ramone, Tony Brown, and Sir George Martin.

Two things differentiate the elite class of engineer/producer from an outstanding first engineer. One is your body of work, and specifically what type of success you have enjoyed, in terms of units sold for the records done. The second is what you earn, which can be ten to one hundred times more than a first engineer, because at this stage of your career, you are in demand. Elite engineer/producers may even command a percentage of an album's earnings, if you are really hot. You still may perform many of the same tasks you did when you were an established first. Now, however, you've got the "golden touch." The other skill that an elite engineer/producer develops is the ability to handle the politics and the recording budgets between artists, their management, and their record labels. This is an entirely different skill set, in addition to engineering and producing a great record.

STUDIO SALARIES

What do the gofers earn? And what does an assistant engineer get paid? Here's the scoop.

Gofers earn from $0 to $9 per hour, based on a survey of leading recording studios that are members of the Society of Professional Audio Recording Services (SPARS) conducted in summer 2006. Assistant engineers earn from $0 to $20 per hour, based on the same survey. It should be noted that the salary ranges referenced in this book will vary a bit from region to region. In an area with a higher cost of living, or where there is more competition for good staff, they will be a bit higher. In a smaller market, they will tend to be a bit lower.

I'm sure you've noticed that the two jobs at the start of this career track have a common element—a salary range varying from free to a reasonable hourly wage. Every reputable studio has a steady stream of persons calling, writing, and visiting who will do anything to "get into the business." This never-ending parade of people is willing to sweep the floor, run errands, and scrub the dishes for free. This means that if you want to gain an entry-level position in a recording studio, you have to be willing to work and learn for little or no money until you can prove your worth.

The more knowledge and savvy you can demonstrate, the faster the opportunities will open up for you. Ultimately, every studio manager or owner has to view each employee's contributions to the success of the business in economic terms. "What work did you perform or what problems did you solve for me today?"

This leads to the question of how to support yourself and pay for the basic cost of living, if you are working for free.

One option is to save up a nest egg and take on the job with a finite time frame, for instance, enough to work for six months at entry level. If you determine that you can't afford to work for free in a studio forty hours a week, perhaps you can work part-time, nights, or weekends, and hold down a paying job (the inevitable "day gig") so that you are able to meet your basic living expenses.

A first engineer makes $15 to $50 an hour, with the potential to even do a little better at the upper end of the experience and competency scale. That's quite a spread, salary-wise, with the upper reaches being at very established facilities for top talent with a steady clientele of A-list projects.

First engineers are likely to have variations in earning if they are paid on the basis of how many sessions they engineer. In a slower month, they may earn $2,000 to $3,000. However, with some overtime and weekend sessions—"The masters are due at the label in five days! We have to work extra hours to finish the mix!"—a busy first may log as many as two-hundred billable hours, or close to fifty billable hours a week! In that month, they might earn as much as $6,000 to $8,000. So a number of variables come into play in analyzing earning ranges for first engineers in the studio-recording business. Speaking with successful engineers will aid you in seeing what the salaries are like in your geographic region.

As you move up the technical career track to studio maintenance, what will you earn? According to the aforementioned SPARS salary survey, $19 to $35 an hour. What does $35 an hour equal as an annual salary? Approximately $72,000 a year (before taxes).

If success and a bit of luck come your way, you may make the jump into the rarefied atmosphere of the elite engineer/producer. These are well-established professionals at the top of craftsmanship, who are in demand due to a solid track record of success. They have Grammy awards, walls of multi-platinum hits, Oscars for best soundtrack or film score, and possibly Clio or Emmy awards for their advertising or television mixes. In the music arena, it's the elite producers who are able to have their managers say, "Yeah, we'll mix that single for your artist." And the mixing fee for that single can be as much as a mid-five-figure sum for the very top mixers and producers with a solid string of chart-topping credentials.

There are a handful of these star talents. That's why I like to equate this part of the technical career track to major league baseball. How many kids play Little League? Millions do. And how many players make it to the World Series? Probably twenty or thirty on each team. So it's a long shot, but some people who started years ago as gofers have made it to the top. It's not impossible.

The elite engineer/producer performs daily in the "World Series" of the recording business. This level of success allows them to earn very handsome fees due to the time and effort they have spent mastering their art and craft. In most cases, this is ten to twenty years or more. For someone starting out in the recording or record-producing game, it's great to aspire to this, but you must temper your expectations. Realize that for every few hundred gofers, perhaps one person is going to work and struggle and learn and eventually graduate to elite engineer/producer. Actually, those odds are quite a bit better than major league baseball, aren't they?

Some more examples of elite engineer/producers are Bruce Swedien, Frank Fillipetti, George Massenberg, Shawn Murphy, Bruce Botnick, Rick Rubin, Bob Ludwig, Tchad Blake, and Gary Rydstrom. They each have built a very strong reputation and track record, and can now command top fees for their creative contributions to albums, film soundtracks, and other projects. With respect to their salaries, similar to the first engineers, the range is fairly broad, from $35 to $75 per hour, which equates to roughly $72,000 to $150,000 a year, if they are working at least forty billable hours per week.

TECHNICAL CAREER TRACK: RECORDING STUDIO

Position	Salary Range
Gofer	Free to $9/hour
Assistant Engineer	Free to $20/hour
Studio Maintenance	$19 to $35/hour
First Engineer	$15 to $50/hour
Elite Engineer/Producer	$35 to $75/hour, to "the sky's the limit"

WORKSHOP 5. BUILDING YOUR CAREER LADDER

Pick one of the three "dream jobs" you identified in workshop 3. Using the blank form below, fill in the various rungs on the career ladder that you think will lead from entry level to the most accomplished level in that field. If you're not sure, start with the top rung and the bottom rung for now.

What resources can you use to fill in the career ladder with accurate and up-to-date information?

Career Track:	
Position	**Salary Range**

CHAPTER 6 Career Ladders: Management Track

Next, we'll take an in-depth look at the career path of becoming a top studio manager or owner, which parallels many types of small businesses in the music industry. Remember, these specific career ladders and salary information may not be specific to your area of interest in the music industry, but they demonstrate the level of investigation you must undertake to have a thorough understanding of whatever part of the business you wish to be involved in. More on this later.

Here's the ladder for the management career track in the recording studio business.

No surprise, you start as a **gofer** (or "studio assistant"). You're ordering flowers, putting toilet paper in the bathrooms, scraping burnt coffee out of the bottom of the coffee pot, running errands, and doing whatever it takes to keep the studio functioning. You will likely be doing some fun stuff, too: picking up celebrities at the airport, making script copies for film automated dialog replacement (ADR) sessions, or setting up chairs, music stands, and headphones for large orchestral dates.

The next stop on this career track is that of **receptionist**. What do receptionists do? It's pretty much the same at any business. Receptionists answer phones, take messages, help with paperwork, and keep the flow of communications going throughout the studio. They basically assist those above them with the operation of the business.

What do **schedulers** do? They book time. If I call a studio and say, "I've got a forty-member choir, and I wish to come in and record a Christmas album," and the scheduler books me into a small studio used for voiceover recording, there is going to be a problem. There is going to be a similar problem if I call and say, "I'm working on a film. I've got a 16 mm answer print, and I'd like to look at it and spot some library music to go with it," and the scheduler books me into a room that has VHS and Betacam video playback but no 16 mm film projection. Hence, schedulers must know quite a bit about a facility's capabilities and recording technology to do their job properly.

Where do schedulers come from? Often, assistant engineers who may not have the chops, the stamina, or the determination to pay their dues and make their way to first engineer become outstanding schedulers. Because they've actually worked with tape and time code, and have set up sessions and worked directly with the gear, the staff, producers, and clients, they know exactly what goes on during recording sessions.

That doesn't mean that someone can't learn how to schedule effectively without ever having done any engineering work. However, it's really helpful to know something about what's going on behind the door in the studio when you're scheduling. This knowledge will become even more critical the further you get from music recording and into sound for film, video, television, broadcast, or interactive programs and games.

By comparison, scheduling for music recording is more straightforward. Most albums are recorded in a three-step process: basic tracks, overdubs, and mix down. Each part of the album-making process has its own requirements, but the engineer and all or some of the musicians will be present for the majority of the work. The basic workflow is similar for most commercial albums, even if some portion of the work is done away from the main studio.

As soon as you start scheduling interactive, Internet sound, film, or music video projects, there are literally dozens of variables. Is the video NTSC, SECAM, or PAL (three non-compatible video-playback technologies used in different parts of the world)? What frame rate was the film or video shot at? Do you need Dolby Surround, Dolby Digital, Dolby E, or DTS? Is the talent union or nonunion? Is the source footage on film, video, or hard disk? Will you need library music, and if so, what genres, tempos, and instrumentation? Do you need to do a stereo mix or a separate mix with stems? What about a foreign language version? Splits for M&E (music and effects) and so on? Whew! The only way to learn and stay conversant with the myriad details involved is to immerse oneself into the daily operations of a studio doing this kind of work.

Our industry is heading into a new era of higher resolution digital audio and video consumers with Super Audio CD, Dual Disc DVD-Audio, as well as the two higher-resolution competing DVD Video formats, HD DVD and Blu-Ray. All this new technology creates demand for talented individuals to master the intricacies of producing and delivering entertainment media to consumers. There are opportunities to create a virtual sonic environment with 5.1 channel surround music recordings that will allow new levels of creativity and realism never before imagined. But in general, audio postproduction requires an encyclopedic knowledge of formats, technologies, and trends in broadcast production and delivery technologies. Put simply, there are more "gotchas" in postproduction than in music recording.

The next step on the career ladder is the **studio manager/sales** position. These people act as the right hand of the studio owners. They assign tasks, help navigate the course for the business, and often lead the staff. Studio managers will usually handle negotiations regarding lengthy bookings, any variation in studio rates, as well as personnel issues. It is their responsibility to work in tandem with the owners to see that the studio is showing a profit, so they need to be comfortable with budgets and basic accounting.

The studio manager is in charge of the day-to-day operation and the selling of studio time. When a regular client calls to book time, they usually speak with the scheduler. If a prospective client calls up and says, "Hey, I heard about your studio from another producer. I'm looking for a place to do a new album next year, and I want to know more about your facility," that call will be routed to the studio manager. The studio will invite them for a tour, play some tracks for them, and may introduce them to one of the engineers who calls that studio home. They will build rapport and foster the belief that this is the right place for that specific project. It's a challenging job. There is never a dull moment when you are in charge of a commercial studio operation.

And then there is the **studio owner**. What does a studio owner do today? He or she manages a team of very creative (and sometimes zany or temperamental) professionals, ruminates on the nature of the next swing of the technology pendulum, constantly reviews financial profitability and performance data, and goes down to the studio at 3 A.M. when the studio's burglar alarm has gone off! Those are just a few of the challenges that await the person who aspires to own a successful commercial facility.

When I left Music Annex in 1995, I had made one career decision for myself. After owning my own commercial studio for four years and working at another very successful facility for almost twelve years, I wasn't ever going to start a business where I had to spend more money every month buying, leasing, and maintaining equipment than I could pay myself. You see, owning a commercial recording studio means keeping up with the latest technology investments. Commercial studio ownership is not a career for the faint of heart. If you are to succeed, you quickly learn what it takes to keep clients satisfied and to keep a close eye on your overhead and bottom line.

As owner of a commercial recording studio, you are constantly considering what needs to be repaired, replaced, or upgraded. Will the new investment result in new revenue or simply in keeping your current clients and rates intact? There's not a day that goes by that you're not thinking about issues such as these.

One exception is if you own a noncommercial studio. If you have your own studio (and hopefully, the technology bug has not bitten you too severely), you can say, "Okay, I'm going to get my studio to a certain functional level. And then I will be satisfied for my needs. I can do my songwriting. I can do my demos. I can compose a soundtrack. I can even put out a homegrown CD, or market my music exclusively via the Internet on MySpace.com, PureVolume.com, or other free music sites." You aren't faced with adding more tracks, more vintage gear, a bigger lounge for the clients, a security guard for the parking lots, etc.

Today's savvy home-studio owner has the option of knowing, "When I am ready to make my magnum opus album, I'm going to go to XYZ studio to do the parts that I can't do at my studio. They've got a bunch of great mics, a concert grand piano, a boat-load of the finest reverbs and signal processors—it's all there. And I'll rent the use of it for the hours or days that I need it. But I don't need to own that very expensive gear year-round."

Heresy? No, just the voice of experience. Listen back to the *Sgt. Pepper's Lonely Hearts Club Band* album by the Beatles, and remind yourself that it was recorded forty years ago by some very creative musicians, engineers, and producers on 4-track equipment that was Stone-Age in comparison to most of the home recording gear available today.

The chart on the next page, based on the 2006 SPARS Salary Survey, gives an indication as to what salaries might be expected on the studio management ladder.

If you compare the earning power of these positions to the ones on the technical career track, one thing is immediately apparent at the early stage: there are far fewer unpaid positions in the management track.

The second difference is that there is a much greater range from the low- to the high-salary range for each position. That is due to two factors. First, the size of the studio business: larger studio operations will generally be able to pay more. The second factor is location.

A successful studio in one of the top markets will offer a more attractive compensation package to attract and retain top talent on their business team. Commercial studios in smaller regional markets will not be able to offer as much.

In a top market at a successful studio, a scheduler can expect to top out at around $55,000 in annual salary, while a studio manager may earn as much as $100,000 or more managing a top multiroom Hollywood, New York, or London studio. And then we have the owner. What is his or her salary range? Whatever they can pull out of a business that demands an incredible amount of attention, financial investment, and personal commitment. Some studio owners drive Ferraris and others drive Toyotas. There is no formula other than following careful business practices, and relying on the advice of finance and legal experts when needed to ensure that the commercial studio generates as much profit as possible in any given year.

SIMILAR BUSINESS STRUCTURES

No matter what sector of the music or entertainment industry you pursue, you will find very similar ladders of increasing responsibility, challenges, and rewards, in both the technical and the business arenas.

For instance, if you decide that you would like to be head of A&R at a record label or program director at a top radio station, you will need to do the research necessary to map out a career ladder similar to the ones outlined in the previous chapters. Determine the specific job titles, responsibilities, and earning potential on the career track leading to your goal. Researching and understanding the nitty-gritty details of the career ladder will help you avoid investing in a career path that may never meet your expectations for creative or financial development. Create a chart with the salaries, titles, and anticipated time frame for promotions before you dive fully into a career path. Doing so will help you to understand what it will take to get to the top in your field of interest.

MANAGEMENT CAREER TRACK: RECORDING STUDIO

Position	Salary
Gofer	Free to $8/hour
Receptionist	$8 to $16/hour
Scheduler	$12 to $26/hour
Studio Manager/Sales	$20 to $52/hour
Studio Owner	Feast or famine; it's up to you!

WORKSHOP 6. HOW MUCH WILL YOU EARN?

Researching salary information is one of the most challenging parts of your career planning and preparation. Fortunately, there are a few useful resources that we will look at more closely later in the book. Here's a starting list of resources that you can use now to check on entry-level salaries for your "dream job." (If your job is extremely specific, for instance, Front of House Mixer for a major touring act, you may find little salary information published and must rely on networking with current professionals to get a handle on current earning potential.)

1. Salary.com. A useful reference tool for basic salary ranges, especially for entry-level jobs such as production assistant, administrative assistant, marketing assistant, etc. Allows you to search by zip code or geographic region. A summer 2006 search for the job "Production Assistant" in the L.A. area revealed the average salary was $28,998.
2. Working Professionals. Do you know someone working in the field you hope to enter? If so, they are one of your best sources for entry-level salary information.
3. Trade organizations. Although we'll cover them in more depth in a future chapter, now's a good time to find out if the area of the industry you hope to enter has a trade association, and if so, whether they publish any general or specific salary or wage information.

Add the information from this workshop to your Career Binder.

CHAPTER 7 Excuse Me, What Do You Do?

This chapter's title is not meant to pose a facetious question. If you don't have a thorough understanding of the skills, responsibilities, hours, pay range, and future prospects for a particular job in the music industry, how can you assess whether or not you have (or can develop) the skills and connections to land that job?

There are two ways to research what working professionals actually do. The first and by far the more accessible method is to read up on a particular job. Keep up with current trade magazines and Web sites covering the segment of the industry that you wish to enter. If you aspire to be a label exec, agent, musician, or producer, then go to the library and check out a few biographies that chronicle the path that various artists or executives have taken to the top. Record producer Sir George Martin, musician Al Kooper, label executive Jac Holzman, and super agent Ian Copeland each have inked compelling autobiographies. Entertainment industry moguls Richard Branson and David Geffen have been profiled in bios, *Losing My Virginity* and *The Operator*, respectively. Richard Buskin's *Inside Tracks* and Maureen Droney's *Mix Masters* provide mini-interviews of many of the most influential record producers of the last fifty years of pop music. *Masters of Music*, by Mark Small and Andrew Taylor, features interviews with a wide range of music industry superstars who reveal how they broke into the big time.

With regard to locating written job descriptions for specific jobs, the Internet is becoming the number one source for finding job descriptions. Many music industry firms are now posting jobs and internships on one or more of the industry-specific career Web sites (see chapter 15). Additionally, the book referenced earlier, *Career Opportunities in the Music Industry*, has useful general descriptions for more than eighty music-oriented jobs.

The second means to find out the details of a particular career path is to network with professionals working in the business (see chapter 14). Depending on what jobs you are aspiring to, most likely, there are working professionals in your area with whom you can make contact. Although this type of research requires more effort on your part, the quality and quantity of information, along with the ability to ask specific questions and the recency of the information, make this a far more valuable resource than simply reading.

If you are enrolled in a school program in music business or recording arts, ask your faculty and fellow students to keep you posted on professionals who may be coming to school to speak or give clinics. Also, constantly seek out industry folk who have been helpful in the past in placing students as interns.

WORKSHOP 7. YOUR DREAM SHEET

This workshop is a series of questions to help you do a basic self-assessment of where you hope to go and what you hope to accomplish in the music business. It should be considered a living document, much like your résumé, kept on a computer disk, and updated regularly.

Fill out your Dream Sheet now, answering the questions by using a word processor or a few sheets of lined paper. When you complete the workshop, print it out and put it into the "My Journal" section of your Career Binder. Mark your Career Binder calendar six months ahead to read and update your Dream Sheet with the information you have learned in the interim.

Keep the earlier copies of your Dream Sheets so you can see how your perspectives evolve over time. A commentary is provided on the pages following the Dream Sheet, but don't look at it until you've completed all the questions in the workshop the first time.

1. What attracts you to a career in the music industry?

2. List, in order of preference, the three jobs you would most like to be doing in the music industry. Although you've been considering your "dream jobs" in earlier workshops, now it's time to focus on the top three and prioritize them.

   A.

   B.

   C.

3. Where do you want to be careerwise in five years? In ten years?

4. Where do you want to be personally and financially (salary range, own home, married/single/family, relocation) in five years? In ten years?

5. How much money do you think you could earn *in the next one to two years* if you landed any of the three jobs you listed above in question 2?

   Write down your best guess in the form of annual income.

   A.

   B.

   C.

6. Identify and list up to three jobs in which you have felt most fulfilled.

   A.

   B.

   C.

7. For each one, identify specifically what made you feel fulfilled.

   A.

   B.

   C.

8. Identify and list up to three jobs in which you have felt the least fulfilled.

   A.

   B.

   C.

9. For each one, identify specifically what made you feel unfulfilled.

   A.

   B.

   C.

10. Pick the number 1 company for whom you would like to work today. Imagine you are being considered for a plum internship opportunity at that company. Write a paragraph explaining what attributes make you the *best* candidate for the internship.

11. State the single, most important thing you hope to gain from a career in the music industry.

DREAM SHEET COMMENTARY

(Don't read this until you have finished your Dream Sheet!)

Question 1: Knowing what attracts you to a career in the music industry is important to help you prioritize the various options and choices you will be faced with during your career evolution.

Question 2: These are jobs that you need to continue researching in order to determine the skills, job prospects, and earning potential for each.

Question 3: Time waits for no one. Setting goals that include a rough timeline is an important part of developing your career successfully. You must also confirm that your objectives and timeline are realistic as you meet working professionals. Revise your objectives as you uncover the story behind the jobs that interest you most.

Question 4: It's a fact that your career development will require a number of years of dues-paying—working long hours for low wages in often underappreciated positions. Find out what people doing the jobs you aspire to do are earning as their careers evolve.

Question 5: You may be surprised to learn that many low-level positions in the industry pay about the same as working in a restaurant. Many students make the mistake of focusing on the top-tier salaries in a given field and don't adequately consider or prepare for making ends meet on an entry-level paycheck. Find out which career areas offer the best opportunities for advancement and salary growth. The best way to find out is to speak with working professionals. The polite way to ask is to inquire what the salary range is for a specific job.

Questions 6–9: Hopefully, you have had a job that you excelled in—one that made you feel that your contributions were important to the success of the company, regardless of what field it was in. Likewise, you may have also suffered through "the job from hell." Reviewing the high and low points of jobs is another important step in assessing what kinds of tasks and duties you have been successful at. Finding the job you love and can excel in is often the most direct path to career and financial success. There's truth in the old saying, "Do what you really love, and the money will follow." Going through this exercise will also help you discuss these points, which are often brought up in job interviews.

Question 10: If you can't articulate your passion for a career in the music industry, you likely will fail to make a lasting impression on your future boss. Every performer, manager, or producer I know drives himself or herself relentlessly to be the absolute best.

Question 11: Is it money, power, fame, or artistic fulfillment? Knowing this will also help you reach decisions when your career comes to the inevitable forks in the road. It's okay to be attracted by fame and fortune; just remember that you have to make ends meet on your journey to the top.

CHAPTER 8 Analyzing Job Descriptions

There is no better way to gauge your readiness for a particular job than to look over a detailed job description or job profile. As when we learned to analyze career ladders in chapters 5 and 6, we'll now dissect two job descriptions so that you are familiar with the job description analysis process. Let's start with a job profile for a record label intern, reprinted from *Career Opportunities in the Music Industry.*[1]

RECORD LABEL INTERN

Career Profile

Duties: Performing tasks in specific departments of a record company while learning the business under the direction of management.

Alternate Title: Trainee

Salary Range: $0–$15,000

Employment Prospects: Fair

Advancement Prospects: Good

Best Geographical Locations for Position: New York City, Los Angeles, and Nashville

Prerequisites: Education or Training: High school diploma minimum; other requirements depend on position

Experience: No experience required

Special Skills and Personality Traits: Eagerness to learn; brightness; aggressiveness; knowledge of music and/or recording business; other skills, dependent on specific position

Career Ladder:

Clerical position
Student intern
Staffer in department

---

1 From *Career Opportunities in the Music Industry, Fifth Edition* by Shelly Field. Copyright 2004 by Shelly Field. Reprinted by permission of Facts on File, Inc.

POSITION DESCRIPTION

An intern working in a record company will perform many of the same duties as other people on staff. The intern works under the supervision of a department head, manager, or director. One of the advantages of obtaining an internship in a specific department is that the individual has the opportunity to learn the ropes from experienced people.

There are interns in almost every department of a record company. In certain companies, one becomes an intern in a single department. In others, the individual's internship involves working in various departments of the company. Duties will depend on the department to which one is assigned. For instance, an intern working in the publicity/press relations department may address invitations to press parties, make calls to check whether various people will be attending press parties, and help make arrangements for the press function. As he or she gains experience, the intern might begin writing press releases, attending meetings to work out publicity campaigns, or calling the media to discuss a good story.

An intern working in the marketing department might work on consumer research surveys, tabulate data, and/or call radio stations and the trades with information about the number of records sold in a specific market. As time goes on, the intern may learn to develop marketing campaigns, go out with field reps, or help the director create a sales incentive program.

The intern usually begins by handling a lot of the tedious work that no one else wants to do. As he or she becomes more experienced, the intern learns how to perform more difficult tasks. Only the simplest of projects is performed without supervision.

Whether or not the intern is getting paid a salary, he or she is expected to function like a paid employee. This includes arriving to work on time and not taking time off unnecessarily. It is to the intern's advantage to learn as much as possible through instruction, asking questions, and just working in a hands-on situation.

The individual is responsible to the supervisor or department head to which he or she is assigned. If the intern is using the internship as part of a college experience, a paper on the work experience may be expected.

A good intern has a fairly good chance of becoming a member of the company staff after the internship has concluded.

SALARIES

Interns may work and not earn a penny. If they do earn a salary, it is usually quite small. An individual who has obtained an internship through a college might receive college credit for his or her work. If the intern is lucky enough to receive a salary, it probably would range from $5,000 to $15,000.

EMPLOYMENT PROSPECTS

Despite the low pay or even lack of pay, many people want to work as interns. Internships can be found in almost any department of every major record company. Smaller labels tend to offer fewer internships, but these types of labels are spread more evenly around the country.

Although many of these internship programs may be located directly through the record company, there are a number that can be obtained through schools and colleges in return for credit and hands-on experience.

ADVANCEMENT PROSPECTS

One of the major reasons so many people become interns in this industry is that an outstanding performance as an intern almost guarantees a job in the record company. After all the training and instruction, the company most likely will want to keep the intern in its employ. The person must, of course, be a good employee and learn the trade. Interns can advance their careers very quickly in most departments. They may first be promoted to staffers, and then become coordinators, supervisors, or directors in various departments.

EDUCATION AND TRAINING

To become an intern in a record company, the only education required may be a high school diploma. If an individual is currently in college, he or she may be able to have the school assist in securing an internship placement with a company for college credit. The person may be working toward a degree in any subject that can be made relevant to a semester or summer in a record company. Majors might include business, advertising, music, communications, journalism, the social sciences, pre-law, etc.

EXPERIENCE/SKILLS/PERSONALITY

Interns do not really need any experience. What is required is the desire to enter the industry and an eagerness to learn all about it.

Individuals who are chosen to be interns are generally bright, articulate, aggressive, and have pleasant personalities. A knowledge of music and/or the recording business is a plus.

Students or recent graduates are likely to start their career path working in clerical positions, before moving to internships. If you work hard, an opportunity may open up to become a staffer in one of the various departments in the label. Locate a copy of *Career Opportunities in the Music Industry* and review other listings for record label positions such as "Staff Publicist" or "Promotions Staffer." Each will reference its own career ladder.

TIPS FOR ENTRY:

- If you are in college, your faculty advisor or the school's career center may know of specific companies that offer internships. If the school has a music business, recording arts, or music-products curriculum, or offers courses, it might have an internship program already established with companies in the music industry.
- Contact record labels and other companies in the music/entertainment industry to see if they offer intern programs or if you can develop an internship.
- If you live in one of the music capitals, you might want to visit the companies personally to see if you can get an internship in one of the departments.
- Interns are often chosen from the ranks of clerical workers in the office. Talk to the head of the department with which you want to work.

If you're serious about a career in the music industry, you must unearth this type of detailed job and earnings information. If you haven't done the research and you just blunder along, how do you know you're going to get where you want? How will you know a job has the potential to earn what you want to earn?

JOB DESCRIPTIONS

Let's examine a job description for a position creating music and sound effects for a computer-game developer.

A job description such as this one helps you to lay out a career roadmap, which is the specific skills, talents, and experience needed to obtain that position and prosper in a particular area of the industry. In tandem with an area-specific career ladder, you then have both the general and specific tools to measure your readiness for that position. By developing a career roadmap, you will be able to know where you're headed and if you have arrived, so don't embark on your career without one.

By developing a career roadmap, you will be able to know where you're headed and if you have arrived, so don't embark on your career without one.

With a job description in hand, take an inventory of the skills and knowledge required to fill the position successfully, and determine the areas in which you may be lacking knowledge.

Job Title: Game sound designer; full-time, salaried position

Position Summary: This person will work with software designers and senior sound staff to create music and sounds for the company's latest products. In addition to maintaining the highest possible audio-production values, the sound designer will be responsible for adhering to the stylistic approach determined for the specific product. Ability to complete work within an established timeline is required.

Job Responsibilities:

- Edit sound effects and synchronize with animation and other interactive elements of the product
- Edit dialog
- Compose music segments, songs, and cues to enhance the product
- Arrange music for the types of synthesizers utilized in PC and Mac computers as well as general MIDI synthesizers
- Review sounds and music to be developed with product-development team and software engineers to ensure playability
- Stay current on various developments in MIDI playback systems for computer applications

Qualifications:

- Ability to compose music in a wide range of musical styles.
- Four-year degree in music or equivalent practical musical knowledge that can be demonstrated through composition and arranging examples.
- Extensive experience arranging music for various types of synthesizers including those commonly used in the general MIDI specification. Thorough knowledge of synthesis techniques, patch editing, and sequencing software.
- Familiarity with digital sound-editing tools such as Digital Performer, Pro Tools, and Sound Forge. Strong understanding of the principles of digital audio and the physical properties of sound. Must know the basic sound properties of the various families of musical instruments (strings, brass, woodwinds, percussion, etc.).
- Experience with Macintosh, Windows, and MS-DOS computers required. Basic knowledge of computer language such as C++ helpful but not mandatory. Practical experience in a recording studio environment is a plus.

Analysis

This job description is clearly written with lots of specific information as to the skills and experience that the employer is seeking to fill this position. Although it's not specifically spelled out, a qualified candidate should have experience playing videogames. Much like film scoring, videogame music serves the needs of the game or story line.

The successful candidate for this position will have a good body of experience as a composer, sound designer, and arranger. He or she will have a strong music and composition background and be well versed in MIDI. Note that although composing is generally a solitary pursuit, this position requires frequent interaction with other members of the software-development team.

In fact, working collaboratively and adhering to deadlines may be as important considerations as innate compositional abilities. Videogame creation requires dozens of creative individuals working in various areas (animation, music, programming, etc.) to work as part of a large team to create a successful product.

In addition to composing and sound design, the successful candidate will also be capable of editing dialog and working in a recording studio setting. This job description makes it easy to create a checklist of the skills that are required and for a candidate to then compare his or her skill set to see if this person is in fact a viable candidate for the position.

WORKSHOP 8. WHAT'S IN A JOB DESCRIPTION?

Use the Internet to find a job description in one of your career areas of interest. Print it out, and take an inventory of what specific skills, traits, experience, and other qualifications the employer is seeking. The more detailed the job description is the better.

Don't worry if it's not exactly the dream job you hope to land. The purpose of this workshop is to teach you how to dissect a job description and summarize the key qualifications the employer is seeking. If you have difficulty locating a useful job description for this workshop, try some of the entertainment industry career Web sites referenced in chapter 15.

CHAPTER 9 Your Marketable Skill Set

What follows is my "Skill-Set Assessment" worksheet—a tool that will help you to achieve your career goals by identifying your marketable skills. For instance, if you are fluent in a second language, that linguistic proficiency is a component of your unique marketable skill set. You have two types of marketable skills. The first type is your foundation skills—the ones you'll need for any job in today's world. Second is job-specific skills that will be required for you to excel in a specific position in the music industry.

If you are at the beginning of your skill-set development, don't tackle specifying your marketable skill set just yet. Instead, read over this section and remember to come back to it after you have spent some time in school or in an on-the-job-training situation, such as an industry internship. Then see how your evolving skills stack up against what you have discovered is needed for a particular music-industry job. Otherwise the exercise may prove frustrating to you.

If you have already developed a number of these skills, jump in and learn how to assess your marketable skill set against the ones required for the positions you are seeking.

> *....when an employer considers whether or not to hire you, they're basically trying to answer one question, "What is this person going to do to make my life easier?"*

To increase your "hire-ability," your marketable skill set should be made up of the skills that a prospective employer would look at and say, "We can use this person's particular set of skills around here." That's because when an employer considers whether or not to hire you, they're basically trying to answer one question, "What is this person going to do to make my life easier?"

That's the single most crucial question you must clearly answer when you set out to create a strong résumé or go for a job interview. What are you going to be able to do to make your next boss's life better and easier, and make the company more efficient and profitable? Your marketable skill set lays out what you're able to do to help your prospective employer.

WORKSHOP 9.1. FOUNDATION SKILLS ASSESSMENT

Taking an inventory of your own marketable skills is a key step in your career development. In today's fast-paced entertainment world, foundation skills are a prerequisite to being considered for most jobs.

Rate your foundation skills below.

	STRONG	MODERATE	NEEDS WORK
Reading and writing	☐	☐	☐
Verbal communication	☐	☐	☐
Listening	☐	☐	☐
Understanding and following instructions	☐	☐	☐
Observing and assessing situations and problems	☐	☐	☐
Decision making	☐	☐	☐
Computer word processing	☐	☐	☐
Computer database ability	☐	☐	☐
Computer spreadsheet ability	☐	☐	☐
Internet navigation and research	☐	☐	☐

Action Item: Which areas need improvement? Decide now on a timeline and a means to improve those areas that will strengthen your foundation skills. Write them down in your Career Binder as a short-term goal, and assign a due date on your calendar for each skill you need to strengthen.

The first six skills are interpersonal skills that most people will have developed some proficiency through school, social, and business situations. The last four relate specifically to computers and the Internet. Today's job seeker must have a basic knowledge of those functions in order to be a productive member of any music or entertainment-industry company.

If you believe you could benefit from strengthening your interpersonal skills, you should see a counselor at your school or local community college and investigate what type of class will help you develop your skills in this area. Speech, language, and writing classes are a few that can help. For computer skills and applications, community colleges offer a low-cost means to develop satisfactory basic skills in each of the four crucial computing areas mentioned in the list above.

ANALYZING A SAMPLE MARKETABLE SKILL SET

As an example, let's look at the marketable skill set for an aspiring recording engineer. Remember, this example is illustrative of the level of detail you need to comprehend for your own industry job, regardless of what area of the industry you hope to work in.

MARKETABLE SKILL SET FOR AUDIO ENGINEER

Foundation Skills

- Reading/writing/following instructions
- Ability to communicate clearly
- Ability to stay calm and cool
- Basic computer skills

Job-Specific Skills

- Critical listening skills
- Audio engineering expertise
- A good "bedside manner"

Here's a breakdown of the critical skills that today's recording engineer must possess or develop.

FOUNDATION SKILLS

1. **You have to be able to read, write, and (yes,) follow instructions.** Why is it critical in a recording studio to follow instructions? Well, you could damage the equipment. You're working with people's master recordings that are the result of thousands of hours and perhaps hundreds of thousands of dollars' investment. More importantly, following instructions means that the studio, the first engineer, or the head tech can say, "Tim, go take care of this for me." That person is not always going to have the time to sit and coach Tim through that activity. So they must be confident that Tim is going to be able to listen, integrate what the request is, and get it properly accomplished. If that's the case, then Tim is a person a studio will want to employ. Because they can teach, mentor, and coach him, they can move him ahead on the career track. They can develop a valuable employee for the firm. Following instructions is critical to learning how to work successfully in any type of a studio or production environment.

2. **The ability to communicate clearly.** Many times when I was engineering a recording session, the producer or an artist said, "It just isn't right. I don't know what it is. It isn't getting me." We often spent hours trying to find out what it would take to "get them." Or you may find yourself working with musicians from another culture or a new genre of music. You have to be able to communicate clearly in order to be as efficient as possible in the recording studio. Many of the delays and problems encountered in the studio are the result of poor or a complete lack of communication skills.

   Knowing *when* to communicate is also crucial. I mentioned earlier the psychology skills an engineer must develop. With practice, you'll learn when to tell an artist, "This isn't working, what if we tried something like..." You also must know when it's more appropriate to remain quiet and allow the producer or recording artist to solve that problem for themselves.

3. **The ability to stay calm and cool.** Artists get emotional in the studio. They're pouring out their whole persona into their performance for everyone to hear. So, they do get emotional. A capable engineer must know how to stay cool when an artist vents their frustration. I've been in sessions where fights have broken out in the mix room between management and the band. People have actually taken a poke at each other. Generally, that's not conducive to the creative process. You have to stay cool, and you have to remember your job is to keep the project on track.

4. **Basic computer skills.** How much computer knowledge do you need to make it as a recording engineer? Many aspiring sound engineers and producers have a good deal of knowledge and experience working on a computer in a sound recording and editing program. That's certainly a plus. The more you know, the more valuable you'll be. But you also need to master the basics such as how to type a letter with word processing software. You must know what a database is and how it works. You must know spreadsheet functions so you can use the computer to add, subtract, multiply, and divide. You must be comfortable with those three basic applications, in addition to the computer's sound recording platforms.

   As mentioned earlier, you can get adequate computer "basic training" at your local community college. A basic computer class covering these applications will teach the fundamentals.

   If you walk into your first day as an intern or a gofer, and your boss tells you, "Go log these fifty tapes into the tape library," and he points you to the computer and you can't figure it out, you're out.

   Should you be proficient on the Macintosh or the PC platform? Good question. Those using the computer for composing, sequencing, and making music tend to use the Mac. The folks who are counting the beans, checking whether the gear has been fixed or not, and managing the business are for the most part running PCs.

   It's helpful to know both. All of the best computer editing software for sound and music initially was Mac-based. However, during the last few years, the PC is coming on strong with respect to music software, and many formerly Mac-based programs now run on the PC platform, too.

JOB-SPECIFIC SKILLS

5. **Critical listening skills.** When I was working as a producer, a computer company came to me and said, "We made this disk of samples with some musical instrument sounds on it for computer users. It shows musical instrument graphics on the screen and then plays that instrument's sounds. We're getting quite a few back with complaints about the sound."

   So they sent me one of the disks, and we loaded it up and played the sound file. It was a little tiny sound file, at a very low sampling rate. (Remember what the videogame "Pong" sounded like?) And it sounded like a chainsaw. I told them, "Well, we don't have the original sound source to do a comparison, but it kind of sounds like a chainsaw."

And they said, "Oh no, no, that's a clarinet!" So the end users were seeing a picture of a kid playing a clarinet on their computer screen, but they were hearing this chainsaw sound. It had been sampled with so much distortion that it didn't even sound like a musical instrument anymore. In the studio, no one was listening to see if the musical instrument samples really sounded like instruments! That's an extreme—but real—example of how critical listening skills could have saved a lot of time, money, and headaches.

If you have not listened to or experienced music in an acoustic environment, you may not know what you're listening for, and you're going to have problems as an engineer. So, you've got to listen to music. And not just recorded music, because recorded music is an illusion of a performance, even if it is a live performance. The well-respected engineer and producer Bruce Swedien encourages up-and-coming engineers to get out and experience every type of music there is in a concert setting, from rock to opera to string quartets to jazz, folk, big band, and blues. Bruce reminds young engineers that records are sonic illusions or sound paintings. In order to become a competent engineer, you have to build up a library in your mind of what instruments sound like naturally—one at a time and in ensembles. Truer words were never spoken.

View your time spent developing listening skills just as you would doing homework. Go out once a week or once a month. Listen to classical, listen to jazz. If you want to be a recording engineer, you need to hear it all. Because one day, you're going to be in a session, and somebody is going to come in with an accordion, a didgeridoo, a harp, or a banjo. You should know how each instrument should sound.

One day, I was engineering a jingle session and the producer brought in a gentleman who said, "I'm a whistler." That was one of the hardest things I ever had to record in my engineering career. I had to experiment with a number of different setups to get it right. But I started by just standing in the room with him and moving around to assess how he sounded in different spots in the room as he whistled, before I even plugged in a mic.

6. **Having audio expertise.** You have to develop a thorough knowledge of audio, such as signal flow, phase, and microphone selection and placement. Whether you are self-taught or went to a recording school, you have to acquire the basic knowledge of how to make a recording, do overdubs, and handle a mixdown efficiently.

7. **Having a good bedside manner.** That's the mood or tone that an engineer sets as they work with a client or artist on a session. Why is that important? The most successful studio engineers I know are the ones that create an environment that is conducive to getting creative work done. The finest equipment doesn't mean a thing if the vibe is not good in the studio. Even if you have a $750,000 recording console, what good is it if when the artist walks in, he or she doesn't feel comfortable? If artists are cared for, even pampered, a good engineer will capture their best performance.

   So now you know the basic marketable skill set required to have a solid career in engineering. When a student asks me, "Keith, what do I have to do to get a job as an engineer?" Well, get those seven things together. The first six, you can learn in school. The seventh, there's only one way to learn it: experience. You've got to sit down in a session and watch other experienced engineers work, in order to observe and learn what's good about their bedside manners. That's why it's a good idea to start out at an established studio that provides some training or internships. That way, you can learn from pros.

   It's also very helpful if you've played music, can read music, or are conversant with the musical language. Know enough about musical structure to understand what forte, ritardando, and the "B" section of a musical chart represent. If you are booked to record a Dixieland band next week, go to a record store or online and buy a couple of well-regarded Dixieland records. It won't break your bank account to spend a few bucks and a couple of hours listening to them to understand how the instruments blend and how the solos sit in the mix.

   Then, when that Dixieland band walks in and you meet the musicians, you've already got a point of departure to build a rapport. You can say, "Yeah, I bought a Turk Murphy recording, and I was checking out how these guys sounded together." The band will think, "My engineer took the time to learn something about what we do. All right! Let's make a great recording."

WORKSHOP 9.2. JOB-SPECIFIC SKILLS ASSESSMENT

Look back at your Dream Sheet from Workshop 7, which should be copied and resident in the "My Journal" section of your Career Binder.

You identified three specific music industry jobs that interested you (question 2). For each job, it will be up to you to uncover what specific key skills are necessary to enter that career path.

Now, log the skills that you uncover and determine which ones you need to develop. Photocopy this page for each job, so you can start to assess what job-specific skills you'll need to build on top of your foundation skills.

Marketable Skill Set: Job-Specific Skills Assessment

Job Title: ______________________________

SKILL LIST	HAVE	NEED
______________________	☐	☐
______________________	☐	☐
______________________	☐	☐
______________________	☐	☐
______________________	☐	☐
______________________	☐	☐
______________________	☐	☐
______________________	☐	☐
______________________	☐	☐
______________________	☐	☐

You may not be able to identify all the skills required for a specific job all at once. Keep each sheet updated as you speak with working professionals, review job skills, and read interviews with persons doing the job you are researching. In a very short time, you'll have most of the key skills identified.

Next, identify the career progression in the chosen field you are researching. (Add second column on right for salary ranges.)

Entry-level position: ____________________ Salary range: __________

Advances to: ____________________ Salary range: __________

Advances to: ____________________ Salary range: __________

Advances to: ____________________ Salary range: __________

Advances to: ____________________ Salary range: __________

Here is a sample completed job-specific skill assessment sheet for a recording engineer job seeker named Jan Carlson.

MARKETABLE SKILL SET:

Job-Specific Skills Assessment for Jan Carlson

Job Title: Music Recording Engineer

SKILL LIST	HAVE	NEED
Critical listening skills	☑	☐
Practical audio knowledge, signal flow	☑	☐
Recording session experience	☑	☐
Knowledge of music and instruments	☑	☐
Microphone and mic placement knowledge	☑	☐
Analog record/edit skills	☐	☑
Digital record/edit skills	☑	☐
Computer, MIDI, and music software skills	☑	☐
Good bedside manner with clients	☐	☑

Next, identify the career progression in the chosen field you are researching.

Entry-level position: *Gofer, Studio Runner, or Assistant* Salary range: *Free–$9/hr*

Advances to: *Assistant or Second Engineer* Salary range: *Free–$20/hr*

Advances to: *First Engineer* Salary range: *$15–$20/hr*

Advances to: *Elite Engineer or Engineer/Producer* Salary range: *$35–$75+/hr*

RESEARCHING VARIOUS JOB SKILL SETS

Using the marketable skill-set workshops ("Foundation Skills" and "Job-Specific Skills") in combination with an employer's job description will allow you to assess quickly and realistically how far along towards a particular job you may be. Don't worry if at first you don't appear to have some of the skills required. Few of us did when we started out, and just identifying the marketable skills you will need to develop puts you a step ahead of the wannabes who spend their time dreaming about the industry job they wish they could obtain. You'll already have identified the skills that will make your own particular music industry career dream a reality.

Use these workshops over and over. When something new occurs to you, you think, "What about Internet radio? What about publishing rights—perhaps I can go into that?" Never throw out your completed sheets. Put them in your Career Binder for future reference.

At the bottom of the Job-Specific Skills Assessment Workshop page is the particular career path. While you're completing this part of the workshop, it's also time to do some basic salary research.

You've started researching music industry salaries in a previous workshop. Now it's time to learn about the earning potential in various jobs. Talk to people in the field, and look at what is available in print. You have to be able to survive while you build your career. If you haven't done your earning homework and later find out firsthand that you can't get by on what the lower rungs of your career ladder pay, you may be setting yourself up for early failure.

Your completed marketable skill-set workshops will come in handy in the next chapter, as you begin to build your résumé. Knowing what skills are required to be an A&R assistant, a music publicist, or a booking agent will help you craft a résumé and cover letter that demonstrate that you have invested in building the necessary skills to tackle the job duties required for success in that position.

Although you can find a lot of valuable information in books, I strongly encourage you to then review the workshop data with a working professional in that field. It's important to validate your findings not only on salary ranges, but also on key skills and the career path as you have researched it.

A final point about your research and completion of the marketable skill-set workshops. Although you can find a lot of valuable information in books, I strongly encourage you to then review the workshop data with a working professional in that field. It's important to validate your findings not only on salary ranges, but also on key skills and the career path as you have researched it. Checking and verifying these facts will help you to attain some peace of mind as you begin the career journey ahead.

CHAPTER 10 Building a Winning Résumé

JAN N. CARLSON

36362 Shining Star Court, Fremont, CA 94538 • (H) 510 767-1111 • jncarlson@yahoo.com

Objective

To obtain an entry-level position as an assistant sound engineer in the film/music industry

Work Experience

Staff Engineer, Bill Smythe Creative Services
2002–2004
Oakland, CA

Assisted leading composer of film scores with engineering, session setup, and all aspects of studio productions. Engineered over 12 film and video soundtracks. Planned and executed upgrade of new MIDI studio including drawings, wiring, and installation, saving the cost of hiring an outside installation firm.

Technical Manager, Audio, San Francisco State University Technical Services
2004–2005
San Francisco, CA

Coordinated all sound reinforcement work done on campus. Worked with artists and management to determine sound reinforcement needs for each show and supervised setup, operation, and teardown for 52 shows. Set up maintenance tracking system and student repair teams to lower amount of equipment out of service and speed up repairs, resulting in increased productivity of department and letter of commendation.

Education

San Francisco State University
2001–2005
San Francisco, CA
BA, Broadcast and Electronic Communication Arts

Other Skills

- Own and operate Pro Tools–based home studio for personal projects
- Ten years experience playing the guitar
- Ability to read, write, and understand music
- Working knowledge of MIDI and Macintosh sequencing software, knowledge of Macintosh, Windows, and MS-DOS

Professional Memberships

- Associate member of NARAS
- Student member of AES, Treasurer of SFSU Chapter

Hobbies & Interests

- Backpacking, camping, fishing, and collecting blues recordings

References available upon request.

THE CHRONOLOGICAL RÉSUMÉ

The most important document you will develop over the course of your career is your résumé. Whether it's a one-pager when you're getting your career started or a two- to three-pager for a grizzled veteran, your written résumé has to effectively communicate everything you can bring to the workplace. It must stand out from a pile of résumés on the desk of a potential employer.

Résumé Example: Take a look at the Carlson résumé, modeled closely on that of one of my former students who is now working in the audio post-production industry.

This is a *chronological résumé.* What does that mean? It's laid out in the order of time, from the most recent accomplishments to the older ones. This is also called reverse chronological order. We'll look at another type of résumé shortly.

Remember, your professional résumé is a marketing tool designed to secure the next step in the job acquisition process, usually an interview. It is not your autobiography, your life story, nor must it include every job or volunteer activity you've engaged in. The more directly you can explain to a prospective employer what you are seeking with respect to your career, and make the case for why you are a qualified candidate, the more likely it is your résumé will result in interviews and job offers.

In both sample résumés, job objective is narrowed down to one sentence or statement. Candidates at the entry level should be saying, "I'm here to learn; please teach me." Those with more experience should highlight their relevant experience for the position they are applying for. The position sought in our sample chronological résumé, Assistant Sound Engineer, means they are looking for a specific job in the film/music industry. It's broad but not *too* broad. They didn't say "the record business, recording." As you read further down this résumé, you can see whether or not this person's **work experience** supports the career path listed in their job objective. In this case, it does. They've already taken some important career development steps. They've assisted in recording film scores and have done engineering and rudimentary sound design. Their résumé points to a likely career path in audio production for film and video soundtracks.

This person's **education** is listed as well as some interests and activities. She stated her degree as briefly as possible, listing the school, the course of study, degree conferred, and when she was enrolled. You need not list anything else. Specifics about course-work completed or your GPA may be shared during an interview, if necessary, unless the employer specifically asks you to include this information on your application or résumé.

Other skills are an important category on this résumé. For this person, it's a clear-cut way to list some of her other marketable skills, demonstrating experience with technology and music.

Two affiliations are noted under **professional memberships**. A few **hobbies and interests** are listed on the sample résumé to help the candidate stand out from the competition.

The sample résumé's overall presentation is very solid, tight, and has an extremely clean look. It uses white space effectively, thereby avoiding the overly crowded, difficult-to-read document many students develop. Toss it in a pile of résumés, and it's got name recognition as well as simplicity to help it stand out.

THE "OTHER" RÉSUMÉ—A FUNCTIONAL RÉSUMÉ

Another way to present yourself is via a functional résumé. It lists accomplishments in the order you feel best represents your qualifications for a particular career path. In which instance would you consider developing a functional rather than a chronological résumé? Usually, a functional résumé is most appropriate when you either have gaps in your timeline or you're changing careers.

Maybe you've worked as a legal clerk for the last five years. Prior to that, you worked in radio, and you're ready to get back to broadcasting. You don't want the very first thing a screener reads under experience to be your clerking for a large law firm. Because when they get that over at K-101, they're going to think, "H-m-m-m, she's a law clerk wanting to get back into the business." Probable destination for that résumé: shredder pile!

In this scenario, use a functional résumé to highlight your skills. In the radio/law example, you'd lead with your radio experience and accomplishments and list your legal work later in the résumé. That's the difference between chronological and functional. But I would estimate that more than 90 percent of the time, a chronological résumé is the best approach in the early stages of your music industry career.

Here's an example of a functional résumé that would be effective in the scenario just described. Note that the current law job only occupies one line of space on this résumé.

MARYANN L. JOHNSON

422 E. 8th Street, Apt. 4B, Tacoma, WA 98523
mljohnson404@yahoo.com • (253) 317-0488

Job Objective

Contribute to the success of a radio station through my skills in sales, marketing, and customer service

Qualifications

- Five years experience in radio station sales and operations including both commercial and college stations
- Outstanding people skills, including conversational Spanish, as well as strong written and oral communication skills
- Comfortable in fast-paced, multitasking environment; adept at team building and problem solving in a business setting
- Success at regularly meeting and exceeding sales goals as an inside ad-sales rep for FM 104.1

Professional Skills

- Proficient in running MS Office, ACT contact management software, MS Access database, Photoshop, Dreamweaver, and MS Publisher
- Operations and on-air experience at college station KPLU radio; Class III broadcasting license
- Supervisory experience co-managing staff of 20 at KPLU

Employment History

- Legal and Research Assistant, Baron, Bowles & Smithers, LLC; Seattle, WA—9/2001 to 6/2006
- Inside Sales Representative, FM 104.1 (Champion Broadcasting), Seattle, WA—6/1999 to 8/2001
- Assistant Station Manager, KPLU Radio, Pacific Lutheran College, Tacoma, WA—8/1998 to 5/1999
- Sales Manager, On Air Talent, KPLU Radio, Pacific Lutheran College, Tacoma, WA—8/1996 to 8/1998

Awards and Achievements

- Inside Sales Rep of the Year, FM 104.1, 2000–2001
- Three-time recipient of Tacoma volunteer "Star" award for planning, organizing, and leading three successful canned-food drives (1998–2000)

Education

B.A. in Humanities, Minor in Spanish; Pacific Lutheran College, May 1999

References Available on Request

Note that this functional résumé really drives home the point that this candidate is someone who is well versed in radio-station operations and sales, and has a measurable track record of success in the broadcasting industry. It goes a long way toward leading the résumé screener to see her past successes and how the skills and talent are likely to be transferable to a current job in radio.

How should this candidate handle the five years outside radio working in the legal field? The best way will be in person during an interview, and most often, the direct approach is best. State why you changed fields; what you hoped to achieve, what changed your mind, and why you believe you are qualified for the current job.

"I was considering going to law school and before making that investment, I thought I'd work in a successful law firm to get a better understanding of how lawyers work. Although I learned a great deal and enjoyed my time in the field, I realize I'm not cut out for practicing law, and I realize that my first passion, radio, is what has always been the most exciting to me."

Don't copy either of these résumés directly. Rather, look at what is in each, the phrases used, and how it clearly states a case that this person would be a valuable asset to a company in her respective industry. References to these sample résumés will be included over the following chapters, so leave a bookmark near it so you can quickly flip back to them.

MAKING YOUR RÉSUMÉ A "HIT"

There are two sayings about songwriting that apply equally to your résumé development. One states, "A song hasn't been written until it's been rewritten." And another, that songwriting is "10 percent inspiration and 90 percent perspiration." Just like a hit song, the best résumés have appeal, hooks, and are very easy to digest. They leave the reader with a memorable impression. They are compact and use the minimum number of words to make the maximum impression. Accomplishing these goals requires a serious investment of time and commitment. In the semester-long class I teach at Pacific, students spend five weeks writing and rewriting their résumés until they are presentable to an employer. As your résumé evolves, you will continually massage it, trying to figure out a way to boil a paragraph down to ten words. Tighten your career objective from thirty words to twelve words. That's the nature of the task.

A colleague of mine who is a senior human-resources executive once shared an interesting fact with me. I had always been under the impression that the people who screen résumés, especially at larger firms, looked for the strongest résumés of those submitted. I was surprised to learn that it's often actually the opposite case.

In many larger companies, a résumé screener's job is to look for mistakes: to take as many résumés as they can and justifiably put them in the shredder. Why? "This one is full of misspellings." (Buzzzzzz … goes the shredder.) "This one says she only will work in A&R." (Buzzzzzzzz.) "This one says he wants to be the president of the label." (Buzzzzzzz.)

In a large organization, the résumé screener's job is not to pick the strongest résumé; it's to leave a pile of non-offensive résumés for their supervisor's review. That's why you cannot afford the slightest error or mistake on your résumé. It can quickly eliminate you from consideration.

So, your first task in the résumé quest is to commit yourself to developing a résumé without negatives and errors. You'd be surprised at how many résumés I have seen over the years in which people stated, "I really hated this job, so I quit," or something to that effect, right on their résumé! We've all had a job we didn't like, but please, don't put that on your résumé.

It's critically important to make sure that your résumé is read and proofread by other people—ideally a professional, such as a career counselor at your school or college—before you send it to a potential employer. What does it say about you and your attention to the details of life and work if your résumé includes typos, spelling, or grammatical mistakes?

Your résumé must be compact, concise, typed or word processed, well laid out, and clean looking. If you have access to a computer, you can generally lay it out on your own. If you don't, go to a shop such as Kinko's and rent computer time. Type up your résumé after you have developed a handwritten draft and proofed it (with the help of some extra eyes) a few times. Be sure to save your résumé electronically, and keep it handy, perhaps on a portable hard drive, so you have it available to update it regularly. Your résumé should be a tool you continually enhance and improve as your entertainment career develops.

NEVER UNDERESTIMATE THE POWER OF A STRONG RÉSUMÉ

A well-crafted résumé is a strong statement of why you are a leading candidate for a prospective opening. In many cases, it will be the *only* chance you have to sell yourself to your future boss in the initial efforts by an employer to fill a position.

Let's say there's a job opportunity in New York (and you live elsewhere), and you hear about it through your network. What's the first step you take? You should call up and confirm that the company is looking for someone with some of the same qualifications you possess. They'll say, "Send us your résumé." Well, are you going to fly there to give it to them? Probably not, unless you're heading for a senior-level position.

You're going to mail, fax, or e-mail them your résumé. This piece of paper represents you: your life, your skills, your value, your net worth, your total marketable skills to date that relate to that job or career path. Will it be the best, strongest, tightest document you can create or a quickie that you copied out of a résumé book you picked up the night before?

In this same scenario, another candidate simply mails in a naked résumé. You sent in a résumé and a well-written cover letter. Your cover letter is another opportunity for you to highlight the key points on your résumé, point out things that you have done that have created value in the past, and show that you have some knowledge of the company and the position the employer is looking to fill. All these things will separate you from the pack, and help you avoid the hungry résumé shredder. So always make the time to write a solid cover letter. (You'll learn how to craft a knockout cover letter in a few chapters.)

YOUR RECIPE FOR A TOP-NOTCH RÉSUMÉ

It's time to roll up your sleeves and develop a résumé that will set you apart from the competition. As you read the following pages, refer back to our sample résumé frequently to see how it stacks up to these criteria. After reading the building blocks of your successful résumé, you'll do a workshop to get you started crafting the first draft of your own hit résumé.

ELEMENTS OF YOUR RÉSUMÉ

Identity: The first thing your résumé must denote is who you are—literally. You have to clearly and boldly state your identity. Your name must be at the top. How big should you make it? I recommend 14- to 18-point type if you're using 10- to 12-point in the body of your résumé. Visualize twenty résumés on a table. If your identity is bigger than the rest, but not too big, you've got a little bit of an edge.

Should you use distinctive fonts? No. Often, when it comes to résumés, especially at larger companies like major record labels, your résumé will be scanned. And if you used a bizarre font called "Antediluvian," your name may appear as a black splotch when scanned or faxed. So it's good to rely on traditional fonts such as Times, Century, Courier, Helvetica, Arial, or Tahoma.

The only exception might be if you are applying for a position as a graphic designer, in which case it may be appropriate to show a tad more design sense in your résumé. But even then, don't go overboard. Let your portfolio show your creative flair, and let your résumé explain verbally why you are the best candidate for that graphic-artist position.

Job objective: The job objective answers the question, what do you aspire to do? For instance, if an individual aspires to become an established songwriter, a good relevant job choice might be at a music-publishing or performing-rights organization in order to learn more about the business of songwriting. In this case, an effective job objective might be:

> ***Sample Job Objective***
>
> *To obtain an entry-level position at a music publishing company to learn more about the publishing industry.*

That's a good job-objective statement. And you can adapt your objective from opportunity to opportunity. That's the beauty of word processors. That's why you've got your résumé ready to update or customize on a moment's notice.

What if you don't have a specific job objective yet? Then identify a segment of the industry that you have an interest in, such as A&R, sound reinforcement, or artist management, and start with that.

> ***Sample Job Objective***
>
> *To secure an entry-level position at an artist management company.*

I believe it's essential to list an objective on each résumé draft. If you know you want to be in the studio business but you're not sure where, you should say so.

> ***Sample Job Objective***
>
> *To land an entry-level position in an established recording studio to expand my recording knowledge and skills.*

Although it's generic, it gives the reader a sense that the candidate has a goal in mind.

Experience: This part of your résumé gives you the opportunity to detail some of your accomplishments. Many people get intimidated when it comes to listing experience on their résumé. The simple rule of thumb on listing experience on your résumé is to emphasize your strongest accomplishments, no matter where you were employed. As your career evolves on the music industry path of your choice, your experience should reflect your career development in your chosen area.

The Saga of the Pizza Man

One of my former students started working in the eleventh grade for a pizza parlor in San Francisco. He was just finishing up his four-year degree in broadcasting and had been working at the pizza shop for six or seven years. At that time, he was assistant manager with a broad portfolio of responsibilities, including cash management, hiring, and training new staff. He came to me and said, "My goal is to work in a recording studio, so I'm not going to mention this stuff" (i.e., his pizza business experience).

I replied, "You're shortchanging yourself if you omit this valuable experience. Look at all the skills you've developed. You're fiscally responsible, and you hired and managed a staff of ten people. You've developed menus. Those are all important business skills. Put them down on your résumé. You don't have to write volumes, but include what you've accomplished that's noteworthy and that contributed to the success of your employer. Every business owner wants to hire someone who has proven to be a responsible employee."

He did just that and landed that job at a leading post-production studio in Los Angeles shortly thereafter, where his organizational and leadership skills were appreciated.

Never forget to tell your prospective employer what problems you solved or profits you helped create in a previous job. The majority of your competitors will only list the dates and title of the jobs they held. Too bad for them! They miss a tremendous opportunity that you must take advantage of to explain the *value* you created in your previous and current job.

Education: How important is education in the music industry? Increasingly so. There are hundreds of schools and colleges that offer pre-professional training in the music industry. Such training provides future employees with a basic understanding of the industry, how various market segments such as the record industry, artist management, concert promotion, recording arts, not-for-profit arts administration, and the music products market segments operate, to name just a few areas. Studios, labels, management companies, record labels and other firms that recruit entry-level employees rely on programs such as these to provide candidates with a rudimentary knowledge of the business. Completing a successful internship at a music or entertainment firm is another way to build your skills and knowledge and enhance one's hireability.

When it comes time to start your job search, your educational background will definitely help you. What if you don't have an education in the music or entertainment industry? It's still important to list your educational qualifications. If you have a high-school diploma, list it. If you took college courses but didn't graduate, specify the general area of study and number of years or credits completed successfully.

Prospective employers want to know that you are literate. Remember that being able to read, write, and follow directions are important components of your marketable skill set. Documenting your education and background is important. Unfortunately, I've received far too many résumés that failed to list any educational accomplishments. That's a mistake. Today, one must list some type of educational background to be considered seriously for almost any position.

Background and interests: Why would you want to put these down on your résumé? Because more often than not, landing your dream job in the music biz means building a rapport with the person who will hire or work with you. And if you have some common interests, be they antique cars, home-brewed beer, or cycling, it's liable to not only go a long way by breaking the ice, but more importantly, separating you from your competition.

Background and interests provide an excellent means to differentiate you from the pack. Let's say you have a huge album collection of a specific genre of music, and the label at which you're applying is developing artists in that genre. You learned of the label through a few articles you discovered in *Billboard* or *Spin* magazine, so there appears to be a nice fit. Your interest in this genre of music may become a plus if you are applying for a position at that label.

Background and interests provide you with a chance to strike a chord with someone. Let's say you're into backpacking and the person who is interviewing you is also a backpacker. Backgrounds and interests allow you to differentiate yourself. If you have any meaningful Awards or Achievements, you might consider listing those rather than Background and Interests. The functional résumé example uses Awards very effectively.

Personal interviews are often a bit like the start of a recording session with a new artist. You and your interviewer may be a bit nervous. Your interests may prove to be a good icebreaker. And the fact that you have some interests beyond your career goals is a healthy sign that you value a well-rounded life.

Avoid mentioning any interests or activities that are highly charged, religious, or political in nature. Stick with pursuits and interests that do not offer any chance to upset a prospective employer. Be careful to never lie or invent any information on your résumé. Chances are it will come back to haunt you and in some cases may prove to be grounds for dismissal. Recent situations where CEOs of publicly traded companies have had to resign because they provided false information on their résumé point out how important it is to never lie or even "stretch the truth" on your résumé.

References: Should you list character references on your résumé? The answer is no. You may, however, choose to add a line at the bottom, *references available upon request.* You must then remember to actually secure reliable references that will vouch for you, because they are likely to be called upon to do so.

Who makes a good reference? Anyone with whom you have worked in a professional capacity. If your experience so far has been only as a student, use your instructors. If you're really in a pinch, use anyone who knows you well, except for family. That's the only taboo on references. Attorney, minister, former boss at the pizza parlor: those are acceptable, too. At some point, you're going to need references, so start planning who will provide this important service for you and ask their permission to use them as a reference in your job search. Some interviewers don't ask for references. Companies are starting to do so more and more often, especially for positions of responsibility. Another reason is that the cost of mis-hiring—that is, having to dismiss and then reopen the hiring pool, re-interview and rehire another employee—has become substantial to all businesses.

PROGRESSIVE CAREER GROWTH

As your career and résumé evolve, take the time to clearly delineate the various examples that show your progressive career growth. This is a prime indicator used by prospective employers to measure the development of a job applicant. Simply put, progressive career growth shows how you have advanced in job responsibility and value to your current and previous employers. Ideally, your job titles will have changed to more clearly demonstrate this, but if you have not had a job title change, but your duties and responsibilities have expanded, be sure to specifically cite this progressive career growth. It's also wise to emphasize your progressive career growth in cover letters that accompany any résumé submissions.

PRESENTATION

What about your résumé's presentation? You should make it easy to read, and carefully check and recheck for spelling or grammatical errors. As noted earlier, with respect to the sample résumé, leave some white space. Do not cram the page so full of information that the reader's eye is overwhelmed; leave it a bit airy. You should also avoid colored paper and nonstandard fonts. If a résumé comes in and it is so packed with words that the reader doesn't know where to start, you've got a major problem. If your résumé is running long or looking crammed on a single page, go to another page. Better yet, get a friend, teacher, or mentor to help you edit it down. Leave some white space. I repeat that point, because it is so often ignored, but critically important in aiding your résumé's view-ability.

If you are ready to vie for an entry-level position in the music industry, there is rarely a need for your résumé to run any more than a single, well-organized page.

A FINAL THOUGHT ON RÉSUMÉ EDITING

Students often inquire, "Should I revise or edit my résumé for each job opportunity that I uncover as my job search gets into high gear?" The answer is, "No!"

I don't advise overhauling your résumé for every single job opportunity, because you're liable to stray from the carefully crafted document that you spent so much time developing. The basics of your education, your experience, and your talents will not change from opportunity to opportunity. And your basic qualifications and worth points (we'll get to those shortly) shouldn't change either. Over the arc of your career, measured in years, it will change—but not every month.

The one thing that is most likely to change is your job objective. To avoid an overly broad job objective, most candidates customize their job objective to suit each opportunity. You might add a sentence here or there, but the core of a well-crafted résumé should rarely change, in the short term. A well-crafted résumé is a solid document that clearly states who you are. It unequivocally states what you've done—the scope of your accomplishments and the benefits created by you and enjoyed by your previous and current employers. In your interview and cover letter, you can and should amplify specific skills and key accomplishments that are likely to excite your future boss.

If you're constantly doctoring up the basics of your résumé, you're likely to introduce errors and more formatting problems. Once you have a strong résumé that you are justifiably proud of, think twice before tampering with its basic elements.

WORKSHOP 10. BUILDING YOUR RÉSUMÉ

Take the following list and set it up in a word processor.

Review this chapter's discussion and make the initial draft of the ideas and words that will grow into your own "hit" résumé. Once you have some ideas and notes, you'll be ready to start a first draft of your résumé. This will help you avoid that sinking feeling many encounter when tackling the résumé development process.

Identity: List your name, address, phone, and other contact information including fax and e-mail if applicable. Some students list school and home contact information, usually at opposite sides of the top of the page with their name centered.

Job Objective: Don't try to write the perfect job objective; instead, simply note a few of the job objectives you aspire to at this time. Most entry-level candidates have a number of dream careers they are interested in investigating. List as many as come to mind. Don't agonize over the wordsmithing now, as you will have time to perfect and fine-tune that later.

Work Experience: For now, list it all in reverse chronological order (most recent items go first). Include part-time and volunteer positions. Pay special attention to any jobs for which you received commendations, raises, promotions, or other identifiable accolades.

Education: Keep it short, but don't omit any special training or internship that strengthens your résumé.

Other Skills: Start a list of all the skills you can think of that may be valuable, especially skills such as foreign language proficiency, negotiating skills, and telephone and computer skills. Even the ability to drive a truck may prove handy. Once you have your list going, poll your close friends and family members to expand your list. Again, in this early phase of résumé development, it's far better to have a wider range of choices and to narrow it down later.

Professional Memberships: If you don't have any professional affiliations yet, perhaps now is the time to do some homework and identify one or two organizations that may interest you. Even if you can't afford the dues, you could become involved as a volunteer.

Hobbies and Interests: Start with every one you have and pare down later.

References: Although you don't need your final list of three non-family character references yet, it's not too soon to identify who your top candidates will be.

CHAPTER 11 Make Your Résumé Sparkle With Worth Points

> *Worth points represent the single, most effective means to quickly convince your prospective boss that you are a candidate worth serious consideration.*

A "worth point" is a well-written, concise statement that will differentiate you from your competition. Worth points are worth their weight in gold, so take the time to learn how to incorporate them into your résumé. Worth points demonstrate why you will be valuable to an employer. They make your résumé shine and glisten.

Worth points clearly state what you accomplished and the results your actions created for your previous employer.

Worth Point Example:

Organized and managed volunteer student committee to raise funds for repair of homeless shelter, resulting in achieving 200 percent of financial goal.

Notice that the example incorporates two action verbs in it: organized and managed. It also clearly states that your efforts exceeded the goal or expectation that was established before you tackled the job.

Remember the worth point statements in the model chronological résumé from chapter 10:

Worth Point Example:

Planned and executed upgrade of new MIDI studio, including drawings, wiring, and installation, saving the cost of hiring an outside installation firm.

That's a strong worth point that uses two powerful verbs: planned and executed. The résumé could have simply stated, "installed a new MIDI studio," and missed a valuable opportunity to make a much stronger, active statement as to the value created for the previous employer.

A worth point is also included under the school job listed on the sample résumé in the previous chapter.

Worth Point Example:

Set up maintenance tracking system and student repair teams to lower amount of equipment out of service and speed up repairs, resulting in increased productivity of department and letter of commendation.

The studio manager who is looking at this résumé carefully is likely to observe, "This person is technical enough so that I wouldn't have to contract out as much freelance technical help. I'd have more tech power in-house. And he has organized repair teams and kept equipment running."

That well-stated worth point is very likely to move the sample résumé up near the top of the select pile of "must contact" résumés.

Use this workshop to develop a few of your own worth points.

WORKSHOP 11. WORTH-POINT DEVELOPMENT

A "worth point" is a well-written, concise way to give yourself an edge when someone is reviewing your résumé. Worth points demonstrate why you will be valuable to a prospective employer.

Here's an example: "Planned and managed 5,000-person walk-a-thon fundraiser for local food bank, resulting in achieving 100 percent of food donation and cash contribution goals." Notice the two action verbs: planned and managed.

To develop worth-point "winners," start by listing three accomplishments that you are proud of.

1. ______________________________

2. ______________________________

3. ______________________________

Now, turn them into worth points by using the following formula. A good worth point uses two phrases. The first describes specifically what you did; the second, its results.

Convert your three accomplishments into worth points.

1a. What you did:

____

1b. What was the result of your action?

____

2a. What you did:

____

2b. What was the result of your action?

____

3a. What you did:

____

3b. What was the result of your action?

____

Take your time and go over your work and volunteer experience. See how many of the job actions you have listed can be "energized" by conversion into a worth point. This is one of the most challenging aspects of crafting a strong résumé that will sell you strongly as a serious contender for your dream job. If you don't have any measurable worth points in your portfolio of accomplishments, consider getting involved with a community organization where you could make a difference and earn a valid worth point to add to your résumé.

The bottom line is that any résumé with well-written worth points jumps out of a stack of competing résumés! Invest the time and effort to see that your résumé has at least one.

Worth Point Case Study

Here's another example of success that could become a worth point. During the course of the summer internship at a radio station, "Terry" is asked to reorganize a tape library, which contains previous radio spots, live broadcasts, and other recordings. During her three months on-site, she comes up with a comprehensive system to organize the spot library, using a computer database and tagging all the tapes by sponsor and air date. She put a great deal of effort and some weekend time into the project. The system was a huge hit with the traffic department and station management.

Now, it's the fall semester of her senior year of college, and she's drafting her résumé.

Ineffective Worth Point: Internship, Z100 Radio, organized tape library.

That's a simple statement of an activity. Turning that into a worth point, she energizes it as follows.

Effective Worth Point: Intern at Z100 Radio, developed computer database system for advertising spot library resulting in 50 percent time savings to traffic and production departments.

See the difference? Terry's résumé will have much more impact because she took the time to develop this worth point. First, it states she developed a functional system using a computer. Second, she had responsibility for an action. And third, Terry's actions led to a clearly stated benefit, saving the station and her employer half of the time it previously took to complete a daily task.

That's how to take an action and turn it into a worth point. If you can do that two or three times in your résumé, and then remind them of those worth points in a targeted cover letter, I promise you, yours will usually be in the top 10 percent of the résumés under review.

People rarely take the time to restate what they've done action-wise with a worth point. Why? It takes time, effort, and extra thought to refine an action into a worth point. But the benefits are huge. If you haven't been in the working world very long, volunteer activities are perfectly acceptable to use as worth points.

ACTION VERB LIST

achieve
administer
affect
aid
analyze
apply
assemble
assist
attain
budget
calibrate
change
check
coach
collect
communicate
compile
compose
compute
conduct
consolidate
coordinate
create
critique
decide
demonstrate
determine
differentiate
dispense
document
earn
educate
edit
establish
evaluate
execute
expedite
facilitate
forecast
fulfill
generate
guide
hire
identify
implement
influence
initiate
illustrate
inspect
install
instruct
integrate
interpret
invent
investigate
judge
launch
lead
lecture
lobby
locate
lower
maintain
manage
measure
mentor
motivate
negotiate
operate
organize
participate
perform
persuade
plan
prepare
present
prioritize
produce
program
promote
propose
provide
publish
question
raise
recommend
record
reduce
reference
repair
replace
report
represent
research
review
rewrite
save
secure
select
sell
serve
set up
solve
speak
speed
streamline
strengthen
succeed
supervise
teach
train
translate
update
upgrade
verify
write

Action verbs sell, in a résumé. They tell your potential employer the things you accomplished and the results that you achieved. The more assertive you are and the more confidently you can state your accomplishments and results, the better your résumé will be viewed. Sales grew, money was saved, accounts were opened, records went up the chart, or hungry people were fed. Each can be represented much more effectively as a worth point. Take a moment to skip back to the sample résumés and see if they incorporate action verbs effectively.

Don't shortchange your résumé. Include worth points whenever you can, and you will be amazed at the difference in the response from prospective employers. You will also find that these worth points will bring you value for a long time as they shine in your résumé and cover letters. They make the case that you are a valuable asset to an employer. Remember to use them in discussions when you move on to interviews. Worth points represent the single, most effective means to quickly convince your prospective boss that you are a candidate worth serious consideration.

CHAPTER 12 How to Write Effective Cold and Cover Letters

What's the difference between a cold letter and a cover letter?

A cold letter is one that is submitted, with or without your résumé, in the hopes of securing an interview with a company that interests you. A cold letter is one that you send into the unknown, often blind, as you may not know if the company is looking to hire new staff or not. Simply put, it's a shot in the dark.

A cover letter is written to address an existing opportunity at a company. Let's say you spoke to someone in the human resources department. They said, "Yes, send us a résumé. Here's our address." A well-written cover letter starts by referencing that this submission is being sent in response either to a specific job opening or to a company's request to review your résumé and qualifications.

The cover letter accompanying your résumé for a specific opportunity should also state why you believe you are qualified for the position in question. Don't assume that the résumé screener will proceed far enough into your résumé to the location where your carefully crafted worth points reside. Restate two or three key attributes and worth points in your cover letter, and end on a positive and enthusiastic note. Remember that the same care that went into your résumé should be invested in your cover and cold letters. Be sure that there are no typos, use good grammar, leave a little white space, and include your name and contact information on the letter, as it may become separated from your résumé. Keep your letter to a maximum length of one page.

Following is a sample of a well-written cold letter I received a number of years ago. I took the time to read it and the attached résumé, which looked promising. But this person never secured a phone or in-person interview with me. Why? She never took the next important step. She never made the follow-up call to see if I would give the time for an interview. Her letter said, "I look forward to meeting with you and will be calling you in the next few weeks to arrange a mutually convenient time."

That call never came. It may have been due to the huge number of letters she sent out, or that she landed her dream gig. But if you take the time to write a strong letter and send it out, you should budget adequate time to do at least one follow-up call for each submission.

Although I wasn't hiring at the time, I would have given this person time for an informational phone interview based on the quality of the letter and the attached résumé, and that would have been a positive learning (and networking) experience for her.

Remember, often the people who have valuable information may not hire you today, but they could refer you to someone else in the industry that is hiring. So invest the time and effort to make your cold and cover letters strong, concise communicators—especially if they're aimed at what I call "Targets of Opportunity," which we will investigate in the next chapter.

Dear Mr. Hatschek,

Your name came up in my research of the music business in the San Francisco region as someone whose effectiveness and influence on the industry has been exemplary. You are clearly an individual whose knowledge and experience would be invaluable to anyone hoping to enter this highly competitive and relatively closed field.

I am a musically literate, well-spoken, and enthusiastic recent college graduate whose greatest passion in life has always been music. Please be assured that I do not expect you to know of any specific positions in your or other companies. Rather, I would welcome the opportunity to meet with you briefly to discuss the business in general and get the benefit of your comments and advice.

In addition to a lifetime of collecting and listening, I have worked extensively with local acts in both promotion and staging, and am myself a singer and a songwriter. I would be happy to discuss this and other work experience in more depth when we meet.

I look forward to meeting with you and plan to call in the next few weeks to arrange a mutually convenient time.

Sincerely yours,

Jane Doe

WORKSHOP 12. WRITE A COLD LETTER

Identify a local company that interests you as a potential employer in your area of interest. Research to whose attention you should send your inquiry. Keep in mind that small to medium-sized companies are the best size firms to approach, as large, multinational companies generally will not respond to a cold letter such as this.

Using the following outline, write a cold letter to introduce yourself and request an informational interview. Be sure to mention:

- Who are you and why are you writing? (Do you want a job, an informational interview, or information on the company and its products or services?)
- How you found out about the company.
- What is it about the company or the work it does that interests you.
- How are you preparing to enter the industry? (school, independent study, internship, etc.)
- A restatement of what are you requesting, (informational interview, tour of studios, etc.) and how you will follow up.

As always, make sure it's well written and to the point. You'll mail or drop off the letter along with a copy of your résumé after you finish up chapter 18, which will prepare you for interview success.

A FINAL THOUGHT ON ORIGINALITY AND ACCURACY IN COVER LETTERS

I'm often asked, "Once I have one really good cover letter, can I just use that as a form letter for all the jobs I respond to?" No, you must always customize each cover letter. It doesn't matter if you have thirty jobs you're responding to this week. Break it down into short-term goals for that day. Write a letter. Carefully double-check the accuracy of the spelling and the address. Pay special attention to the name of the person to whom you are sending the letter. If you are unsure of any of the contact information, call the company. "Hi, I'm sending a letter to Keith Hatschek. I just want to make sure I am spelling his last name right. Is it H-a-t-c-h-e-c-k?"

Receptionist: "No, it's got an 's' in there and no 'c' at the end."

"Oh, thank you, H-a-t-s-c-h-e-k."

You accomplished two things during that phone call. You have gotten your prospective boss's name right, and you made an impression with a person at that firm who is likely to remember that you took the time to call and find out how to spell the boss's name correctly. People remember things like that. So the cover-letter originality and accuracy are very important to serious job seekers. You can and should use some of the same sentences and bullet points for similar jobs, but don't fall into the trap of sending out a generic cover letter. You're missing an opportunity to further separate yourself from the pack if you take that path.

CHAPTER 13 Why Most Music-Industry Jobs Are Rarely Advertised

TRACKING DOWN JOB OPENINGS

Do recording studios, management firms, production companies, videogame developers, or music products companies advertise open job listings in the relevant trade magazines covering these particular business areas? Rarely, if at all. The reason is that they don't want to be inundated with hundreds or thousands of résumés. And of the hundreds a firm may receive if they were to advertise, how many do you think might qualify as top candidates? Perhaps a few dozen, maybe none. The other reason that only a small percentage of jobs are listed or advertised is that a qualified candidate referred by either a colleague or an existing employee is a much more efficient means to locate a new hire.

Today, a small number of positions are in fact advertised, and with the growth of effective Internet job banks, which we'll look at more closely in chapter 15, the chances of locating relevant job openings has increased in some measure. However, even with the number and caliber of job listings on the Web growing, the vast majority of music industry hiring goes on via referrals. Web listings, by their very nature, are exposed to a potential job seeker universe numbering in the tens of thousands. Finally, the freshness or recency of Web job listings may be very poor.

So the music industry job sleuth has a problem. If only a small percentage of the jobs are advertised and each job seeker is dead set on developing a career in the music industry, what should one do?

Go to an employment agency? Don't go to a local employment agency and say, "Hi, I really want to be an A&R assistant. Can you help me find a position?" They cannot help you.

Instead, try networking, mingling, and/or joining some trade organizations. Those kinds of activities will put you on the proper trail to uncovering a wealth of unadvertised job opportunities. It's a simple fact that the entertainment industry is entirely relationship based. In my own case, every job I have taken or developed in the last thirty years has been based on a personal or professional relationship I had developed in an earlier job.

> *...the entertainment industry is entirely relationship based.*

Don't overlook the value of basic research in identifying job search "targets of opportunity." Let's say that in this week's issue of *Billboard* (which you stop by the library to read, if you are unable to afford a subscription), you identify a company that's involved in your area of interest. Now the fun begins for a dedicated industry detective.

As a first step in your research, you have identified a company you may want to work for. Next, you dig out the name of the hiring or personnel director by calling that company. You also soak up all the information you can about the company from the Internet. Then send your résumé and a carefully crafted cover letter explaining your interest. You'll be surprised how this detective work will improve your odds of landing interviews and other potential job leads.

With each résumé and cold letter submission, a good detective always asks for something in return. "I'd like to know if I might arrange an informational interview with you or so-and-so in person, or request a brief tour of your facilities." If you don't ask, you definitely won't get one. Even if they decline, the people reviewing your submission will see you are serious about your interest in their company.

What if you find out that a particular company that interests you doesn't offer informational interviews?

The next best tactic is to network with the employees. Large companies have large employee populations. For instance, here in the San Francisco Bay area, videogame powerhouse Electronic Arts has hundreds of employees that work in its various departments including sound, music, video production, and so forth. A major record label has thousands of employees around the world. A large multiroom recording studio complex may have from ten to fifty employees. They belong to trade associations, shop at local equipment dealers, attend conventions, and so forth. If you're a student in a music or entertainment-industry program, it's likely that a recent graduate may even work there now. Your assignment as a sleuth is to utilize your network to locate and meet an employee of the firms you want to learn about.

Perhaps you've heard of the "six degrees of separation" concept. Each of us knows someone that is a few times removed from a target company or individual. The reality is that if you want to make a connection badly enough, you will probably uncover a means to do so. You'll strive to quench that "fire in the belly" that must be satiated with information, because as a committed music industry sleuth, you are on a continuous information quest.

Anytime you learn of a career seminar, workshop, or job fair related to your area of interest, get involved. There will be people attending from companies or labels you may want to work with or, at the very least, add to your network. Get it together and go. You have to put yourself out to get a return.

As more music industry firms begin to post some job openings on relevant Web sites, consider mining those job listings for the number of positions at each firm, the specific skills and talents that are in demand, and the location of the open positions. This will give you an overview of "where the action is," with regard to the types of jobs and firms that may be your best current leads to finding your dream job.

Another value of such open position listings will be evident as you continue working on the job-specific skill-set workshops for a particular career track(s). The qualifications listed in the open-position listings let you know what skills employers are looking for in a new hire today. Don't overlook this excellent guide to confirming the specific skills employers are seeking and then checking your résumé and cover letter to see that you clearly demonstrate which of these skills you can bring to bear on behalf of the employer.

Remember, your marketable skill-set workshops are the tools and building blocks you can use as you create or modify your résumé. Picture a job candidate walking into an interview and saying, "This is my marketable skill set." That won't work. However, it—and any help-wanted listing or job descriptions you locate—will provide you with a blueprint for your résumé development. With tools such as these, you can ensure that you have developed and can communicate that you have the necessary skills and attributes employers are seeking.

Here are a few examples of some open job listings and some decoding of the requirements listed in each.

HELP WANTED

Fast-growing, Manhattan-based distributor needs administrative assistant. Assistant to the president, experienced A/P, A/R, computer literate with letter writing ability.

That's a clerical job with some financial experience required, most likely found in a smaller company.

HELP WANTED

Assistant sales manager, telemarketer, with three years record sales experience to wholesale accounts required.

If you don't have the experience for that one, you shouldn't apply.

HELP WANTED

VP promotion, growing record company. Must have campaign experience, strong contacts with radio and press, country preferred but not necessary. No rookies.

If you don't know what campaign experience is, you'll need to find that out. Say it's January, and an artist is going to be releasing an album in April. The label is going to break the first single in March and head out on tour in May. The tour will last May through October. The many activities and promotions that are carefully combined to promote a release and the artist are combined into a campaign to benefit the label for whom that artist records. The hiring firm is clearly looking for a candidate with some substantial industry experience.

Help-wanted listings and online job postings can help you assess the skills necessary for a particular job. They're a way for you to test your marketable-skill-set workshop for that position, if you have developed one. Do the skills you think you need to do that job in the A&R department match the ones they are looking for? Because if you think it's skills A, B, and C, and three different companies are advertising for skills Q, R, and S, your marketable skill-set workshop is probably incomplete or inaccurate, based on what the marketplace is seeking. In that case, regroup and develop a more accurate assessment of the marketable skill set that is required for a specific job by talking further with teachers, mentors, or working professionals in your area of interest.

MEETING THE RICH AND FAMOUS

I've been asked, "Why can't I just go up and introduce myself to a top producer, director, engineer, or label exec and offer to intern for them?" Here's why:

Every person who is already successful has a support team in place. You're better off trying to network with people whose star is on the rise—the up-and-comers who are hungry and open to making new contacts. History has proven that you are much more likely to hook up with someone on the way up than with someone already at the top. It would be difficult, if not impossible, to cold call and speak directly with a top-level artist, producer, or studio or label honcho. They don't take anonymous phone inquiries.

In the event that you do connect with a superstar in your area of interest, it's important for you to know that many, if not all, usually have justifiable concerns about their security and privacy. It's far better if a trusted associate can introduce you. With respect to the top talent that I have had the pleasure to work with, it would be extremely intrusive to be called at home on a day off by someone that they don't know and hear, "Hey man, I love your stuff, I'd really love to work for you." You will end up with a big zero for your efforts.

Remember one of the oldest sayings in the record business: *To get ahead, it's not just what you know, it's **who** you know.*

Instead, if you really want to connect with a top talent or executive, then find a way to be introduced by a member of their team. You want to find someone who can say, "Jim, this is somebody who really is into some of the same music we are, and I think you both have quite a bit in common." That makes all the difference in the world. Remember one of the oldest sayings in the record business: *To get ahead, it's not just what you know, it's **who** you know.*

WORKSHOP 13. FINDING UNADVERTISED JOB OPENINGS: A FIELD TRIP TO AN INDUSTRY EVENT

The surest means to identify unadvertised industry jobs is meeting and maintaining contact with working industry professionals.

Based on your geographic location and the specific area of interest you are focusing on, research the trade association that serves that market segment. For instance, for record labels, the respective trade associations that intersect the record business include RIAA, NARM, AIM, and to a lesser extent, NARAS. Find out where the nearest upcoming event, conference, meeting, seminar or other event that you might attend will be. Then develop a plan to get in contact with that organization and ask if you can attend one event to check out the association. You might also offer to volunteer to assist at the conference or workshop. The goal of this workshop is to start the process of meeting working professionals in your area of interest. These are the very people who will be capable of tipping you off to unadvertised positions once you have met them and made a positive impression.

CHAPTER 14 Schmooze or Lose (Secrets of a Networking Guru)

> *Starting today and continuing for your entire career in the entertainment industry, commit yourself to spending a portion of each day building and nurturing your network.*

The most important tactic you can use to develop key industry contacts is networking. Starting today and continuing for your entire career in the entertainment industry, commit yourself to spending a portion of each day building and nurturing your network.

Since most job openings aren't directly advertised, it's only through networking that you uncover "hidden" opportunities. You have to consciously build and work to maintain your network. I recommend students invest two hours a week on network development. *That's only seventeen minutes each day*. Like other aspects of your career development, networking is work. If you don't hustle and sweat while you are building and maintaining your network, you won't achieve the necessary results to get ahead. The choice is yours. Net-"work," or sit back and hope your dream gig falls in your lap.

How do you manage your network? Make phone calls. Attend industry meetings, seminars, trade shows, and events whenever possible to multiply your contact with people in the business. Remember to bring your business cards. (You don't have a business card yet?)

Correspondence is an important part of your network maintenance, too.

Here's a letter I received last year.

Dear Mr. Hatschek,

I read an interesting story about your public relations firm last month in *Billboard*. I am completing my studies in studio management at XYZ University and will be visiting San Francisco this summer. I would like to see if I might stop by to introduce myself and ask for a few minutes of your time to discuss my career objectives in the music business.

Sincerely yours,

Jim O'Hara

P.S. I'll call two weeks prior to my trip, to inquire if you will be willing to make an appointment to speak with me.

Letters such as the one above will help you to get your foot in the door. The letter would have been even stronger if there was a referral included, "Joe Jones (someone who knows me professionally) recommended I give you a call while I am in San Francisco." If a professional acquaintance is willing to help make an introduction, you have a real leg up over your competition.

Such a visit may not lead to a job offer. Maybe you're not looking for a job at this stage, especially if you are still in school. But you've just widened your network. You've got another professional contact in your database or index file. You've got another person who knows you and you know them. Your range of possibilities just increased. That's how successful networking in the entertainment business is done, day in and day out by networking gurus. With a steady investment of time, effort, and follow-up, pretty soon you'll be a networking guru too.

Networking is not a one-way enterprise. To be successful, you've got to "give" when you "get." How you do that is by being an information sponge.

For example, if you are living in L.A., there is a celebrity or charity music business event almost every weekend. You may not meet the head of each record label, but you will meet some of the staffers at those labels. One example is the TJ Martell Foundation, which was founded by members of the music industry and has been very active for more than twenty-five years raising funds for leukemia, cancer, and AIDS research. They regularly host charity events in L.A. and New York.

Find out when and where these and other events are being held, and volunteer at a few of them. In L.A., the weekly magazine *Music Connection* has a "Heart & Soul" column, which regularly lists upcoming charity events such as concerts, celebrity auctions, and tennis or golf tournaments, each offering an excellent opportunity to the savvy network builder to get out and start adding to their network. With the investment of a few minutes' research, a few phone calls, and perhaps a brief personal interview, you can be working with and helping out industry pros at a charitable event.

HOW TO USE YOUR NETWORK

Let's say you begin with a network of twenty-five people. That's a good start. Consider them your "team." One day, you make a career decision that you would prefer to work at a record label rather than a recording studio. Each person in your network may know somebody who works at a label.

Successfully working your network means that you send out an e-mail to your network stating, "Hey, I've decided to jump tracks and try to land a gig at a label, ideally one that is into hip-hop music or electronica. Do you know anyone at a label to whom you might be able to introduce me to gather more information?"

In this example, if each of the members of your network in turn has his or her own network of 25 persons, you now have a potential 625-person universe (25 x 25 = 625) in the music business to ask questions of. In this scenario, it's likely that you will get one or two positive responses to your inquiry. Your team will ask themselves, "Who do we know in the electronica and hip-hop music biz? My friend really wants to learn more about that part of the biz."

Soon, you receive three e-mails back, suggesting you check out a certain label, or introducing you to a new contact at a particular company. That's networking, par excellence.

GIVING BACK TO YOUR NETWORK

How do you reciprocate and give back value to your network? Here's how. Let's assume that you have landed that job at a hip-hop label in L.A. One day, your boss mentions that the company needs to locate a campus rep in New York City. You mention that you could send out an e-mail to your network (which, by the way, has now grown to fifty persons). Soon, a number of résumés are received by fax and e-mail. Just like that, you transitioned from job seeker to a job referral source. That's how a person continues to grow, give back to, and nurture their network.

A well-tended network should grow like a garden. It's unlikely that you will intimately know most of the people in your network. That's not important. What is important is that you manage and grow information and support those with whom you network. Doing so gives you access to an unmatched source of up-to-the-minute inside information.

When I managed my marketing and public relations firm, Keith Hatschek & Associates, we had more than 1,000 active contacts in our immediate network of associates, editors, vendors, and business acquaintances. Through them, we had the ability to communicate indirectly with another 5,000 or more people involved and interested in the industries we served. That's a potent tool. As an example, when someone needed a photographer in Nashville, a member of our staff simply searched our database for the names and numbers of various photographers in Nashville. If a publicist in London was needed to assist a client with a UK project, we'd e-mail or fax one of our London contacts and inquire as to who might be an appropriate referral. It doesn't matter if you have not met any of these referrals personally. So long as they are introduced through a referral by a known colleague, they were every bit a part of our company's network. That's how the business of networking in the music industry works. It's powerful, potent, and creates a lifelong web of knowledge and information available at your fingertips.

Networking represents the most surefire method to gather information about a position, industry, or company in which you have an interest. And it's the most effective means to plug into a job that's never going to be advertised. Trade associations, which we'll discuss in chapter 16, offer another important avenue to build your network.

Remember, there's a big difference between networking and interviewing. Interviews place you in a position to learn directly about a specific company or a specific job opportunity. Networking is the investment you make to meet people and share information about common career interests. Networking is the free exchange of information, usually done informally in conversation over coffee, via e-mail, or in a phone chat. You must view networking as an ongoing, constant flow of information within your network.

To excel at networking, think of it as a numbers game. Invest the time and effort to make new and different contacts. Set a goal. "I am going to network with four new people every month..." or whatever you see as being a realistic goal. Don't be afraid to push yourself—to set a goal that is just a little higher than you think you can achieve. Write it as your goal, then work towards it, keeping a scorecard to measure your progress. It is important to set and achieve short-term goals, especially with respect to growing your network.

Once you get started, you'll find it's not that hard to build up your network. Go to industry events such as seminars, open houses, and workshops that have an informational agenda. Volunteering and involving yourself in trade associations and industry organizations provides the fastest, easiest, least stressful way to expand your network resources. In San Francisco, the local chapter of the Recording Academy stages thirty-five to forty events a year. Volunteer in any capacity, even if you're making nametags and cleaning up after the event.

If you have any kind of a family or personal connection, now is the time to use it. "My uncle is divorced but his ex-wife has a job in finance at Capitol Records. I'm going to see her at a wedding next month." Don't be shy. If you've got your résumé ready to go, pass her a copy of it in an envelope and ask her if you can follow up to see if she might introduce you to someone in personnel. Never waste a family connection, even if you have to gather up your courage to take advantage of it.

If there's any ethical edge you have to get a foot in the door, use it. Remember, even if that particular person is not able to assist you now, ask them who they may know that might be able to. Just because they may be family, don't expect them to treat you differently. Be professional; tell them what you can bring to the table. Explain that you are serious about a career in the business. If you are in school, explain that you are studying, learning, and networking, and are dedicated to finding a way into the music and recording business. That's critical.

Two-thirds of music industry job seekers secure their first industry job through active networking. Never underestimate the power of networking, no matter how far up the career ladder you climb. Even if you aren't the most talented individual that is pursuing your particular career path, if you are a maestro at networking, you're liable to do well.

Two-thirds of music industry job seekers secure their first industry job through active networking.

Musicians often have "call files" they use for subs—musicians who have filled in for them, or they have filled in for the subs. Your call list is a great place for you to start networking.

If at first you are a bit uncomfortable networking, don't worry. Many others have been, too. Remember this principle of networking: If you are giving and getting information, and you are not a pest or a nuisance, you are successfully networking. Start with a simple introduction and alert the other person to what you are interested in. "Hi, I'm Jane and I'm looking for an internship with a record label."

On the next page is a networking workshop to demonstrate to you that you already have the building blocks of a basic network. Fill it in before finishing this chapter. When you are done with the workshop, pick three members of your network and ask them who they may know that could be a possible referral to help you learn more about your current career areas of interest. You may be surprised at how quickly your network starts to expand.

WORKSHOP 14. NETWORKING

Most people actually have between 100 and 250 contacts in their extended network, although they may have frequent contact with 25 to 40 persons (the so-called "inner orbit") each week. Identifying and nurturing those "outer orbit" members of your extended network is a great way to start expanding the usefulness of your network.

Family members

Alumni/Teachers/Mentors

Friends

Business Contacts

Clubs/Organizations

Classmates/Bandmates/Etc.

What can you do to expand your network? Which areas of new connections are likely to be the most fruitful with regard to industry connections?

CHAPTER 15 Digging in the Dirt (Or How I Learned to Love the Internet)

Successful job seekers hone their research and detective skills to a fine edge. And never has there been a research tool with the speed, power, and access afforded by the Internet. Using the Internet as a primary research tool, today's job seekers can uncover a wealth of information to aid their career development. Ten years ago, putting that information together would have taken weeks or months, if it could have been located at all. However, the Internet also has the potential to lull job seekers into thinking that simply registering with a few job search engines and doing some online research will be effective in helping them land their dream job. The truth is quite different, as the Web simply broadens your access to a wider pool of job listing information, but does little to move job seekers closer to landing their next job.

A number of top career consultants advise that no more than 30 percent of your career-development time be spent reviewing Internet job sites. Old-fashioned networking, informational interviews, visiting with mentors, and reading relevant trade magazines are all equally valuable in identifying job opportunities.

In this chapter, we'll look at a full range of career research methods including libraries, directories, trade magazines, personal contacts, and the Internet. (A separate section listing a host of relevant Web sites is in appendix E.) Using the broad range of tools has proven to be the most effective way to uncover the best job opportunities and put you in a position to compete for them.

WHAT ARE YOU SEEKING?

One of my mentors said, "If you don't have dirt under your fingernails from digging to discover new things, you're never going to uncover the treasure." For job seekers, doing so requires identifying your chosen career path and embarking upon it. So be cognizant that it's up to you to do the necessary detective work to become well versed in your area of interest. Knowing as much as possible about your career focus is a necessity. Only when you become extremely well versed in this area will you be able to compete effectively, represent yourself as a serious student of that field, and make good career decisions when the time comes to do so.

MAGAZINES MIRROR THE INDUSTRIES THEY COVER

Today's music industry trade magazines offer a fast way to get a glimpse at the companies, trends, and trendsetters that are making news in a particular industry segment. Many of the periodicals listed in "Selected Resources" at the end of this book offer online editions and a few offer complimentary subscriptions for the print edition upon request. Some are available at a larger, well-stocked newsstand. Larger book chains such as Barnes & Noble and Borders carry some music industry trade magazines, too. I would suggest you go and buy a copy, or investigate a good-sized library to get your hands on the ones that cover your area of interest.

Who's hot? What styles of music are on the way up? Which ones are on the way down? Which recording studios are hot? Which record labels are coming on strong? Which videogame developers are coming up with the most innovative products? Trade magazines will answer these questions and many more. They give you the dish on the latest tools, techniques, trends, and success stories. Some of the online editions of these magazines will often have extended or exclusive Internet-only content not found in the print edition.

You must invest time on a regular basis to mine this critical information. Set up a regular reading schedule for the trade magazines that interest you. For instance, every Saturday morning, you might spend from 9 A.M. until 12 noon reviewing relevant articles and editorials. Whether you are at a library that has a good number of industry trade magazines or prospecting the magazine's online edition, take notes, identify leading personalities and companies, and consider what type of work most interests you.

If you are at a library, be sure to sit down and skim through the back issues. You'll likely find a number of articles that interest you. Photocopy them, and add these clips to your Career Binder. Until you're working in it, reading about the business is the easiest way to begin to learn about the industry. At the outset of your career development, this is the closest thing you have, unless you have a job or a mentor in the industry, to finding out what's going on in the music industry. If you are interested in a different facet of the business—for instance, touring, artist management, radio programming, or film sound—find out what magazines cover those segments and review them religiously.

MAPPING YOUR CAREER INTERESTS

Would you try to drive cross-country without a map? Your career search requires the same kind of planning that a lengthy journey would necessitate. You've got to have a map and know a little bit about the landscape. Well, the way to begin to develop a career map and to get your bearings is to dive into the print and online editions of the trade magazines that cover your area of interest and the Internet. The entertainment industry continues to embrace the Web in a big way. For instance, many entertainment firms maintain extensive Web sites that feature a wealth of information about their artists, the company, and their direction. The other fascinating part of the Internet is its global scope.

You may discover a company on the other side of the world that is involved in an area of interest that you share. And increasingly, entertainment companies are taking a global view of their business, in part because the Internet has broken down many traditional borders, and secondly because entertainment programming and products have a much longer product life cycle if they can be marketed around the world, rather than only in the U.S.

If you don't have Internet access at your home or school, call your local public library. Most libraries now offer free or low-cost Internet access.

ADVANCED SLEUTHING

Becoming a detective requires shifting your mind-set. I've had students who have actually photocopied pictures of Sherlock Holmes to place next to their computer. It graphically reminds them that one is always digging for information about topics and jobs of interest. Only a dedicated detective will uncover and exploit the best job opportunities.

If you'd like to be promoted from amateur detective to senior sleuth, then begin to read the bible regularly—not the King James version, but whatever "bible" is for the entertainment-industry segment that fascinates you. For the record industry, *Billboard* is the weekly bible.

Billboard is valuable because it tracks the pulse of the record and entertainment industry. Although it primarily covers the record business, it also covers film soundtracks, home video, intellectual rights and music publishing, mobile/ring tones/videogame music, downloads, various musical genres, music distribution and retailing, artist profiles, and it even manages to review new records. *Billboard* gives an excellent snapshot of the industry segments it covers. Another useful news source that covers the record and broadcasting segments and is available online is www.hitsdailydouble.com.

Well before the multi-platinum *Titanic* soundtrack became one of the biggest success stories in the industry, *Billboard* had identified and tracked the relationship between hit record albums and other entertainment properties such as movies, TV shows, and videogames. TV shows such as, *The OC, One Tree Hill, Smallville*, and movies such as *Spiderman I* and *II*; *O Brother, Where Art Thou?*; and *8 Mile* are driving hit records. Without soundtrack albums, the record business would be in trouble. Soundtrack albums such as those mentioned are keeping some record companies afloat. Those companies and executives who read and absorbed what a source like *Billboard* reports were aware of this trend early, took advantage of it, and surfed the wave as it developed.

So, identify what the bible is for the industry segments that interest you. If you're into recording technology, *Mix, Tape Op, EQ*, and *Pro Sound News* are some of the bibles for the recording studio segment. For songwriting, *Performing Songwriter* and *American Songwriter* are two of the best magazines. To determine your "bible," you'll need to join the right network of people working in that segment. For a songwriter, it could be a regional songwriters group or one of the performing-rights societies, ASCAP, SESAC, and BMI. The people working in that segment will tell you what they rely on as their bible. Those performing-rights organizations also produce very informative magazines for their members.

Reading your bible regularly provides a senior sleuth with up-to-the-minute information on what's happening in the market segments they are interested in. They also often provide another important insight: what entry-level jobs are open and what qualifications are required.

WORKSHOP 15.1. FIND AND USE YOUR INDUSTRY NEWS SOURCES

Identify two print magazines that provide the best glimpse into the industry area that most interests you.

____

____

Identify two Web publications that offer up-to-date, insightful news and commentary on the industry area that most interests you.

____

____

Develop a schedule for you to update yourself on the latest industry news from these four sources.

____

ASKING THE RIGHT QUESTIONS

Being a detective means learning to ask the right questions. Asking good questions means you must be knowledgeable before you can know exactly what to inquire about. Many people I've interviewed have actually asked me, "Mr. Hatschek, can you tell me what you do here?"

Unfortunately, a question like that is the kiss of death for a job seeker. I do everything I can to end that kind of interview in three minutes or less. If someone hasn't taken the time to at least find out what business occurs at the firm they're interviewing at, why should an interviewer have any interest in investing any time in them? Forget it. It's over.

Become a monster detective, if you're serious about wanting to have a career in the music industry. Why? Competition. Other people are doing their detective homework. If you don't do your research and your competition does, they're going to have a big edge when it comes time to interview and impress the future boss with their savvy and intelligence. The person who hasn't done their detective work will often appear to be just another wannabe. Few things impress a prospective employer more than an articulate job candidate who has a basic knowledge of the hiring company's business activities. Having a few well-thought-out questions or observations to bring up in the interview is another way to make a strong positive impression.

An extensive listing of useful research books, directories, industry Web sites, and job listing Web resources may be found in appendix B at the end of this book.

WORKSHOP 15.2. CAREER HOMEWORK

Part 1

Visit the nearest library that has a good collection of the business and industry directories such as Plunkett's, Hoover's, Ward's, etc. Dive in to investigate what information is available on some of the leading companies in your area of interest. Take notes on the company size, its overall revenue, where the company is located, who the key company officers are, and so forth. Then, use one of the online database services that may be available at the library such as Lexis/Nexis or Factiva to investigate any articles that have been written recently about the company and its latest efforts.

Part 2

On the Internet, visit Vault.com and RileyGuide.com. Look over the various topics from interviewing to negotiating salary. Pick two articles from each Web site that you find most helpful and print and add them to the Clipping section of your Career Binder. Get in the habit of tapping your own network, as well as online career resources when you have a career-related question or problem that needs solving.

CHAPTER 16 Alphabet Soup: All About Trade Associations

In today's music industry, there's a veritable alphabet soup of trade associations. Dozens are involved in the entertainment industry and provide excellent resources to those looking to join the business. (An appendix of some of the leading trade associations is found at the back of this book.)

It's up to you to identify, locate, and involve yourself in these organizations on a local, regional, or national level. Most have some type of dues structure. Some offer low-cost student or trial memberships. These organizations produce newsletters, events, trade shows, and seminars, and almost every one of them has a Web site loaded with inside industry information.

What are you waiting for? Some of the most important associations for the music industry—the Recording Academy (NARAS), the Audio Engineering Society (AES), the Music and Entertainment Industry Educators Association (MEIEA), and the Society of Professional Audio Recording Services (SPARS)—are listed in appendix C. Check out their Web sites, and see how you can get involved in their activities and meet their members.

These trade associations provide you with a direct link to working professionals and offer a ready-made pipeline to quickly beef up your network. As an example, in the San Francisco region there are quite a few active trade organizations: the San Francisco chapter of the Recording Academy, the student section of the Audio Engineering Society at San Francisco State University, Stanford, Ex'Pression Center, as well as the regular AES members' section, the West Coast Songwriter's Association, the Society of Motion Picture and Television Engineers, the American Federation of Musicians (AF of M), the local chapter of AFTRA/SAG (American Federation of Television and Radio Artists /Screen Actors Guild), and others. AF of M, SAG, and AFTRA are unions of working professionals providing additional benefits to their membership. Every one of these organizations presents an opportunity to grow your knowledge and build your network. How many exist in your region? It's up to you to make contact today and use the organizations to expand your network.

Most of these trade associations regularly host events and maintain a mailing list. Get on that list. Attend the events. If you can't afford the admission, see if you can volunteer in exchange for attending. Tapping into trade association resources is as easy as volunteering. If you volunteer for a trade association, you will gain information and contacts. How much easier can it be? They may not need a volunteer today, but when they do, you've got to make sure you're at the top of their volunteer list. Bring your business cards, get involved, make yourself an asset to the manager of the trade association, and before you know it, your network will be ten times its current size! But once again, you have to put in the effort to get the reward.

Some also offer job referrals, open position listings, and informal news of positions that become available.

Get involved and see what types of information and resources are accessible, or you'll likely miss out on dozens of potential unadvertised job and internship opportunities.

The sheer number of trade associations can be daunting. After a while, they may begin to blend and look like the aforementioned alphabet soup, so pick one or two to get you started and see what develops. Remember, trade associations exist to provide information and resources to their members. Participate in them and you will move ahead much more quickly than your competitors who choose to not get involved.

The last point is that these organizations provide one of the surest means, other than a personal referral, to locate working professionals who may be willing to educate and mentor you in the ways of the business. And there's no way to put a price on the value of that treasure.

THE ROLE OF MENTORS

Webster's Dictionary defines a *mentor* as "a wise and trusted counselor." Another way to think of a mentor is as a "coach" in a specific area of your career. Close your eyes for a moment and consider, "Who is my music industry mentor?" Securing a mentor to help guide your own career development is arguably one of the most impactful ways to advance your career. A mentor—someone with extensive industry experience, knowledge, and connections—provides insight that newcomers to the industry would take decades to develop on their own. Learning from a mentor is an invaluable aid to fast-tracking your own career knowledge and development.

Where does one find a mentor? Look to teachers, family friends, and the aforementioned industry events, often sponsored by various trade associations. You may also decide to send out an e-mail blast to your network asking if anyone knows of an experienced industry person in a specific area who might be willing to chat with you about careers in their field. You don't have to call them and ask them to become your mentor right out of the box. Instead, simply ask for a few minutes of their time to speak about your career interest and their experience. If the chemistry is right, you may have just added a mentor to aid you in your career development.

WORKSHOP 16. LOCATING A MENTOR

If you don't already have a relationship with an industry mentor, now's the time to approach possible mentors and start a mentor-mentee relationship. Make a list of possible candidates for your mentor and determine the best way to approach them to ask if they would consider helping you to learn more about the industry.

Each of us has to develop a pitch that we feel comfortable with. Sometimes asking someone you may barely know to serve as a mentor may seem to be reaching. If that's the case, instead, simply call or e-mail and ask if they might have twenty to thirty minutes to meet and chat about the music industry. Based on the chemistry at that meeting, you'll have a good idea if that person might be willing and available to continue meeting or corresponding from time to time.

CHAPTER 17 Goal-Setting Skills

No matter what you tackle in life, setting and achieving goals is a key to becoming successful. And setting goals is really as simple as defining various long-term, mid-term, and short-term goals. A goal must be written down and have a date by which you will complete it. Getting a job is not a goal, because you have no control of when and if you will be hired.

As an example, let's say that your eventual goal is to become a successful songwriter. Right now, you're working at a bank. But your long-term goal is to write Top-10 pop songs. You also need a mid-term goal, because it's unlikely one can go from being a bank teller to a hit songwriter overnight. So what might be a good mid-term goal? Perhaps a mid-term goal is to be a published songwriter and have two to three songs recorded on an artist's album. Pretty darn good; you got a paycheck. That's a very realistic mid-term goal.

One short-term goal is to study and learn the craft of songwriting. For instance, you discover (via detective work) that there will be a master songwriting class going on at Berklee taught by a well-known songwriter over a three-day weekend. You beg, borrow, and steal the money to go to it. Take time off work. Borrow a car, if yours is a clunker. You get there because you're determined. Other short-term goals include practicing and learning your craft.

The craft of songwriting requires you to constantly be recording. At one point, you'll be ready to put together a demo. You don't need to hire a symphony orchestra for your demo. If you work with one good musician/arranger, you can do just about anything that's required at this point. This demo may be a short- or mid-term goal, depending on where you start your songwriting odyssey.

How about identifying and subscribing to key trade magazines? That would be a short-term goal. Another is to locate a teacher/mentor. Say you attended a songwriting workshop given last year, and you began to correspond with one of the teachers via e-mail. Perhaps he would take on a student like yourself because you can learn so much in the right mentor or teacher relationship. Even if he is writing in a different genre than you are, the craft of songwriting is nearly identical across styles and genres. And being exposed to those who are further along on your intended career path, no matter what it is, is essential to speeding up your learning process.

This is how developing your own short-, mid-, and long-term goals will help you to chart a path towards your ideal career. Let's say you identify four short-term goals and set a six-month window to complete them. Your mid-term goal mentioned above—getting songs onto a record—is your one-and-a-half- to four-year window. And your eventual goal of writing a song that goes up the charts is your five- to ten-year goal. Break it down into bite-size chunks, and you will have a clear roadmap to take you to your long-term goals.

Don't just stay up every night biting your fingernails worrying, trying to write that magical hit song. You may nail it, but your odds are so long it's like playing the lottery. Don't lose sight of your overall goal and timeline. Make your goals concrete with a chart in your composing room. Review the short-term activities in process now that are going to take you to your long-term goals.

It's human nature to want to avoid setting goals and timelines. However, without using this tool and others like the marketable skill-set workshop and the interview workshop, careers in the music industry seem distant and out of reach. You won't know if your short-term goals are in sync with what's required to make it on a particular career path if you haven't researched your area of interest. Desire alone will not make your dream a reality.

If you want to be a program director at a major-market radio station, you've got to know what it takes to get there. What skills, experience, salary, and geographic moves will be required? All that information must be at your fingertips. When you have that information, it will be crystal clear to you whether or not that is the right career path for you. If you don't do your detective work, you may spend months or years pursuing a career path that really isn't what you want from life. Don't make that mistake.

That's why goal setting is so important in this industry: everybody is following their star and chasing their dream. Almost everyone wants to write, record, sing, produce, promote, or engineer that smash hit. But how do you put yourself in the situation where you're actually working with the artist who can write those hit songs? How can you work with a Tony Brown, Glen Ballard, or Quincy Jones?

Defining and achieving the little steps (short- and mid-term goals) will help you achieve your long-term goals.

So to recap, you need to identify attainable goals and set a timeline for accomplishing each one. Review goals as often as possible. Use the two one-year calendars in your Career Binder to track your progress. Update your goals as you move forward. Some will be completed and you can cross them off. New ones will become clear to you as you continue your career development.

Finally, remember to be patient. Be sure to print out and keep your career goals visible—for instance, prominently posted near your computer or in your personal rehearsal space. Doing so reminds you daily of your goals, nudging you to gauge your progress to achieving them. Maintain and update those goals, pat yourself on the back when you accomplish each one, and let the goal-setting process work for you. If you are diligent in maintaining your goals, you have a much better chance of achieving long-term success.

A SONGWRITER'S ROAD TO SUCCESS

Short-term goals	**Mid-term goals**	**Long-term goals**
6–18 months	1½–4 years	5–10 years
• Subscribe to trade magazines • Enroll in songwriting classes • Find a teacher/mentor • Join a trade association	• Publish songs • Begin building relationships with publishers, artists, managers, producers • Two to three songs recorded • Get involved in a performing rights society • Investigate co-writing options • Regularly record demos, write, and pitch new material	• Record a Top-10 song • Have songs placed in films • Collaborate with leading artists and lyricists • Win Grammy for song of the year!

WORKSHOP 17. SETTING YOUR GOALS

Identify your ultimate career goal, and list a few of the short-, mid-, and long-term goals that you believe will help you attain your ultimate music industry career goal. Don't ignore personal, life, recreational, and financial goals. Successful music industry pros with long careers understand the value of prioritizing both personal and professional career and life objectives.

List your Short-Term Goals: 6–18 months

List your Mid-Term Goals: 1 ½–4 years

List your Long-Term Goals: 5–10 or more years

CHAPTER 18 Preparing for Interview Success

THE VALUE OF INFORMATIONAL INTERVIEWS

Informational interviews help you gather information on a company or a position without being in the potentially high stakes situation of an actual hiring interview.

Before we look at how you can secure an informational interview and then craft the questions that will elicit the most useful information, remember that in today's increasingly hectic working world, professionals you will approach may often have difficulty making time for such activities. Don't be dismayed if your requests for informational interviews occasionally result in turndowns. By asking your network and mentors for referrals and getting involved in conferences or trade associations, you will quickly find opportunities to land informational interviews. If you are hidden at home, you can't very well meet people who can help you. Only then will you discover the wealth of information that such an interview can bring to your job search.

If you will be approaching a company or person "cold" for such an interview, here's the most effective approach.

Introduce yourself via letter, phone, or e-mail. If you have just met someone at an industry event, or heard them speak at a panel or workshop, you may also approach them immediately afterwards. Explain briefly who you are and what you are interested in learning about from them. If you are approaching a firm cold, ideally, you will have the name of the person with whom you would like to meet. That person might be the studio manager, head of personnel, tour manager—whomever you feel might be a good information source. Be sure that you are professional and polite. Enlist the help of the person answering the phone in getting an "at bat" to request an informational interview. Do not antagonize the receptionist or assistant, also known as the screener. If they have to put you on hold, say it's "no problem" for you to wait until they can get back on the line.

If you actually are connected with the person you wish to meet, or the assistant, once again be clear about who you are and why you are calling. Now is the time to clearly state that you are asking for a brief appointment (ten to fifteen minutes is a good length) to find out a bit more about the industry and the company. If they say no, then remember to ask if there is another person in the company who might be able to share a few minutes, either in person or by phone. Another option is that the person to whom you are speaking may know of another working professional they believe may be helpful for you to contact. Always end with a polite thank you for each person's time, no matter what the outcome is.

Once you land an informational interview, brush up on the following workshop, listing some of the basic questions to ask. Be sure to bring a pocket note pad and jot down their key comments.

The speed at which valuable information will be coming at you during such an interview will make taking notes very helpful. You won't have the luxury of calling them back to check a fact, name, or phone number. Take your time, and when an important point is made, repeat that point aloud to confirm that you understood exactly what's been said.

WORKSHOP 18.1. INFORMATIONAL INTERVIEW GUIDELINES

You're in your interview… now what? After outlining briefly—in one or two sentences—why you are there and your career goals, use this list as a guide. Be sure to start the interview by asking how much time your interview subject is able to share with you. Then stick to that timetable.

1. What do you look for when you are hiring a [target job]?
2. Will I need special training or education?
3. If so, where is the best place to get such training?
4. Is specific job experience required? If so, what kind? More importantly, how would you recommend getting such experience?
5. Is there any way to break into this field without on-the-job experience?
6. These are the skills and abilities I have developed.
7. (Briefly outline your basic skills and/or hand over your carefully crafted résumé.)
8. What do you think my chances are of being hired as a [target job]?
9. Do you have any suggestions for me to increase my chances for being hired as a [target job]?
10. Do you hire people in this capacity often? What's the supply-and-demand situation in terms of job seekers and available jobs in this field?
11. To what level can a person hired at the entry-level advance?
12. What is the usual starting salary range? After two years?
13. Does your company offer internships?
14. Can you suggest other companies or people to contact in your field?
15. What is the most important attribute that someone wishing to enter the field today should possess?

This list will result in a lengthy interview, if all the questions are discussed. If time is tight, you will have to prioritize these questions for each informational interview you secure. Another question that can be illustrative of early-stage careers is to ask how they got their start in the industry.

Your informational interview subjects will pass on a wealth of information in the short time that you are with each of them. Their answers will serve as a roadmap to fine-tune your career development and job search. Your focused inquiry will say to them you are serious in your approach about entering their field, often impressing them enough to create more opportunities for you.

It's only going to take two or three productive informational interviews to understand exactly which skills are requirements for success for a given job and whether or not you are currently employable in a particular position.

Are such informational interviews easy to obtain? No. Why? Everybody has twelve hours of work to do in nine hours. How are they going to get it done? Many executives and middle managers are just too busy to even consider such interviews. That's why nurturing your network to get an introduction when you are ready for it is so vital to your career development.

If you can't approach a person or a company directly, you may connect with them at a professional meeting, seminar, conference, lecture, or class. In that setting, professionals will often say, "I enjoyed speaking to the class (conference, workshop, etc.) today, so here is my e-mail address if you have any other questions." If you don't write that down and send them an e-mail, you are squandering a prime opportunity. Even better, if you ask for that speaker's business card, you should follow up with a handwritten thank-you note. You'll make a strong positive impression by doing so.

Every time you have an opportunity to network with a working professional, take it, regardless of whether or not that person is directly on the career path you see yourself taking today. You never know when having a wider network may help you. You've got to have access to fresh, reliable industry information to make the most of your career opportunities. In addition to what you will learn from magazines, books, seminars, and classes, networking provides the best source of locally relevant information for someone on a career search.

What else do you bring to your informational interview? Two résumés and some business cards. When you get home from that informational interview, promptly write a thank-you note. Thank them for their time and the information they shared.

THE JOB INTERVIEW

Let's assume you've submitted a résumé for a position that is advertised or that you've learned about through your network, and you've been called in for an interview. How do you maximize this opportunity?

Here is a checklist of what you should do in advance to prepare for the interview.

PRE-INTERVIEW CHECKLIST

		YES	NO
1.	Your résumé is in tip-top shape.	☐	☐
2.	You know something about the company and, if possible, the person with whom you will be meeting.	☐	☐
3.	You have a handful of your business cards.	☐	☐
4.	You have practiced the interview workshop on the following pages with a friend or family member. If the interview is for a particular job opening, use the list on page 120. If it is an informational interview, use the list on page 115.	☐	☐
5.	Dress neatly and present yourself professionally.	☐	☐
6.	Plan to arrive a few minutes early, especially if you are traveling there for the first time.	☐	☐
7.	Jot down a few questions about the company, its activities, and the requirements for an employee's success in that company. Make a note to ask these questions during your interview.	☐	☐
8.	Bring a notepad and pen.	☐	☐

During the interview itself, just concentrate on being yourself and answering questions as directly and honestly as you can. If you are at the entry-level stage of your career, the person interviewing you doesn't expect you to have all the answers. What they are looking for is intelligence, a positive attitude, and whether or not they feel there will be a fit between you and the company.

Take the time to look around the company offices and take a few mental notes. Are the offices neat, bright, and pleasant? Do the people working there smile and address you directly? Is this the kind of place you would like to come to each day? If not, no matter how good an offer, you should consider these factors. Also, if there are pictures of sailboats in the office of your interviewer, and you happen to have a family member who sails, take the initiative to mention that point and use it to build a rapport.

How should you dress for an interview? Dress appropriately for the company. Determine appropriate dress by doing your homework. If you're going for an interview to a company that does concert production and sound reinforcement, their stock in trade is building, moving, and maintaining big, heavy pieces of equipment. You definitely don't want to be wearing an Armani suit. However, if you're wearing a pair of khaki pants and a neatly pressed shirt with a collar, you will look professional and neat. If you are interviewing at a well-known Madison Avenue entertainment law firm, you would wear a suit. The impression you make with your dress, your manner, and your questions and comments set you apart—to your benefit or your detriment. The choice is yours to make. So take the time to rehearse carefully so you are as comfortable and confident as possible.

Now let's look at the interview drill workshop on the next pages. It will allow you to build your confidence by practicing aloud the types of questions that you are likely to be asked during an actual job interview.

It's important to spend some time thinking about and writing down your answers to these types of questions. Equally important is practicing the interview drills aloud with a friend or family member. Do it more than once. The more familiar you are talking about yourself, your qualifications, and your worth points (how you have created value for your employer in the past), the better the impression. Be prepared to the point that discussing your interests and skills is second nature. Doing so will give you the confidence to present yourself at your best.

WORKSHOP 18.2. SEND YOUR COLD LETTER

Remember the cold letter you drafted in the workshop in chapter 12? Now that you've practiced interviewing with friends and family, put a current date on that letter, proofread it one last time, and send it out to secure an informational interview!

WORKSHOP 18.3. JOB INTERVIEW PRACTICE

You wouldn't show up for a gig with your band without adequate rehearsal, would you? Don't shortchange yourself in an interview. Rehearsal will allow you to be at your best.

Start by looking carefully at the questions below, and write down your answers. You will have to do some thinking. Don't expect to draft perfect answers on the first attempt. Interviews can be tense for all parties, and practicing will build your confidence! Once you have answers that you feel comfortable with, it's time to enlist the help of a friend or family member to drill you and strengthen your interview skills.

Job Interview Practice Session

Your interviewer is a human resources coordinator for Big Time Records.

Questions:

1. How did you learn about this position and our company?
2. What do you feel qualifies you to work at Big Time Records?
3. In your past work experience, what have you enjoyed doing the most?
4. What part of your working experience was least enjoyable?
5. Where do you see your career taking you over the next two to four years? (A variation on this question is to lengthen the timeline to five to ten years; use your published goals to help answer this question.)
6. If we don't have any openings for paid positions at this time, would you consider an unpaid internship?
7. Are there any other skills or accomplishments that you feel qualify you to work here?

Remember to thank your interviewers for the time they have spent talking with you. Time is the most precious commodity any busy professional can share.

Use this workshop again as a review before you go out on an actual job interview. Answer questions in an even pace, and take a minute to think about your answers. Above all, if you don't know the answer to a specific question on an actual interview (especially if it is a technical question), don't be afraid to answer by saying, "I don't know the answer, but I'm sure I could find out."

How is your body language? Try not to be tense and nervous, and remember to speak clearly. It is important to show enthusiasm and make eye contact with your interviewer.

Remember that any interview is, first and foremost, your best opportunity to make a positive impression on a potential employer or a referral to employment. Make the most of each interview by being well prepared and ready to answer basic questions such as these. If possible, secure the full name and accurate pronunciation of your interviewer's name in advance. Bring at least two copies of your current résumé, and have some current information about the company at your command so you can show you have done some research.

Review these questions and practice your answers aloud at least three times before going on any interview. Do your homework before you step into that office, and your interviews will bring a handsome reward!

The questions in the interview practice session are similar to those that you're likely to be asked if you're actually applying for a job. If you don't practice answering them, odds are that you may say something that you regret.

If an interviewer asks, "What do you think qualifies you to work at XYZ record label?" be ready to answer that with some of your worth points. Do your preparation on the company in advance. Know something about what they do and mention what you know about the company and their business in the interview. Before you go on the interview, practice stating your worth points and the information you have dug out about the company. Practice speaking in front of a mirror, and then practice with a friend. It makes all of the difference in your delivery. Remember not to speak too quickly, and try to enunciate your words. Ask your rehearsal partner to grade your speed, delivery, and intelligibility. Speech patterns make a difference. If you are enrolled at school, there is likely a career center that may offer to do a mock interview and critique with you. By all means, take advantage of this to further strengthen your skills.

Also, practice both sitting and standing. Be aware of your hands and facial expressions. Overactive hands can be a distraction. However, using your hand or hands to help make a point occasionally can strengthen your communication. Likewise, don't stare at your knees or look at the floor during your interview. You don't have to lock eyes with your interviewer, but make eye contact from time to time, and keep your head up and focused in their direction. Be aware of your legs and avoid playing with your clothing, shoes, hair, etc. Women, be sure to wear clothing that will not embarrass you if you sit on a couch or deep chair. If you have tattoos on your arms and legs, it might be wise to cover them up for the interview—at least, until you can observe the culture of the workplace.

You may have an unconscious habit that could become distracting in an interview. Find out in your practice session and get it under control. Above all, be tidy, organized, professional looking, and prepared for success.

In addition to your enthusiasm, experience, and qualifications, which should be evident from your personal demeanor as well as your well-crafted résumé, your interviewer is trying to determine, "Will you work hard, do you know a bit about the business, and is there prior job performance that shows you are stable and trustworthy?" On the business side of the industry, your presentation will be more important. Do you look professional? Do you sound articulate? Are your communication skills displayed to your advantage? Will you be comfortable representing the employer in person and on the phone? Your interviewer may say, "Bill, come to my desk and pick up the phone. We want to ask you a few questions over the phone." Or they may ask you to take an aptitude test to measure your ability to follow directions, do simple math, and assess your command of the written word. One of my students just applied for a job at a leading Hollywood entertainment PR firm and at the start of her second interview, she was shown into a conference room and asked to draft a short news release using pen and paper from a one-sheet scenario. Be prepared to show your skills to your best advantage.

Practice makes perfect, so don't shortchange yourself by going into an interview unprepared. Be just as prepared for informational interviews, because you never know when an informational interview may turn into a job interview.

CHAPTER 19 Learn Before You Earn

Internships can offer an effective bridge to a job in the music industry. A good internship position puts you in a working environment where professionals are practicing their craft in your specific field of interest. An internship also allows you to observe and participate meaningfully in the firm's day-to-day business operation.

Although I am a strong proponent of internships, since they provide an unparalleled real-world learning experience, they also may tax your financial health. Many entertainment industry internships are unpaid positions. A few paid internships do exist, and they are competed for fiercely. A growing number also require intern candidates to be enrolled in a for-credit college course. However, even an unpaid internship can be extremely valuable to your career development if you plan for it properly and set specific goals for what you plan to learn.

To get the most from an internship, expose yourself to as many facets of the company's operations as possible. Avoid no task or activity that can help you grow. If you see the company president is hosting a golf tournament, volunteer to help. The more you can rub elbows with the movers and the shakers, the more benefit you will receive from your internship.

Learning how to set up a recording session, mail out a press release, or make travel plans for your boss properly isn't the only thing you want to master. Many benefits accrue for savvy interns who network with the employees they meet.

Another way to maximize the benefits from an internship is to widen your exposure at the company. As an example, if you intern three days a week at a record label, perhaps you could come in one of the other days and observe operations (often called "shadowing") in another department. That way you will learn more about what's done in say, the business affairs department, the marketing department, or the promotions department.

My bottom line on internships is that they provide outstanding opportunities for a person who wants to learn and get established in the industry. But there are exceptions—situations where a few companies may take unfair advantage of so-called "interns" to get free labor, with little or no learning or mentoring offered in the exchange. I've known interns who were faced with requests for unpaid activities that, frankly, were way above and beyond the call of duty for what amounts to a volunteer position. My advice to those facing such a situation is to use common sense in judging whether or not you should commit to a seemingly inappropriate or overwhelming task. To learn about a firm's business and its operation, you should be exposed to more activities than simply operating a copy machine or making coffee. Be upfront before accepting an internship and ask for specific information as to what parts of the firm's business and operations you will be exposed to. Explain what areas of the industry you have an interest in and ask for guidance and mentoring in that area.

If you find yourself in what appears to be an abusive internship situation, or one in which you are continually told to "read a magazine" until we have something for you to do, be it paid or unpaid, bring your concern to the attention of the supervisor or boss. State your concern calmly and listen carefully to the supervisor's response. What's the worst thing that might happen? They may let you go. If that does happen, don't fret. You probably aren't going to have a career at a firm that does not value every member of its team, even a "lowly" intern. If you are enrolled in a college program for internship credit, you have an advantage in that your faculty sponsor will also act as an advocate for you, and usually will contact your workplace supervisor to confirm that your enrollment is predicated on doing meaningful work, albeit at an appropriate level, at their firm. And the faculty sponsor should also emphasize that a key component of every successful academic internship is a workplace supervisor who gives regular feedback to the student on his or her performance.

Don't be too apprehensive about landing an internship. There are thousands of fabulous internships hosted by firms who understand the value of offering an introduction to future industry members via an internship. Remember, many school programs in music business, music products, entertainment law, the recording arts, or other areas of the industry, maintain records of internship opportunities that have been tested by previous students and recommended by faculty. This is an excellent approach to landing the right internship that can be your stepping stone to a greatly expanded professional network and in some cases, even your first job offer.

One studio manager at a leading world-class recording facility candidly remarked to me, "The first place we look to fill an opening is our pool of current and past interns. They know our business and what we expect in an employee. More importantly, we have seen them in action and have a good idea as to how quickly they will be able to get up to speed with clients and the rest of our employees. Proving yourself as an intern is the fastest way to be considered for a staff position at our studios."

ON THE JOB/YOUR INTERNSHIP

Once you arrive at your internship, a new level of learning begins. Although academic training is important, there's only so much you're going to learn in a classroom environment. When you've got an artist breathing down your neck demanding, "Where's the guitar track that I just played?" your motivation to learn quickly is definitely heightened. When you're in a classroom environment, there is a different dynamic. When your boss has instructed you to have the new portion of an artist's Web site up and functional by week's end so that the band's new video can be previewed there as they launch their national tour, it changes the stakes and your investment in succeeding in a big way.

What will make you, as an intern, valuable to your future boss? That's the golden question that interns perennially seek to answer. Here are the key attributes that employers look for most when hiring.

MUSIC-INDUSTRY EMPLOYER'S WISH LIST

1. **Problem-solving ability** is very important. Bosses generally are bosses because they're the best at dealing with a thousand-and-one problems. So if you develop problem-solving skills, chances are you're going to go a long way toward impressing your supervisor. The best way to develop your own problem-solving skills is to take on new challenges or work study positions, or volunteer for interesting and exciting roles at school or in your community.
2. **Technical skills** also play a part, too—especially if you've charted a career path on a technical track. Don't overlook the fundamental computer and Internet skills that many baby-boomer aged employers rely on your generation to provide.
3. The ability to **responsibly complete assignments** is a critical skill. Employees who can work effectively in a self-directed manner are a big asset.
4. There are not "white-coated operators" standing by at every music industry firm waiting for job assignments. There are just enough people to get projects completed and sometimes not quite enough people to get by. So, to succeed in this industry, you have to **hustle**. You will occasionally stay until midnight to complete an important job. It's the nature of the beast. The entertainment industry is not like the banking industry, in which retail banks are open from 9 A.M. to 6 P.M. and then everyone heads home. Weekends? Prepare to sacrifice quite a few of them over the course of your career.
5. **Perseverance** keeps turning up as another key attribute. Early in my career, a very successful magazine publisher told me, "Keith, you've got to be in the right place at the right time... and that means being aware of what's going on in all the areas you have an interest, all the time."

   What he meant is that if you're serious about a career in the music industry, you have to get plugged in so that you have constant access to the information that relates to your interests. You have to be ready to network every minute of every day, even if you've got a nonmusical job. You may be pleasantly surprised to discover that someone in the company at which you work has a kid or a nephew or an uncle who works at a label, a booking agency, a theme park, or a film studio. Let people know what your aspirations are.

Not to the point of annoyance, but it's good to voice where you are headed in the long run to those you feel close to at your day job. "I enjoy working here, but I'm also writing songs every chance I get and studying how to become a successful songwriter." You may be pleasantly surprised to find out that a distant relative actually turns out to be able to help you make a key career connection.

6. **Integrity** is a key component of your success, not only as an intern, but all the way to the top. When you say you're going to do something, do it. If you say you're going to do something and you realize you can't, don't be afraid to go back and say, "You know, I really can't do that." People will respect you for that far more than if you hide under a blanket and think, "I hope they forgot I said I was going to do that."

   Your boss and coworkers are not likely to forget your failure to live up to your promise to perform. The entertainment industry is surprisingly small and most people have good memories. It's okay to regroup and say you can't deliver, but it is a huge liability to just blow off an assignment, no matter how trivial it may seem to you. Integrity is an asset that once damaged proves extremely difficult to repair.

FINANCIAL SURVIVAL FOR INTERNS

Once you have identified a prospective internship that appears to provide you with the right learning opportunities, the final hurdle appears. The last concern prospective interns have is usually the biggest one: that is, the lack of pay from the employer even though, as an intern, you must make a firm commitment of time, effort, and energy. If a studio calls up and offers an internship and it doesn't pay, you may have to do a little finagling, especially if you have a full-time "day gig" to pay your bills. You may have to ask the boss at your day gig if you could work flexible hours for the term of your internship. That's why it's helpful to let people know a little about your long-term quest to be successful in the music industry. Most people want to see others succeed in the long run.

The worst thing that can happen is that your day job boss will say, "No!" and you'll have to choose to decline the internship or look for a different day gig.

The best internship programs are ones in which your role as an intern is managed. This means that when you are interviewing to learn about the opportunity, the employer can lay out, "Here's what our internship offers you and what types of work you will be doing." On the other hand, if your internship description is vague, uncertain or consists mostly of "clean up and setup, make coffee, stock the bathrooms, wait for assignments as they come up," you might want to look for a little more structured learning environment. Ask a few more questions, because a successful internship is a two-way street—a give-and-get proposition, and the best internship host firms understand they are your teachers for the duration of your time with them.

A good internship program should offer you numerous learning opportunities, which may come in all shapes and sizes. You should have the opportunity to "stretch" your knowledge and skills beyond your current comfort zone. This type of internship should include some moments of revelation where your understanding of the industry takes a leap forward. It's this type of learning that greatly enhances your value in the job market as a music industry professional-in-training.

In the pre-internship discussions, you should be interviewing the intern managers as much as they are interviewing you. "Mr. Studio Manager, if I intern at your studio, would there be some learning opportunities for me? What would they include?" If you get a good answer to that, it's a very positive sign. However, if you don't, or if the manager hems and haws a bit, that's a warning sign.

Find out if there will be an opportunity to ask questions of the senior staff at some point. Will you be able to attend staff meetings? Will you have contact with clients (if appropriate)? If they don't have an answer to these questions, you've likely got an internship host that does not understand the learning paradigm required for the best internship outcomes. If you have to do any errands or traveling, will you be reimbursed for gas? It's smart to ask those kinds of questions up front.

A few internships, usually with the larger companies such as record labels, actually offer minimum wage to interns, as they understand the mutual benefit of actually offering a paycheck, however small.

Why is that? The intern, even when receiving a small paycheck, is often more committed. And the employer, since they are actually paying, thinks, "It's a resource. We're paying for it," instead of saying, "She's an intern; she sits and reads *Billboard* for four hours and only does fifteen minutes of work, but it has no impact on my bottom line." So ask questions and if possible, speak with a current or past intern to hear what they learned during their internship.

Another key is to network with your friends and acquaintances. Let your friends who have similar interests know, "I did an internship at such and such company, and they're looking for more people now!" If you're in a school program, network constantly with other students who have completed internships. Your faculty advisor should also be able to tip you off to the firms that in the past have offered the best internship opportunities.

I really believe in the value of internships. However, try to find one where you really believe you've got an opportunity to learn. Prepare yourself, since you may need to work a part-time job or save up enough money to focus on your internship. Earning will come later in your career. Do not mistake your internship as an earning opportunity. It is a way to enhance your "hire-ability" as soon as you absorb what knowledge you can.

Remember, an internship is temporary. Go into an internship knowing that it is not your permanent station in life. Secondly, in a good internship, there's a balance between learning and earning: completing meaningful work for your intern host firm (earning) and your boss, and learning the ins and outs of their business, which will enhance your marketable skill set, including your area-specific industry knowledge.

Not all internships lead to your next step on that career ladder. A former student called to say, "Oh-h-h-h, that internship was a nightmare. I had no idea what an entertainment-industry public-relations firm did. I was stuffing press kits and envelopes and running a copy machine in a tiny, hot room. I was sorting hundreds of pieces of mail and clipping articles with an X-acto knife. I was there until 2 A.M. because there was an ad campaign breaking, and we had to assemble and hand out goodie bags to 10,000 people at an industry event at 7 A.M. the next morning. At the conclusion of my three-month internship, I knew that this end of the business wasn't for me."

Guess what? That was the second most valuable type of internship that person could have had, at that point. Why? Because they now know for sure that they are not cut out to work in entertainment public relations. The most valuable internship is one that leads to a strengthened professional network and marketable skill set in your number 1 area of interest.

WORKSHOP 19. DESCRIBING YOUR IDEAL INTERNSHIP OPPORTUNITY

If you're considering an internship, take this opportunity to make a list of what types of internships might be the best stepping stone for your own career development. Next, add to that list the types of jobs, duties, and responsibilities you think you might be engaged in on an ideal internship. This is a handy exercise and goes a long way to preparing you for a prospective pre-internship interview. Be sure to be realistic and remember that the best internships are ones that combine some of the necessary grunt work with the opportunity to observe and learn from the key employees at the internship host firm.

CHAPTER 20 Preparing for Your Job Search

Let's assume that you have at least one marketable skill-set workshop completed. You've got a career path and a ladder that you've investigated and that really interests you. You've done a bit of research on the job, divining the earning potential from grunt to big cheese on your chosen career path. You even have a plan to survive financially while you do an unpaid internship. You're at the career starting gate, ready to dive into your preferred segment of the music industry. What is your next move? In this chapter, I'll help you to get the greatest results from your forthcoming job-search efforts.

YOUR ATTITUDE WILL DETERMINE YOUR ALTITUDE

I can't overemphasize the importance of bringing a positive attitude to your job and to your job search. Why? Because no one wants to be around folks that are grumpy or out of sorts. Work is tough, full of stress and challenges. You have to be able to come in and say, "Okay, how can I contribute? How do I create value for the company? How do I make my bosses more successful?"

That's really what you should be thinking about when you're heading into an interview or a potential job situation: What are you capable of doing to make that company measurably better?

And when it does come to an interview for a prospective internship or job, having a positive attitude will make it easier for you to communicate what you've done elsewhere in the past. Even if you haven't had any big career successes yet, be sure to highlight the noteworthy accomplishments on your résumé. You can work at a local level. Volunteer at a local organization. Anyplace where you personally helped make a change is a notch in your career belt, and that's the information that you need to present clearly in a job interview. Having a positive attitude goes a long way in making the impression that you are someone that would be valuable to an organization.

INVESTMENT IN YOUR SEARCH

You're going to have to invest in your job search. The first investment is time, one of the most precious commodities anyone has. You must invest time regularly to do your career "homework" and educate yourself about all aspects of the area of the industry you plan to enter. Next, some cash investments are required—none too large, but it may be essential to invest in some organizational tools, such as contact management software, and also budgeting for whatever clothing is appropriate or any travel that may be necessary.

On the subject of research, it's clear today that the Internet is an essential resource. I am continually amazed when I'll ask, "I wonder what this company does?" and I'll tap, tap, tap, tap, tap on my computer keyboard until the information comes onto my screen. By and large, the information is out there, if you're willing to look for it. Don't neglect the annual business directories mentioned earlier. Your local or university reference librarian is also a valuable resource.

If you aspire to be a songwriter, you need to get yourself on the mailing list of every songwriter's organization there is—local, national, and international. Learn about performing rights societies and how they can help your career. (The leading performing rights societies are ASCAP, SESAC, and BMI, listed in the appendix.)

If you want to be a recording engineer or producer, you should become a member of the Recording Academy (NARAS). Learn too about SPARS and the AES—organizations that serve the recording studio, engineer, audio technology, and producer communities (also listed in appendix C).

If you want a career in broadcasting, you've got to seek out similar associations, such as the National Association of Broadcasters. If videogames are your thing, you should investigate E3 (Electronic Entertainment Expo) and their annual trade show featuring the latest in interactive entertainment, and continue to make connections to appropriate trade associations and conferences that serve this field, including the Computer Games Developer's Conference, and other similar events. Get involved. It's vitally important to continually meet people and learn. Invest the time and membership dues to participate in a pertinent trade organization that is on the career path that interests you the most.

TOOLS AND INFORMATION RESOURCES

What are the basic tools you're going to need to do your job search?

First, your résumé. You'll need that soon enough, but not in the research phase.

How do you learn about companies? Start by utilizing the tools that everyone has access to: the telephone, the library, and the Internet.

Many books are updated every four to five years. In terms of the freshness of the information, they are not as current as a trade magazine or the Internet. Business directories are updated constantly, and although the printed version may be published once a year, their online directories may be updated more often. Print and online editions of trade magazines provide fresh information daily, weekly, or monthly, depending on their publication schedule. Major daily newspapers in New York, Los Angeles, and Nashville regularly cover the entertainment industry, so searching their Web sites for recent articles often uncovers a great deal of information about local companies, trends in the market, local or regional trade associations, and the names of leading experts in various fields.

The Internet provides access to information that is often updated daily. Even if a label Web site is primarily aimed at consumers, record buyers, and fans, there's usually other information about the label to be found on the site. Many major and Indie labels often post job listings online.

What else will you need to invest in your career development? Time. You need to make a commitment to set up a very specific time budget. When you first moved out of your parents' house, you had to figure out what you could spend on rent, car insurance, food, clothing, etc. In the same way, you need to set up a time budget to succeed in your job search.

Can you afford to spend ten hours a week? Can you afford to spend two hours a week? More importantly, can you afford *not* to?

The most important aspect of your career-development time budget is to be consistent and stick with it every week, be it ten hours or one.

Make your time-budget allocation based on how close you believe you are to being prepared to compete for a paid position in your area of interest. If you're in your second year of a four-year college program, you might devote one to two hours per week. If you have completed a relevant internship and will be graduating in a month, you should be spending eight to ten hours or more a week. Once you have a time budget, keep a log of your time. For example, "On November 15, I invested one hour." The most important aspect of your career-development time budget is to be consistent and stick with it every week, be it ten hours or one.

Many trade magazines now have online editions that you can check up on frequently. Personally, although online editions are convenient, I prefer print editions because I can also take two to three trade magazines with me on a flight or overnight at a hotel and browse through them, updating my industry-specific knowledge for that market area.

Another place to mine information is company literature. If the company is publicly traded, you can locate their 10K statement. This lists the officers of the company, what state they are headquartered in, how many employees they have, and their annual report. You may also find much of that information on their Web site.

Some basic organizational tools have proven to be effective for me. I use business-card sheets that each hold 20 business cards back-to-back and fit in a three-ring binder. I also have a small Casio electronic pocket organizer, a precursor to the Palm Pilots and Blackberry devices of today, but that stores 300+ personal and professional contacts for me. Other alternatives are the Filofax or Day Planner organizers. These help you keep track of contacts, appointments, to-do lists, and the like.

Whenever you get a new contact's business card, have a routine that you never deviate from for storing and accessing that information. Whether you tuck it into a page of your business-card organizer or enter the data into your Blackberry devices, be sure to capture it in a way that you can quickly access it when you need it.

Each time you do an interview, make some notes about what you discussed or learned. It's also a good idea to write down the name of the receptionist or the secretary of the company that you interviewed at on the back of the interviewer's business card. Then, if you go for a second interview, you've got that card, and you can bring it with you. You can know that the receptionist's name is Mary or Jim, and you will make an impression that you are sharp and personable. That impression is crucial to separate you from the other interviewees.

Your own business cards are a must. I strongly encourage you to invest in them as soon as you're ready to begin your job search. Office-supply stores such as Office Depot, Office Max, or Staples can design and print 500 simple business cards for less than $20. Other options include free online business-card providers such as VistaPrint.com, which can provide 250 free business cards for a $12.95 processing and shipping fee, delivered in seven days. Another option is to purchase Avery business-card stock that is perforated and ready to use on either a laser or ink-jet printer. You can download a free business-card template from Avery.com and print your own cards up 8 to 10 at a time on a high-quality printer.

Business cards are something job seekers often overlook. Have them made even if you don't have a job or internship yet. They set a professional tone with anyone you interact with. Even if you are working a day gig, you don't have to list your day gig on your business card. It can just include your name, address, and contact information. Most of my current students follow a simple format for their short-term business cards, which are the ones they will use until they land their first full-time industry position. They include their name, cell-phone number, e-mail address, and a campus mailing address or P.O. box, if they have one. Some only list the e-mail and cell phone. Don't worry about a job title or career track. A few students know they will be going into a certain area, such as recording engineer, songwriter, or artist manager, and put that on the card as well. One student planning to attend law school, put "Lawyer-in-training" on her cards, which was a memorable way to differentiate herself from other interns looking for summer internships at law firms. Whether you go the name, phone and e-mail route, or add an area or job of interest, just get your cards in hand.

The final benefit to having a business card is that when you meet someone, you can give that person your business card. Most of the time, they will pass their card back to you, so you have another contact to add to your growing universe of industry contacts.

WORKSHOP 20. CAREER INVESTMENTS

Using a piece of lined paper, list the organizational, research, and career tools mentioned in this chapter you plan to invest in. Keep in mind that greater cost is not an indicator of any better chances of success. Many have done extremely well staying organized using binders, 3x5 cards, and notepads.

Next, set up a time budget for the next thirty days to invest time each day in your own career. Your time should be invested in a variety of activities such as networking, research, phone and e-mail contacts, attending public events, working on your own materials, etc.

CHAPTER 21 Are You Ready to Hit the Streets?

If you've done your detective work, performed the workshops outlined earlier in this book, developed a rock-solid résumé, and started to build your network of contacts, then you're probably itching to hit the streets and put your new career-building skills to work.

Hold on for a bit, please, before you head out onto the streets. Before rushing out the door or to your telephone to begin calling prospective employers, read, review, and implement these tips, techniques, and strategies that will help you be more successful in finding, keeping, and growing in your music-industry dream job. First, here are some attributes that have proven to be essential to long-term career success.

Enthusiasm is essential to making a favorable impression on your future boss and coworkers. It's hard to convince your future boss that you're the best person to hire if you don't display confidence in yourself. Building confidence requires you to practice communicating effectively with those in the industry.

If you play a musical instrument, you wouldn't perform unprepared. Likewise, if you're going to an interview, whether it's informational or a final interview for the job of your dreams, don't do it without first practicing. Chapter 18 provides a blueprint to develop your basic interviewing skills. Rehearsing your interview will give you confidence. That confidence will translate into enthusiasm and the ability to communicate your skills, attributes, and career goals to those you meet, whether it's at an industry event or an interview. This will make a tremendous difference in the quality of your interview experience. Critique your practice interviews honestly. We all have areas in our interviewing skill sets that can be strengthened with practice and assessment.

What else will help you build your confidence? Start with a good résumé. Regularly practice your interviewing skills. Dig up information on the company with which you have an interview or tour arranged. Be ready with well-prepared and intelligent questions that show you have a basic grasp of the company and their business. Succeeding in your career search requires you to be enthusiastic, knowledgeable, practiced, and confident. The way to accomplish that is **adequate preparation**.

The next key to getting that job is to clearly communicate the **results** of what you've accomplished so far in your working history. Remember, making the best possible presentation on your own behalf in any type of interview requires selling yourself. In sales lingo, that means you need to highlight the "benefits" and not the "features" you offer an employer. Here's an example of the difference between features and benefits.

Say you live in Palm Springs or Orlando. Every car should be equipped with air conditioning in such hot climates. If I'm a car salesman and I say to a prospective buyer, "This car has air conditioning. It's really nice," I've merely told a prospective buyer about the A/C *feature*. I'll be much more successful in getting my customer to want that air conditioner if I communicate, "Remember last week when the temperature reached 102 degrees? This nicely air-conditioned car will keep you cool and comfortable, no matter what the weather is like." The comfort that the buyer will experience illustrates the **benefit** they will get if they purchase an auto with A/C.

Think of yourself in terms of the benefits you can create for your prospective employer. Can you make their life easier, more profitable, and more comfortable? If so, how will you communicate this to them? Will they have more free time because of your competency? Less worries? Can you increase their bottom line because of what you can do for them, say, using your Web skills? You must communicate the **benefits** that they are likely to enjoy if they hire you.

Practically speaking, there's no better way to accomplish this than by stating your worth points in your résumé, your cover letter, and most importantly, in person during your interview. Skip back to chapter 11 and read your sample worth points aloud. They clearly state the benefits you created in a no-nonsense manner.

Go back to the worth points in the sample chronological résumé found in chapter 10. This candidate can use her accomplishments in organizing the tracking and maintenance of the sound equipment at school as a perfect way to illustrate the benefits (less downtime, faster repairs, and more gear available for shows) that such organizational skills can bring to an employer. Even if it's a different type of company, not one in the live sound field, the skills demonstrated by the worth point discussion are completely transferable to any technology-related company. If you are using a functional résumé, be sure to emphasize the transferable skills that will benefit your future employer. Now is the time to go back to the worth-point chapter, and if you haven't developed a few that you can incorporate into your career package, reinvest the necessary time and energy into finding something you have done in the past that demonstrates your ability to create some type of measurable benefit.

Be careful not to overstate or overhype your accomplishments. No employer wants an overblown, narcissistic employee. But if you state your worth points and demonstrate how you can contribute to the company, you will have made a favorable impression, one that is likely to land you in the top tier of candidates for the job you seek. To convince them, you must demonstrate you are the *best person available* for the job at that moment. Worth points are one of the most effective ways to accomplish this task.

Another key action after you've completed an interview is to *follow up* in writing. Re-emphasize the key benefits you believe you can contribute if hired. At some point during your interview, take a moment to ask your interviewer the following question: "I appreciate the time you've spent telling me more about the company and what kinds of job opportunities exist here. Could you identify what are the two or three key attributes it will take for a person to be successful at this job (or in this company)?"

Listen very carefully to the reply, and make a note of what the interviewer says. Then, you can write a thank-you note. (You did remember to ask for a business card, so you are sure to use the correct spelling of the interviewer's name and title, didn't you?) Now, you're in a position to not only thank this person for the interview, which demonstrates your professionalism, but you can also briefly restate how your marketable skill set will make you an asset to the company. If you are interviewing for a specific position, you can state that your skills, worth points, enthusiasm, and experience would be an excellent fit with the company... based on what you learned during your interview.

It's your responsibility to communicate with your prospective employer why you are the best choice. Employers will rarely read between the lines on your résumé and cover letter. They don't have the time. However, if you've done your homework and arrive prepared with many of the things outlined in this book, your prospective employer is likely to think, "This person seems articulate, informed, and has relevant job experience. They also took the time to find a little bit of information about us." When you hit them with a follow-up letter that restates your experience, worth points, and your sincere interest, you score a few more points.

Should you follow up by e-mail? I suggest you use paper. Generally, if you're still in the running for a position, the company is likely to add your follow-up note to your file. If it's e-mail, they may not print it out. Also, I believe that e-mail is still a bit ephemeral in today's business world. Always save a copy of your follow-up correspondence.

As your career develops, it's important to demonstrate your *progressive career growth.* That is, how you have increased your skills, your responsibility, and the value you created for your employers over time.

For instance, if you are climbing the technical track of the studio career ladder covered in chapter 5, you probably started off sweeping floors, running errands, and making coffee as a gofer. Then you moved up to making tape copies and soon were assisting on sessions, setting up the tape machines and microphones in the studio. That's progressive career growth. It shows your progress and represents a very powerful method to sell you to your next boss as someone on the way up. You've missed a very important opportunity, if all you communicate on your résumé is that you "worked in a recording studio."

Progressive career growth shows a prospective employer that you've evolved. That's one of the career keys your next boss really wants to see. Over time, you will develop from a one-page to a one-and-a-half-page résumé. You will be able to communicate verbally and in writing the way that you have developed and the specific areas where you have created benefits (don't forget those!) on your previous gig. Use as many action verbs as you are able. Employers are much more likely to hire people who are able to demonstrate that they are on the way up.

Sell yourself by showing the *solutions* you've developed in the past. Once again, I cannot overemphasize the importance of investing the time to develop the worth points that were covered in chapter 11.

Show a prospective employer the benefit of your actions, not just the action you took. This is the single, most powerful attribute you can communicate as you search for your job.

Keep these four tips in mind:

1. Bring enthusiasm.
2. Communicate the measurable benefits previous employers enjoyed due to your efforts.
3. Follow up religiously.
4. As your career develops, highlight your progressive career growth.

Doing these four things now and throughout your working life in the entertainment business will help you get to the head of the class as you develop your career.

MAKE TIME FOR ONE LAST MONEY, GEOGRAPHY, AND GUT CHECK

At this point in your music industry career game plan, I recommend that you conduct one more "reality check." Based on correspondence with some of my former students, there are three important factors that you should check about the specific job you have targeted.

Salary: Is there the potential to earn the kind of salary you need both to survive in the short term and to prosper in the long term? Remember the earning range on the technical career track in the recording studio? It may take a person two to three years or longer to make it to the role of a first engineer. Ask yourself if you are willing to work and sacrifice at the salaries you have researched to make the climb up the ladder.

Geography: If your family or best friends are all in your hometown, are you ready to move on to one of the major urban centers where the entertainment business is percolating? Prepare for new surroundings, new stimuli, and if you are moving to New York or Los Angeles, a significantly higher cost of living. Are you willing to make the move? To succeed as a songwriter, many move to Nashville at some point in their career.

If you want to flourish as a recording engineer for film, television, or postproduction, you likely will be in L.A. or New York, and maybe even London. If you have deep roots in your hometown or perhaps your wife or husband has a solid career there, now is the time to really consider the "G" for geography factor. Are you willing to spread your wings and move?

Use the Internet to gauge the cost of living in the various cities or regions you are investigating. Since the cost of a similar apartment can vary by a factor of five times from Manhattan to Austin, you need to do the same kind of research on the prospective cost of living that you performed on the various career paths that interested you. (Remember, Craigslist.org provides a quick reference to housing costs in many U.S. cities.) Put those detective and Internet research skills to work. Don't forget possible higher car-insurance premiums, parking, and other costs unique to a big-city environment, if that's where your career path seems to be headed.

Gut Check: Have you prepared yourself for the rejection involved in working your way into the entertainment business? There are tens of thousands of persons seeking employment in the industry, and that competition makes it easy for prospective employers to sometimes treat those who are seeking a job with little or no respect. Unfortunately, it's probable that you will have the door slammed in your face, literally or figuratively, many times in the course of your job search.

Get yourself ready for it. You will experience negativity. You'll have people tell you (as they did me), "Why pursue this career? You'll never make any money," or the ever-popular, "Why don't you get a real job?"

If you don't have a burning desire, that fire in the belly, pushing you to embark on an entertainment industry career quest, I strongly urge you to look at other career options.

But if you have it, then I encourage you to dedicate yourself to your quest, develop the necessary skills and information, and go for it. But be prepared and be armed. Equip yourself with as many tools, as many advantages, as much information as you can dig up in order to increase your chances of success. Ultimately, that's the core message of this book. It's a very competitive industry and you'll need every scrap of drive, determination, and knowledge—plus a bit of luck—to make it to the top. But you *can* do it as others have before you. In fact, these same methods, which have been used by my students for more than a decade, have proven to work for dozens of different career paths in everything from videogame production to financial management for superstar artists.

Make the most of each opportunity when you find a responsive company, interviewer, or mentoring figure—be it a teacher, guest lecturer, or conference panelist.

Even with proper research and preparation, a fabulous internship experience, strong worth points, and a mentor or two in hand, your career path may not go exactly as you plan. Ask the people who you know and trust if your expectations and your marketable skill-set assessments are realistic. It's far better to learn now rather than later if you are basing your plans and expectations on faulty, inaccurate, or out-of-date information.

Most successful recording artists make no bones about keeping a day gig until they can earn enough money to maintain a decent, if simple, quality of life as a touring or recording musician. Not doing so would, in the end, be counterproductive to a long career in the business.

I'm not suggesting you shouldn't "shoot for the stars," because if you don't aim high, you limit your own growth. But be realistic. If you dream of becoming a hit songwriter and crafting a series of top-ten hits, go for it, but develop a career "Plan B" as well. Make sure your alternate plan realistically allows you to make a living and survive as you pursue your dream. The longer the odds of accomplishing your dream, the more important it is to have a career Plan B in place. Don't forget: only one-half of one percent of the recordings released by major labels each year break even. The rest lose money for their record label. Most successful recording artists make no bones about keeping a day gig until they can earn enough money to maintain a decent, if simple, quality of life as a touring or recording musician. Not doing so would, in the end, be counterproductive to a long career in the business.

Even after you have identified your target career path and started investigating companies, it is crucial that you continue to be an information sponge—someone who is hungry for every piece of information on their chosen career path. This is why reading the trade magazines, even if you can't afford to subscribe to them, is so critically important. Keeping up with the periodicals and Web sites that are the "bibles" of your targeted industry will give you a big edge in your job search. Don't get lazy and give up that edge.

If you go for an informational interview and see a stack of trade-magazine back issues, take the opportunity to politely inquire what the company does with them. It's likely that they recycle them after a few months. Offer to pick their discards up once a month and tell the receptionist that you are trying to learn all you can: "May I stop by once a month to pick up the out-of-date back issues?" If you get the green light, then congratulate yourself! You just got a pile of the magazines you need to be reading on your area of interest for free.

Be resourceful with respect to information gathering, especially if you're operating on limited resources. Each magazine sells for $5 or $6 on a newsstand. A subscription to *Billboard* is approximately $300 a year. Remember to check for online editions, use the public or school library, and budget and invest a set amount of time each week to be an information sponge. If you do, you will be pleasantly surprised at how much useful information, jargon, and details you retain about a variety of industry companies and careers. Photocopy and keep the most important or insightful articles for your Career Binder. All of this will help you position yourself as a well-informed job candidate, ask intelligent and relevant questions during interviews, and upon getting hired, be a much more valuable member of your employer's team.

MAKING YOUR MOVE

When you are armed with your résumé, including as many worth points as possible, when you've done your homework by developing your marketable skill-set workshops for the jobs that most interest you, and when you find that your gut, geography, and salary checks all come back positive, then you're ready to make your move.

In the next chapter, I'll reveal the three tactics that have proven to be the most successful in seeking and obtaining a position in the entertainment industry.

CHAPTER 22 The Three Best Means to Land a Music-Industry Job

History has proven that effective networking—identifying and approaching firms that represent targets of opportunity in your career areas of interest—and applying for specific open-job listings are the key methods used to secure employment in the music industry. We'll review each method in this chapter. Now that you're ready to present yourself in the best possible light, take advantage simultaneously of the three most effective means to identify and land your dream job. In this chapter, you'll learn how to maximize your job search by:

- Effective use of networking
- Identifying and approaching company targets of opportunity
- Applying and following up to open position listings

1. NETWORKING

Although networking was covered extensively in chapter 14, here are a few more networking tips to use in combination with that chapter's content.

Networking tips:

- Be courteous and gracious to everyone, even if they may not be able to help you today. You never know when you may be able to support them, or they you, in the future. Remember, various segments of the music industry are small markets where most professionals know one another.
- Carry your business cards with you all the time, even at the health spa or at a church picnic.
- If you see someone in your network who doesn't recognize you, take the initiative to go up and reintroduce yourself. Never ask, "Do you remember me?" Instead, say hello, and then mention when you met and what you have been up to lately. Be sure to ask about his or her latest activities and interests, as well.
- Always return calls and e-mail within twenty-four hours or the next business day.

- Nurture your network. I try to contact one person each week that I haven't seen or chatted with recently. I also try to have lunch monthly with a person I have not seen in six months. Investing in your network will help you reap the benefits of the diverse range of interests and contacts your network members have.

2. TARGETS OF OPPORTUNITY

As part of your ongoing detective efforts, your mission is to identify any target of opportunity, a company that is established, or one that is hot and on the way up in your area of interest. A proactive career sleuth always must be hunting for new companies that are targets of opportunity.

How do you find them? Hearing about such companies through your network is the best method. You can also scan the magazines covering the industry segments that interest you most.

After identifying target companies, what's the next step? Let's say you've identified ABC Records as a hot company. Your next step is to dig up all the information you can about that company. Surf the Internet, review magazines and articles, gather clippings, stop by the library to research articles in any business or trade publications, and carefully read any interviews with executives of that label. Don't forget to check search engines such as Lexis/Nexis, if the company is a market leader.

Visit the company's Web site regularly so you know what work they are doing. Get every scrap of information on that label that you can. Collect it, read it, and understand it. Know it backwards and forwards.

Next, check around your network to see if anyone may have a contact inside ABC Records that you might be introduced to. If so, you are ready to approach that person with your referral. If not, then you're ready to send the label a cold letter, one that's well written and demonstrates your worth points, along with your knowledge of their activities and your enthusiasm for the business.

Next, follow up with a phone call to investigate whether or not you might be able to secure an informational interview. Better yet, find out if they are trying to fill any positions for which you may be qualified.

The worst thing you can do with a potential target of opportunity is to get in contact without being prepared to present yourself in the best light.

Better to be prepared so you can…

Get ready (identify companies that interest you)

Take aim (do the necessary research to understand the company and what it is doing)

Fire! (open a channel of clear communication to present yourself to the company)

Anything less than that is doing yourself a disservice and is not likely to get you in the door.

Why is that? If you represent yourself poorly a few times, you're quickly diminishing your chances to make a favorable impression and to build your network with the people in the industry that could actually do you the most good. If you're in a secondary market such as San Francisco, Boston, Phoenix, Denver, Minneapolis, or Austin, this is even more critical since the prospective number of industry employers and mentors is smaller than those found in the entertainment capitals.

Be especially aware of any information that indicates growth or new areas of development for a prospective target of opportunity. Suppose one of your targets is a record label that has been very successful in r&b and now they're branching out into movie soundtracks. Let's say you are a songwriter and have just placed one of your own songs in a locally produced film. You could write a letter to their A&R department, introducing yourself and stating your qualifications, desire, and go-getter attitude. Mention the story in *Billboard* that alerted you to their new soundtrack division. This company may be a good target of opportunity.

Remember, for this kind of approach to bear fruit, you have to include a value statement or worth point that clearly answers the question, "What can this person do for me today to improve my position in the marketplace?"

Good firms are continuously on the hunt for new talent. Any company that's growing is always looking for new people. They may not be hiring that day, but savvy managers are always keeping a résumé/tickler file of people with good skills. So don't ever be put off when someone says, "We're not hiring now."

Be prepared to answer that statement with, "I've studied your company, I am very interested in what you do, and I would like to ask you to please keep a copy of my résumé on file in the event you need someone with my skills and enthusiasm in the near future."

More often than not, they will accept it and may even annotate it to say, "This person has moxie or chutzpah." Bingo. At the very least, you've got yourself on file at that target of opportunity.

Remember, the cold letter approach is your last option. The most effective way to approach a target of opportunity is through a member of your network who is familiar with the company. If you don't have a personal connection, you should also find out what local, regional, or national trade associations the firm's employees are involved with. This is yet another way to meet and network your way into an informational interview. If you can't gain access by any other means, then complete your research homework on that firm, and initiate a direct approach via cold letter and résumé submission. You may find yourself invited to an informational interview.

3. OPEN JOB LISTINGS

Traditional help-wanted listings in the daily newspapers and music industry trade magazines are becoming an anachronism as more and more industry employers harness the power of the Internet to advertise open jobs. By regular research of a range of online industry job posting sites, you can see what types of jobs and skills are advertised. An open-job listing can help you to identify which skills are required for a certain position and also what types of positions are most needed.

The frequency of listings encountered is directly related to the type of job advertised. If you're planning to become a record producer, you are not likely to see any open job listings. For a songwriter, it's liable to be the same story. However, you will find open job listings for administrative assistants, label sales reps, royalty clerks, distribution support staff, marketing and PR assistants, and many other positions at the mid- and entry-level.

Recording studios usually rely on word of mouth and recording schools to fill entry-level positions. For senior staffing, a referral, recommendation, or letter of introduction is more commonly employed by those seeking employment. Employers may promote from within their own company, or use their network to identify prospective candidates already working in the business.

It pays to regularly look at the open job listings. Refer to the list of music and entertainment online job-listing sites in appendix B. Remember, open job listings usually generate a large number of responses. When responding to a listing, be sure to include a brief mention in your cover letter that you are responding to a job listing in a particular Web site and use the job ID number if one is listed.

Tune up your cover letter, and send your response as soon as you see the listing. This shows you are able to respond in a timely manner. It shows that you're aggressive. Always have someone proofread your cover letter. If a fax or e-mail address is listed for submitting your résumé and cover letter, use it, and mail a hard copy as a backup, if they list a mailing address.

Keep your cover letter as short as you can make it, and as long as it needs to be. If this is a job that you believe offers you a perfect fit, a full page is not out of the question. Why? What should you include in the cover letter? Again, include your worth points, your experience, and what makes you a uniquely qualified candidate. (See chapter 12 for more about cover letters.) Paint a word picture that positions you as the best-qualified candidate for that job. If you do, you'll reap the rewards!

If your cold or cover letter gets too wordy and overly long, there is more potential for you to hit a potential "hot button," which may be a turnoff to the person reviewing it. Remember the one-page-or-less rule when it comes to the length of such letters. Always ask yourself if you can make your points in a shorter letter. The same care that you used to prune down your résumé to a tight, hard-hitting document should be spent on your cover letters. Cover-letter editing and fine-tuning are like many of the career skills provided in this book—acquired skills. The more you labor at it, the easier it becomes to craft strong, well-written documents that will help your submissions stand out.

By now, you know what your worth points are. Incorporate those that clearly communicate why you will be valuable to your next boss. Demonstrate your experience. Showcase your progressive career growth in light of your increasing levels of responsibility.

State specifically which of your qualifications meet the job requirements detailed in the company's open job listing. This makes it easy for the screener to see that you have the required marketable skill set they are seeking.

You might use a few bullet points that clearly demonstrate how you meet the advertised criteria. State specifically which of your qualifications meet the job requirements detailed in the company's open job listing. This makes it easy for the screener to see that you have the required marketable skill set they are seeking.

Always use short paragraphs, no more than three or four total, each covering a key point you wish to emphasize. Your job is to ensure that the person reviewing your submission thinks, "Oh, he or she has experience in this area, created value here—put this one in the pile of people that we are going to call back." Following these simple guidelines will help your submission make it into the select pile that avoids the dreaded hungry shredder!

In addition to the careful wordsmithing needed, make a good visual presentation, with no typos. Make sure you don't smear the ink when it comes off the printer. If you can computer print or type the envelope, do so. If you handwrite the envelope, do so neatly. Take your time. If you smudge it or miswrite a word, get another envelope, and make it perfect, because first impressions count for a lot.

About a week after your submission, make a follow-up phone call, if you have a number on file for that firm. Keep it short. Ask for "personnel" if the company has a personnel office. If it's a small firm, explain that you are calling to follow up on your résumé submission for an advertised position. Ask to confirm receipt and what your next step might be to keep in touch regarding the opening. Be polite and upbeat, and respect the time of the person with whom you are speaking. The fact that you cared enough to follow up is usually viewed as a plus at small- to mid-sized firms.

For larger firms, it's usually not practical to make a follow-up phone call, so if you have a Human Resources e-mail address or employment Web contact, follow up approximately two weeks after your submission, simply asking if the firm might share a progress report on the open-position number you applied for. Don't be surprised if you learn that no decision has yet been reached, as larger firms sometimes take more time to review and interview than smaller firms.

Some firms, however, have a strict policy of not responding to any inquiry calls relating to open position listings or résumé submissions. Once again, the exposure that music industry open position listings have via the Internet makes any response to follow-ups a perceived waste of resources for most firms. In that case, console yourself with the knowledge that your hard work has resulted in presenting the strongest possible case for your candidacy via your well-crafted cover letter and rock-solid résumé. You can then invest the time you would have spent on following up with firms that don't allow follow-up, getting back to the important work of nurturing your network and identifying your next ripe target of opportunity.

At the early stages of your career, look to open job listings, both as opportunities that you may be able to apply for immediately, and as road signs directing you to new companies and marketable skill sets that those companies are willing to pay for. It's reasonable to expect that you will most likely have to apply for dozens of open positions before you get responses from a few employers. The access that so many job seekers have to online job postings makes it a numbers game, of a sort. In order to generate results, you need to keep the number of your applications going out as high as possible (of course, without applying for any positions for which you are not even remotely qualified). If you do keep at it, you will begin to see results. If you only wait to apply for the one "perfect" job, you are likely to be disappointed, if you don't get a response to that application.

Working all of the "big three" simultaneously—networking, targets of opportunity, and open job listings—is key to keeping your job search and career development on the fast track.

FIVE FOLLOW-UP TIPS

Picture a long-distance runner as he runs a marathon. He focuses on all the little things such as maintaining an even gait, proper breathing, knowing the course, how much water to take and when to take it, keeping his toes pointed forward, and so forth. Just as that runner has to remember each of these important details, you, as a music-industry job seeker, need to develop and maintain the details of your follow-up system with fierce determination, not casual indifference.

As you develop and expand your network, increase your universe of targets of opportunity, send out applications to open position listings, and begin to secure interviews, you need to also:

1. Attain the monthly goal you have set for expanding your network.
2. Write down your new contacts and add them to your system (card file, Filofax, Palm Pilot, computer database, etc.).
3. Set a schedule for keeping in contact with various members of your network. Set up a section in your Career Binder, card file, or computer database to update each contact with members of your network.
4. Review your Career Binder at least once a month, and add to it weekly as you locate and mine new sources of information.
5. Investigate and make contact with companies, explore new or related career options, and get to know the people you discover through research, reading, networking, etc. That means getting out into your local marketplace, attending events, volunteering, and building relationships.

If you have a computer, you might invest in a contact manager program such as Symantec's ACT, or use a computer database such as Microsoft Access, or even a spreadsheet program, to keep track of your network names and contact information. An example appears below. Include the name, company name, titles and addresses, phone numbers and e-mail, date of last contact, and so forth.

CMPNY XYZ Records
FNAME Janet LNAME Doe
TITLE VP, Human Resources
ADDR1 1234 Main Street, Suite 2
CITY San Francisco STATE CA
ZIP 94124 CNTRY US
IDSTATUS1 Record Label
IDSTATUS2
IDSTATUS3
IDSTATUS4
SEND PHOTO WITH PRESS RELEASE?
PHONE (555) 555-1234 EXT
PHONE2
FAX (555) 555-5678
CEL PH
E-MAIL jdoe@xyzrecords.com
WEBSITE
ASSISTANT
REFERRED BY
COMMENTS "Met at Recording Academy Mixer in SF"
Print this Conta

Don't forget to send important people you encounter a thank-you note whenever appropriate. That really can include anyone who is friendly and supportive of your career journey, be they professional or personal contacts. Performing the five follow-up basics listed above will help you maintain steady progress toward your career goal. Making them a part of your daily and weekly routine will hasten the day you are considering a job offer. So take them to heart, and like the long-distance runner, maintain a steady pace that will lead you to your next goal: landing a job in your area of interest.

As a closing note on follow-up procedures, I'll share a chat that I had with a human resources manager from an Indie record label. She confirmed that more than 50 percent of job applicants who apply for a position never bother to follow up. That's incredible.

Don't be in that silent majority. Always take the time to follow up each application you submit to see if the position has been filled. If so, determine whether the company will keep your résumé on file, and if so, for what length of time. Note that in your follow-up records. If the company is high on your list of targets, keep in touch. The results of your extra efforts may pleasantly surprise you.

WHAT ABOUT YOUR COMPETITION?

Let's review how much competition you are likely to encounter for each of the three job search tactics we have covered in this chapter.

In the case of *networking*, your competition for specific jobs is very low because jobs identified by this method are usually not yet public knowledge. People often learn of jobs through their network well before they are advertised; in many cases, the job is never once openly advertised, so networking is the only means to discover the position.

When you're contacting *targets of opportunity*, the competition will be a little greater, especially if it's a company with fifty or more employees. Such firms are likely to be contacted on a regular basis by savvy detectives (job seekers) like yourself. Take heart, the competition is still much lower than if there was an open listing. If you've done your target-of-opportunity research well, you will be armed with plenty of useful information, a few good questions, and a thorough understanding of the firm and its business, positioning you to make a strong positive impression when you make contact.

When you approach a company in response to an open job listing, your competition will be the greatest, but you also know that it is nearly certain that the company is hiring. One person will be getting a job at the conclusion of that company's search. By following the techniques you have learned from this book, you will have greatly enhanced the chance that it could be you.

Job Search Technique	Level of Competition	Are They Hiring?
Networking	Low	Unknown
Targets of Opportunity	Moderate	Unknown
Open Job Listing	High	Definitely

WORKSHOP 22. JOB SEARCH ACTION PLAN

Make a grid that has three columns and four rows. If you do this in your word processor, you can save and reuse the forms. Put today's date at the top of the page. At the top of each column, write the three methods of locating a job outlined in this chapter. Then use the three boxes under each heading to fill in three current opportunities to network, three targets of interest, and three jobs you applied for (or plan to apply for).

Networking	Targets of Opportunity	Open Listings

Save each sheet, and depending on the amount of time you are investing on your job search, start a new sheet as you fill up each one. Keep the past sheets in your Career Binder.

CHAPTER 23 Careers in New Media and Music Products

HOW INFORMATION AND ENTERTAINMENT ARE BECOMING THE NEW "GOLD STANDARD"

A few years ago, I was surprised to learn that a young Wall Street investment counselor, David Pullman, had begun an investment fund that allowed the public to purchase shares of future earnings (appropriately called "futures") on the songs written by David Bowie.

I was fascinated by what I originally viewed as an oddity, but as time marched on, his New York–based company, the Pullman Group, signed on more and more artists willing to allow investment in their future royalty stream. Artists such as James Brown, the Isley Brothers, Ashford and Simpson, the estate of Marvin Gaye, and Holland-Dozier-Holland have joined forces with Mr. Pullman. That provides a good backdrop to what I believe is rapidly becoming the new currency standard for the twenty-first century: the control and manipulation of information and entertainment. It's truly an exciting time to be involved in the music and recording business.

THE GLOBAL PERSPECTIVE

Roughly 38 percent of the world's population resides in two Asian countries, China and India. In 2006, the United Nations reported that Asia's overall population of 3.66 billion people represented 57 percent of the world population. In comparison, North America represents roughly 5 percent of the world population.

Most people in Asia do not speak English. However, they do listen to western music. They do play western videogames. They do enjoy western movies. According to Plunkett's Entertainment and Media Industry Almanac, the average Hollywood movie produced in America earns more gross revenue overseas than it does domestically. U.S. movies rank number 1 in box-office revenues in Japan and Western Europe. Entertainment today is a rapidly expanding global industry that transcends language barriers.

Tracking entertainment companies such as Fox, Electronic Arts, or Sony on a global basis leads one to a conclusion that I share with many future-oriented business leaders: Information has become the new gold standard.

NEW MEDIA AND GAMING

The same skills that apply to a career path in the music industry will apply to electronic media and information-age careers. Loosely described as convergence, new media and gaming marks the intersection of information, entertainment, and business. It is where the latest technologies for the Internet, computers, cable or satellite television, broadband delivery, movies, and music converge. Job opportunities are exploding just as fast as new companies are born and bought, as the industry races to develop and deliver the most compelling content to a worldwide audience hungry for information and entertainment. Consider how much time you spent today enjoying some form of entertainment, whether it was listening to the radio or music, watching TV, going to movies, reading magazines, viewing videos, surfing the 'Net, or playing some type of game. Chances are, it was more than a few hours in total.

A recent example of how new media is impacting the entertainment industry is Yahoo! Music's video portal, which provides instant access to tens of thousands of music videos from both the world's top artists and Indie bands that have made their own iMovie. They are all available 24/7, anywhere in the world at the click of a mouse. Rather than waiting for a cable TV channel to count down the top videos of the week, fans can simply click on the video of their choice and enjoy it when and where they wish.

Another example of the opportunities rapidly emerging in new media is the overnight explosion of MySpace.com, which quickly went from an underground site that allowed bands and music fans to find out about each other by creating interconnected lists of friends, to a recent acquisition by multinational media conglomerate, News Corp, which had the foresight to see the value in such a successful grassroots entertainment marketing and delivery platform as MySpace.

When it comes to the rapidly growing world of videogaming, in 2005, 76.2 million Americans were playing videogames, growing more than 13 percent from the 2004 statistics. There are thousands of companies involved in the production of videogames, and the production standards for many of these games are coming to resemble movies and television in their complexity.

Let's check in on one such job in the videogaming field, that of a music composer. Forget the old notion of a sequence of a few bad-sounding synth notes repeating in an endless loop as you demolish the bad guys. Today's games, especially those delivered via DVD, offer well-crafted musical scores that can rival that of a feature film in sophistication, orchestration, and playback fidelity.

Music scoring for the leading game companies can be very rewarding financially. With 2005 total revenue for interactive games, devices, and accessories reported at $10.5 billion (source: NPD Group), the interactive game industry exceeds the $10.4 billion 2005 U.S. record business (source: RIAA figures) and the $9 billion represented by 2005 box office revenues in the feature film industry (source: MPAA).

Globally, the console videogame market, as well as forthcoming handheld and online gaming, is expected to grow to $54.6 billion by 2009 (sources: Price Waterhouse Coopers and Paul Kagan & Associates). The blockbuster game *Halo 2* registered pre-orders of more than 1.5 million units and, by the end of its first day on sale, had racked up 2.5 million units equaling $125 million gross revenue. *The Sims*, which has sold more than 10 million copies, has helped to fuel an industry that exceeds either the music or movie business.

Is composing for the game industry right for everyone? Hardly. But if you are a talented composer who is comfortable working with computer audio and MIDI programs, you should investigate your opportunities. Long hours and critical deadlines can lead to some all-nighters for those in this field, but the rewards outstrip those available to the band playing covers in the lounge at the local Holiday Inn.

Staff positions as a music composer at the larger software developers pay in the $45,000–$70,000 range with benefits, paid holidays, and profit-sharing programs. Freelancers working for game developers can also do well on a project-by-project basis.

And not just composers are needed. Any skill or craft that goes into the making of a feature film is likely to be required when a new game is on the drawing board: session musicians, recording engineers, dialog editors, voice talent, computer graphics designers, sound effects editors, production assistants, continuity, video editors, localization experts, and on and on.

An example of how interactive media and the record industry are cross-pollinating may be found in the late 2005 announcement that Electronic Arts, the world's leading videogame developer, and Nettwerk Music Group have formed an alliance to sell original music from EA's successful videogames to Digital Service Providers via online sales. It highlights the overlap between consumer interest in all forms of digital media and entertainment. This is just one example of new career opportunities that are being developed, bridging across traditional and new media enterprises.

Other areas that are growing exponentially include the mobile music and legal online digital music market. More than 42 million personal MP3 players had been sold through the end of 2005. According to the RIAA, ring-tone sales represented $421 million in 2005 domestic sales. Meanwhile, Apple's successful iTunes music store recently sold its 1 billionth download, while the rate of paid downloads more than tripled from 2004–2005. According to Standard & Poor's, projected spending on digital downloads and music subscription services such as Rhapsody and Yahoo! Music will grow from $900 million in 2005 to more than $2.4 billion in 2010.

And don't overlook the $64.6 billion industry represented by TV programming services including the major networks, cable, satellite, and pay-per-view. The expanding universe of content requires new talent to help create and produce programming for the hundreds of channels available.

Consider any media that utilizes audio, music recording, and sound editing. You'll see that literally dozens of new opportunities are being developed each week—for instance the emerging market for ring tones, ringbacks, master ring tones, downloadable TV, and film clips, etc.—all for the booming mobile entertainment market. Dive in and start exploring the possibilities offered by new media.

Another very hot area is the issue of rights administration and protection as an entertainment attorney, paralegal, or copyright administrator. Look for careers in this area to continue to grow at an amazing pace as newer, faster, and more secure technologies emerge. Another growth area will be international relations and distribution deals in a global marketplace where borders and laws are difficult to enforce due to the explosion of the Internet.

Companies are working harder than ever before to maximize the earning potential of each new entertainment vehicle. Movie tie-ins, tour sponsorships, sheet music folios, soundtrack albums such as *Spiderman*; *O Brother, Where Art Thou?*; and *City of Angels*, to name a few recent hits, TV series such as *Desperate Housewives* that spawn soundtrack albums, or made-for-TV movies on the lives of recording artists, all present new and potentially lucrative earning opportunities for a wide range of creative and business personnel.

Force yourself to think outside the box. There's a great big beautiful world in the entertainment industry for those who are motivated to make their mark. Push yourself to look beyond the record company or recording studio and at least explore the potential for what creative and financial opportunities may exist in these exciting new media market segments.

MUSIC PRODUCTS CAREERS: MAKING MUSIC MAKERS

Another form of entertainment is making music, not necessarily for the professional musician, but for the growing demographic of Americans with leisure time and disposable income looking for a hobby or interest that is fulfilling, nonfattening, and enriching. Enter the music products industry. It represents one of the most overlooked sectors in the music and entertainment world.

What are music products? A music product is any instrument, device, object, book, or accessory that someone might need to make, teach, study, create, or share music. Everything from musical instruments such as guitars, trumpets, harmonicas, synthesizers, and grand pianos to sheet music, recording equipment, karaoke systems, music education software, and loudspeakers, to name just a few of the products encompassed by this market segment. Additionally, the millions of Americans that are involved in studying music in schools or in private lessons are also all customers for the music products industry. In the U.S. alone, the music products industry is a $8+ billion a year business, so it is large enough to offer a wide range of career opportunities for those passionate about music.

One of the greatest attractions to a career in the range of market segments within the music products industry is that those working in it are surrounded by peers who make and love fostering the growth of music making. And the mission of every company in the industry—be it manufacturer, distributor, retailer, online merchant or vintage dealer—is to help others make music.

During my own thirty-plus year career in the music industry, I've been active and worked closely with clients in the recording industry, TV and radio broadcast, advertising, film, public relations, computer, medical, education, and music products industries. As part of my work, I would attend trade shows in each market sector regularly. When I attended the trade shows for these various industries, one thing that struck me was that during the dozens of NAMM (International Music Products Association) shows I've attended, no matter where you look, you will see people who are sharing their passion and doing what they love to do as their so-called day gig. Those who are successful in this segment spend the bulk of their time either making or helping others make music, or they provide music making opportunities through distributors, retailers, or other business partners.

Another observation about the music products industry is that unlike some other industry segments, there are a great many owner-operated firms—some that have been managed successfully by the same family for more than a hundred years. As a result, new employees who are passionate about music and dedicated to helping others learn about and make music are valued assets. Unlike some of the recent record company layoffs due to the continual rounds of label consolidation, the music products industry is actually anxious to find talented new employees to continue to grow the pool of professional and recreational music makers in America. Starting salaries in the music products field are generally higher and offer better benefits than the record industry, too. Additionally, the music products industry has proven to be somewhat recession-proof and immune to the peaks and valleys of the overall economy.

For those who may have been attracted to a music industry career because of their own creative aspirations or an interest in working closely with high profile recording artists, jobs within the music products industry offer these opportunities and more. For instance, every major manufacturer of music products has an artist relations department that provides support for the artists using their products. For those who prefer to make music, a position as a clinician or product specialist gives you the opportunity to travel around the country teaching others how to use your company's instruments or products.

The International Music Products Association is the trade association that hosts the semi-annual NAMM conferences where up to 85,000 music makers and music products professionals convene to share information, do business, and enjoy the world of music products. With nearly 8,000 member companies spanning the globe, this trade association provides a window through which the diversity of companies and career opportunities can be viewed. The NAMM show itself is not open to the public, but one of the easiest ways to identify companies in this industry is to visit the association's Web site (www.namm.com) and look at the list of member companies. You may be surprised to see there are quite a few in your geographic proximity.

If you have not yet begun your college career, you might also consider enrolling at a college that is a NAMM-Affiliated Music Business Institution (NAMBI), as one of the professional training paths these schools offer prepares students for a successful career in the music products industry. See the NAMBI Web site (www.nambi.org) for a list of these schools.

WORKSHOP 23. NEW MEDIA AND MUSIC PRODUCTS OPPORTUNITIES

Make a list of three companies in each of the market sectors covered in this chapter. Using some of the research methods you've learned, investigate all six companies to see if they may be hiring, print out any job descriptions, and analyze whether or not they might be able to use someone with your marketable skill set.

TAKING CHARGE OF YOUR OWN CAREER DEVELOPMENT

If you've taken the steps outlined in this book, you're armed to start your trek to the top. Rather than give you a pep talk, here are a few reminders to help keep you focused as you begin your career journey.

- Make sure that your résumé is rock solid. Take pride in knowing that a top-notch résumé sets you apart from the vast majority of job seekers. Take the time to fine-tune a cover letter that clearly states why you are writing and how hiring you can improve your future employer's business!
- Employ all these tactics simultaneously to uncover jobs and companies that interest you: networking, contacting targets of opportunity, researching, and responding to any open job listings that are appropriate.
- Prepare yourself mentally and spiritually for the rejection that comes with any job search. Unfortunately, rejection is a basic part of the weeding-out process that is so central to the entertainment industry. Additionally, with more firms moving to online job application processes, you may find that you receive no feedback, not even a rejection letter. Although many doors may initially be closed to you, it only takes one that's open to establish a career beachhead.
- Maintain a positive attitude. When the going gets really tough, rely on members of your network to help you maintain focus on where you are headed and to remind you of how far you have already progressed.
- Set short-, medium-, and long-range goals and measure your progress towards attaining them. Regardless of whether you have landed your dream job, doing so will give you a sense of accomplishment.
- Learn to ask intelligent questions. When it comes time for an interview or furthering a relationship with a member of your network, you need to be perceived as an asset, not a liability. Learning to research and develop intelligent questions about a career path or an area of interest is a proven means to further set you apart from other job seekers.
- As you network with people and secure informational interviews, you will become more and more connected to your local entertainment community. Members of your network will land jobs, get promotions, and move up. You must keep in touch with them.
- Invest the necessary time required to do research. Become a thorough detective and do your career homework so you become well-versed in your area of interest.

- Identify those companies who are the leaders in the sector of the market you're interested in. Find out as much as you can about each one.
- Locate a willing mentor or sponsor to help you along your career path. That person can be an instructor, teacher, retired professional, journalist, a family member or relative, a neighbor, or an acquaintance who takes an interest in your quest and can provide insight and share life experiences. There is no substitute for a working knowledge of the industry in which you plan to work. Fast-track your career development by getting as much industry and networking experience as you can.
- The last fact to keep in mind is that tens of thousands of other people have gone before you on the road to a fulfilling career in the music, recording, and entertainment business. They've gotten their careers started from a small opportunity. They've made the investment in time, energy, and self-improvement to build a career in one of the most exciting industries in the world. You can do it, too.

PART TWO Views from the Top

To offer additional insights into careers in the music and recording industry, ten professionals have shared their views on career development and requirements for success in today's music recording world.

- Joe Lamond, CEO of NAMM, the International Music Products Association
- Jeanine Cowen, Film Composer and Founder of JMC Music, Inc.
- Chuck Taylor, Managing Editor, Top 40, *Billboard* Magazine
- Alan Stoker, Recorded Sound and Moving Image Curator, Country Music Hall of Fame
- David Jahnke, Vice President of National Sales, Hal Leonard Corporation
- Gary Miller, Vice President of Motion Picture and Television Music, Clearance and Licensing, Universal Music Publishing
- Leslie Ann Jones, Director of Music Recording and Scoring at Skywalker Sound
- Murray Allen, Vice President of Postproduction, Electronic Arts, Inc.
- Gary Gand, Music Retailers and Owners of Gand Music & Sound
- Gregg Hildebrandt, Northern California Sales Rep for the TASCAM, a Division of TEAC of America

Joe Lamond

President/CEO of the (NAMM) International Music Products Association

It's hard to imagine how a young man with his sights set on becoming a forest ranger would end up as CEO of the world's premiere music products trade association. As you'll learn from my interview with NAMM CEO, Joe Lamond, his path to the top was anything but a straight line. In between a few decades spent behind a drum kit, he managed to pick up a host of business and life skills that have prepared him for his key leadership role as one of the world's most visible music advocates, heading up the trade association for the $8 billion U.S. music products industry. In this role, he helps to shape the future of how the art and craft of music making is perceived and supported in America and abroad.

What drew you to a career in music?

Before I answer that, let me preface the answer by saying that one of my goals these days is to be clear. There's so much fog in this world as far as business and communication. What I want written on my tombstone is that "he had a quest for clarity." So my first answer is easy: Girls! I mean, it's not complicated. I was drawn to music to meet girls. I wish there was more to it or some noble cause.

How about your first gig?

I was in a band with my older brother, Jim. He turned me on to all the great music of the day. I'm grateful for him opening the door for me. He played bass and I was the drummer. And so my first paying job was in the fourth grade playing at his junior high school dance. I remember it well. I did a drum solo on Grand Funk's "TNUC," if I recall, on my $45 red sparkle, Kent brand 4-piece drum set.

As your career has evolved, what kinds of skills or training have been helpful to you?

Knowing that it is the nature of things to go from order to chaos, I think the ability to take things from chaos to order has been one of the main skills that I've used. You do that by being organized. You do that by being able to see multiple sides of an issue and find common ground. As far as education, the thing that has been most helpful to me was a background in accounting. In business, you've got to know how everything relates to a balance sheet. The goal of any business is first and foremost to remain in business, and a good accounting background helped with that.

Who were some early mentors?

I had a business professor who basically made me realize this stuff could be fun. All I wanted to be was a drummer, and so anything that got in the way of that was just a hindrance. He brought some of the marketing and business classes alive for me—and I was still pretty young, nineteen or twenty—in a way that probably didn't really sink in until later. I just remember him really having an impact on me.

The next big phase of mentoring to me came when I went through post-performance life and started my business career. I really do look at my life in terms of decades. The decade of the twenties was really fun—you know, playing music—although I always had a day job. At age twenty-eight, I kind of had an epiphany of "what's next?" and I was very lucky to have two good mentors come into my life at that time. One was Skip Maggiora from Skip's Music in Sacramento, and the other was [recording artist] Todd Rundgren. Those two guys were very important to me. I think the idea of having a mentor is critical, especially when you are receptive to the message. Those two guys hit me at the same time, when I was very receptive to a new message.

Could you walk us from the end of that drum solo on "TNUC" until taking the reins at NAMM?

Sure. Basically, I grew up in New York. I was an upstate New York kid who loved the outdoors and loved music—two very different things, in a sense. I went to school to be a forest ranger and discovered after one year that there was a fork in the road; I took music and decided not to be a forest ranger. So I went down to SUNY Morrisville, near Syracuse. My parents always said I had to have something to fall back on, so I got a degree in business knowing full well that was simply a stepping-stone to pursuing music. I moved to California in 1982, from New York, because of a girlfriend. Most of my early decisions seemed to be tied those common threads: music and girls!

I figured again, while I was becoming a rock star, I needed a day job, so I went to all the music stores in Sacramento and got hired at a small store in Sacramento called Andy Penn's Drum and Guitar City as a bookkeeper. Pre-computers—everything was on a manual, dual-entry pegboard system of accounting. Doing the books is one of the best ways to really get in and learn all about a business.

So that was my early twenties. I would say the next period was spent playing by night, pursuing the dream, and holding down a music store job by day—never thinking in a million years that that would be where I would end up. I had the brushes with the big time. My band actually had a songwriting deal with CBS Records, a production deal with Virgin, and then I got the gig as a touring drummer for Tommy Tutone. And then I got hired for extra jobs within Tommy's organization as the band's popularity—this is a Spinal Tap moment—"became more selective," and I ended up doing the bookkeeping and a bit of tour managing as well. That led me to realize doing the books and knowing everything that is happening and being kind of in charge was actually more fun than just being the drummer, who didn't really have much say in things—someone who just showed up to play.

I realized that maybe I could combine doing what I love with what I happened to be good at.

That led me to a couple realizations. I realized that maybe I could combine doing what I love with what I happened to be good at. And it sunk into my thick head that maybe I wasn't that great of a drummer!

So that was in 1989—two big things kind of changed my life. I decided to recommit myself to music retail. I got hired at Skip's Music in a very humble way. I took the lowest possible job available at that store. I like to say that after working hard my first few months, I got promoted to the warehouse—and this was after having been the manager of another store. But it was really good to start over. At that same time, in fact that same month, because of the experience with Tommy Tutone, I got offered the production manager job with Todd Rundgren, who was based out of San Francisco at that time. So for two years, I worked at Skip's—Skip was kind enough to let me come and go—and then I toured with Todd. I would do six-week tours with Todd and then come back and work a few months at Skip's. Both of those guys mean more to me than I've probably told them, and some day I need to go back and tell them. They taught me how to work; they unleashed some of the passion I had for business and for organization and being involved with great music. Both of those jobs were immersed in music. That was a wonderful time, but probably unsustainable for very long because at some point I would have to have chosen one path or the other, and at the same time I met the woman who was going to be my wife through some things we were doing with Todd in San Francisco. Within three months of turning thirty, I made three big decisions: I cut my hair, committed to Skip's as General Manager, and got married. So I became we, and closed that decade of my twenties in a very symbolic and clear way—on to the next phase of life.

At Skip's, I went from General Manager to Executive Vice President and basically was happy as a clam. I thought I could live out my life there. I found out I could buy a house and support my family in the way other folks do. That was a huge realization after having been a musician for so long—especially a drummer. The old saying is that "a drummer without a girlfriend is the definition of homelessness." All of a sudden, it hit me, "Wow, I can actually make money at this." Very exciting.

I could have not aspired to much more except for a pretty fateful phone call, sometime in '96, when NAMM wanted to branch out and expand its market development opportunities. They were looking at Skip's and what we were doing with adult musicians and the Weekend Warrior program that brought older customers back into music by helping them form bands and play a concert. By working with NAMM with the Weekend Warriors program and packaging it for members, I got to know them and I got to work with the people in market development—wonderful folks. And then when their market development director, Bob Morrison, got the nod to come to New York and start VH1-Save the Music, he gave me a call in June of '98 and said, "This would be really good for you. I don't know if you're even open to this, I don't know if it would be something you're interested in or if you're willing to move. I'm leaving NAMM to start VH1-Save the Music." Fork in the road again. Could I have planned for that? Hell, no. But doors were opening, and I was doing the right things along the way: Taking care, being responsible, and being accountable for what we were supposed to do. You'd be surprised that I've discovered that that is a very rare thing. And you tend to rise up to the ranks by the fact that there's not a whole lot of competition; not a whole lot of people who are really responsible and accountable for their actions.

So that July, I was offered the job of Market Development Director of NAMM and had to go home from the Nashville NAMM show with the pretty heavy burden of "what do we do?" I talked to Skip. It was a very tough time for both of us because he had been almost a father figure to me, but I just felt that we did a lot of really strong market development activities within Skip's. We just didn't call it that, we simply called it wanting more customers. It dawned on me that I could do this (market development) on a national level—and although I didn't know at that time, an international level. And I thought I just couldn't pass this opportunity up. Again, no more aspirations than that level, but a great job description of creating more music makers. I didn't have to move. I actually became a Southwest Air commuter, living in Auburn outside Sacramento and flying to the NAMM headquarters in San Diego once a week.

Again, our story could have ended there pretty quickly and we might not be doing this interview. But, soon after coming to NAMM, Larry Linkin, who everyone calls Link, announced his retirement, after nearly three decades at the helm of NAMM, and they began a search inside and outside the industry to find his replacement. Being kind of naïve, I just kept my head down, working on market development and never even thinking about the search for a successor until one day when Link came to me and asked, "Would you ever think of doing this?" I answered, "No." He told me, "You should." In my mind, it was a "No." Time went by and literally a couple months before they were ready to announce the candidate, he came to me and said more forcefully, "Joe, you need to apply for this position."

So he called your bluff?

Yeah, this was January of '01, and they were going to announce in March of '01. It's not like there was a whole lot of time left. I hadn't updated my résumé in fifteen years, maybe since college, because many of the jobs I was taking didn't go through those channels—the traditional interview process. I got them because the person offering me the job knew somebody who knew me or my skills. So I sat down and did a résumé and went through the firm's criteria, which were a series of interviews, things done with psychologists, all these types of things. And then I was offered the job in March of '01. I took over on Link's 62nd birthday in May of '01.

So let's backtrack a bit: forest ranger, backwoods, steel-toe boot-wearin' drummer goes to SUNY, gets a little bit of business background, chases girl to California, follows Mom's advice—always has a day job—has a great time being an irresponsible drummer with just enough sense of responsibility to not be homeless, comes to the point of being twenty-eight and seeing a few grey hairs and realizing "What's next?" has two huge doors open—walks through both of them, discovers through the decade of the thirties what hard work is and how that can pay off and you can become financially successful doing that, and at age forty becomes CEO of the music products industry trade organization and really looks at that as the next decade. To me, this is the decade of the forties, I'm halfway through it. I'm excited about what the fifties may bring! What's next?

So much of what's been going on under your stewardship at NAMM is to broaden the total picture for music makers internationally. You're writing the script as you go. It's very exciting!

My high school counselor did not envision this path and that I would end up being a suit-wearing CEO. That was never mentioned, I don't think. I think he was the one who told me the usual way to address a drummer in a suit, which is "the Defendant!" So that's how we got here. I've never tried to draw that out on a career chart.

Day-to-day, could you describe your job at NAMM?

In many ways, my job is very simple. It is deciding how to best allocate resources to accomplish our long-range vision. I've been given this great opportunity at an organization, which at 105 years of age, has good fiscal reserves, a great team of talented and passionate folks, and an unbelievably motivating mission. Most of my day is spent deciding where resources can best be used for the maximum return to the industry for the members and the fulfillment of our mission.

So when your team comes up with three great ideas, you get to coach them and say they're all good but this is where we're going to get the biggest lift, the biggest bounce.

Yes. I've got to continually have that overview because a lot of them will be seeing it from one slice of the picture. At the same time, I think the second part of my job is to interface with members in the industry as much as possible. I think last year, I was on the road 160 days doing nothing but meeting people, and listening, and hearing their ideas.

It is amazing how everything I've done in the past relates to what I'm doing now. I've applied things I learned on tour with Todd, such as solving a dispute with a union steward in Cleveland or dealing with an equipment problem in Tokyo when no one else spoke English. You learn how to deal with people all along the way. All those experiences shape how I look at things now.

You're five years into leading NAMM—what gives you the greatest satisfaction?

First and foremost are the friends I've been fortunate to make in the industry. The [NAMM] show to me—this may sound cliché—is an absolute family reunion, and you get to know these people over time. You get to know their families, learn about what their kids are doing, their success or challenges in life. I will never forget the people I've met, and I'm grateful to Link and the NAMM Executive Committee who gave me this wonderful opportunity.

Second would probably be to see what an impact our efforts can have: The reward of seeing a kid's music program get saved because of lobbying we did in Congress or research that was funded by the industry, or seeing a New Horizon's Band recreational music class here at the NAMM office for seniors. What we do matters!

My greatest satisfaction overall though is just to see this organization and our industry fulfill its potential. And I think we're just starting to take the cover off this really super race car, and we're just beginning to see what its full potential is, not only here in the United States, but internationally as well.

Obviously, things are shifting so dramatically in terms of the world economy and the world business environment; it's a golden opportunity for NAMM to lead.

I know, scary, huh? I sometimes look around and think, "When are the adults coming back?"

> *I sometimes look around and think "When are the adults coming back?"*

Exactly. What would an entry-level position at NAMM include?

It would be supporting a manager-level staffer. And that would be people involved in the trade show, people involved in communications, people involved in government relations and public affairs, and people related to the market growing activities and market development.

I'm guessing that computer skills, communication skills, and basic business knowledge would be key skills you would look for in a candidate.

Sure, however I think the number one thing at entry level is personality. You want to build a team around people who are energetic and have the ability to throw passion into what they are doing. What we're looking for and I think what most employers are looking for in anything is someone who's excited to be there, has a positive personality, and can work well with others. The other thing to remember is the day doesn't end at 5 P.M.

Does NAMM offer internships?

Absolutely. And most interns have been hired on full time. It's important to us to set an example for our members. So if we can do that, or place them with a member, I think that is important. To lose a talented person out of the industry would be our definition of failure.

What's your sense of the future in terms of music making and the music products industry?

Every society since the dawn of recorded history has made music. Based on historical statistical analysis, one would think this industry has a great chance for future success. It's a wonderful industry and it's going to continue to change as any industry does. I also understand its place in the world, in the larger scheme of things—I've got friends who run companies bigger than the entire U.S. music products industry. But the impact of the music products industry touches everyone. For those of us who have this blessing (or curse!) to have music in their blood, I think this is a wonderful industry and a way "to do well by doing good."

Looking back on your own career, what do you wish you knew at the outset?

On one side, I wish I would have gotten organized sooner. I wish I would have not waited until age twenty-nine to decide to really pursue a career in business because I might be further along. But on the other hand, I would not have traded some of those experiences for the world, like some of those tours with Todd or Tommy, or even those club bands in the Bay Area. They are priceless memories. There's no other way to get those experiences except by doing them. You can't teach them; you can't learn them in a classroom. Those are just some life things I wouldn't have traded for anything. So I'm of two minds. One side says you should have started earlier, and the other side says nope, you did it just right; everything on your journey led to just the right place.

A last thought?

I come across a lot of people in their forties who are trying to get into this business because they followed more traditional paths—what they thought would make them rich or happy and they realized that it didn't. They are just dying to get into something that has meaning and appeals to their passion. So I think it breaks down to those who are lucky enough to be in this business and those who want to get in.

Jeanine Cowen

JMC Music, Inc.

As owner of her own film and video scoring firm, JMC Music, Inc., Jeanine Cowen is uniquely qualified to talk about the dual track career of a composer/entrepreneur. A classically trained percussionist, she first became captivated with film scoring when a college friend asked her to write music to accompany a short film. She loved the nuance and power that music could bring to the art of filmmaking.

Jeanine has resided in Boston for twenty years, tapping the city's exceptional array of musical talent to perform on her soundtracks including members of the renowned Boston Symphony Orchestra. She maintains writing and production studios in Boston and L.A. to service her stable of film, TV, and game development clients. She also teaches Pro Tools for Berkleemusic.com, and within the Music Production and Engineering department on the Berklee campus, and is heading up a new Recording Arts program at the Center for Digital Imaging Arts located at Boston University, which has the potential to link young composers and filmmakers together just as each are beginning their careers.

In this interview, she references the points in her career where she has had to rely on making a "leap of faith." It is clear that for Jeanine, these leaps have led to an expanding range of musical possibilities and accomplishments.

How did you discover your interest in a career in music?

Well, I can't even tell you when I *didn't* imagine having a career in music.

Did you grow up in a musical family?

It's not so much that I had a musical family but that I was always interested in music. I started playing drums at a very young age. My family always encouraged me. The school system I went through had a very strong music program, which was wonderful for me. I started private lessons in third grade and then continued to play from there on out.

You studied classical percussion at Northwestern and then switched over to Berklee. Then you ended up studying at Berklee in music production and engineering, and then also added the film scoring degree?

Northwestern is a fine program and when I went there, I wanted to be an orchestral player. After a few years I realized my passion was really with film scoring. The only two film scoring programs were really at Berklee and USC. Once I landed at Berklee and I saw the MP&E department, it was the best of any world that I could imagine.

What was your first paying job or gig in the music industry?

My first paying gig was playing in the pit orchestra for a local music theater organization when I was in school. I vividly remember getting paid for that first gig!

What kind of shows were you playing for?

Oh, you know, we did *Fiddler on the Roof*, *Joseph and the Amazing Technicolor Dreamcoat*, all of that stuff. This was while I was in high school.

You started playing music at an early age, so as your career has unfolded, what skills have been helpful to you along the way?

Every piece has been helpful to me along the way. Being able to read music has been huge. I started composing when I was in high school—being able to orchestrate and arrange and think about what other musicians need and can do has been important to me, and I think it has led to me being more comfortable in the studio and being able to get out of the musicians what I need from them. The other thing that was actually key for me was my education at Berklee—forcing myself to think out of that classical box and thinking about improvisation and jazz. Having an experience with a lot of different genres of music has led to me being a much more versatile film composer. You never know what you're going to be writing. You need to be able to deliver. You need to be competent in a lot of genres.

So being a film composer or orchestrator is actually a generalist job because every filmmaker comes to you with a different set of challenges.

And you also need to know your own deficiencies, so you can go out and hire or consult with people who will be able to deliver the pieces you can't.

Early on, were there some mentors who influenced you, who helped shape your direction?

My high school band director really instilled a love for music and also the confidence that I could actually make a career out of it.

Beyond that, I think my two private instructors, who were both college educators, had a big influence. They were remarkable because they pushed me to be a better player than anyone else was. It's very important to be the best player that you can be. At Berklee, George Monseur and Danny Harrington, who taught the core music classes, and the entire MP&E department. And then the whole Berklee vibe—that's really where I learned to listen. People don't talk much about hearing and listening but they are critical skills and rightly emphasized at Berklee.

You started freelancing in high school. What's it been like to be the person in charge of your next job... and the next?

I've been freelancing almost my whole career. There was a brief stop when I was employed at a game company. Besides that year, I've been working for myself. It started with an internship with another film composer, Mason Daring, which turned into my first scoring job. Working for him and seeing him work was really an in incredibly eye-opening experience. It informed me as to how you are successful as a film composer.

Working for him and seeing him work was really an incredibly eye-opening experience. It informed me as to how you are successful as a film composer.

So having an apprenticeship with someone already scoring films gave you a good idea that there's more to it than just sitting down at a computer and sketching out scores.

Oh yeah! It's this way in a lot of the industry. Many times, as a film composer, you write something that you normally wouldn't write if left to your own devices. You are, in the end, working for someone else. You need to be able to meld your intuition with what their needs are.

Was it scary leaving school and saying, "I'm responsible for my next paycheck, I've got to find my next client, I've got to open a business bank account?" Was there a point when you thought, "Wow, this is a big challenge," or was it a straightforward evolution?

It was a challenge for a long time! When you're working for yourself and you are really the master of what happens to you, you have to have a leap of faith. You have to be able to say, "I know it's going to work out."

One of the things I learned is that I have to have at least a month or two of living expenses in the bank, so when it comes to the end of a project, I don't freak out and take a project I wouldn't necessarily take otherwise. I think that the payoff of working for yourself is incredible. Being able to guide yourself to the projects that you are more drawn to makes a huge difference. As a composer, you have to write music that comes from within you. Having projects you connect to allows you to do that. If you're writing for a project that you don't truly believe in, you're going to have a hard time being convincing.

That's important in creative careers anywhere. You need to have a sense of passion to go along with each commission.

The one thing that kind of got me through all of that—and it took me many years to realize this—is there are a lot of qualified film composers who on some level you are competing with, but if I write your score, I'm the only one who can write that score.

What is a typical day for you?

My typical day is a combination of writing music but then being an administrator of my business. You have to pay the bills, write the checks, make the calls. And then, there's a certain amount of troubleshooting that seems to happen every single day. If I get to spend half of my day writing music, I'm really happy about it.

Composing is a fundamental part of the business, but it isn't the whole business.

Yeah, and I think that's the difference. You are a musician in a business. You're not a hobbyist; you're actually running a business. And that's the same whether you're working for somebody else or you're running your own business. There are certain things that have to happen because you have clients.

What part of your work gives you the greatest satisfaction?

The struggle is always worth it, but probably the two things that I really love are being in the studio with musicians—making music with other people is an amazing experience, especially when you have this commonality of the final goal—and the other thing is actually seeing that final product and how it really does add to the final experience.

Talk about your first film-scoring gig. How did you land it, how did you find out about it, how did it go, and what was it?

My first film-scoring gig was a feature film called *Home Before Dark*. I got it because the filmmaker had called Mason Daring and he simply didn't have time so he recommended me. It was unbelievable. The filmmaker, Maureen Foley, and I just got along really, really well. It was a low-budget film, but it was done very well. I still listen to the score and I don't know how I wrote it. One of the cues in the score I wrote the night before the session, early in the morning.

Your résumé also includes a bit of work in the videogaming community. Is it a very different kind of composing and client-management exercise from film?

Well, I think it's different because if you're working for a development company, it's much more structured and they have milestones you need to meet. The collaboration is very different because you are frequently working with the visual artists, the animators, and the development team. As much as the film industry is very team based, it's not as much face time. Composing for film can be a very solitary position. And it can be a much longer process.

Composing for film can be a very solitary position.

Talking about a career as a composer, can you identify a few key skills or attributes someone should be strengthening or developing?

An ability just to make deadlines is enormous. You can't be the one to miss deadlines or you just won't get hired again. You really have to have a passion for the music you are writing, so you can't let yourself get talked into writing a score for something you're really not into. You need to be able to figure out a new angle. If the client wants something you are just not willing to deliver, you need to figure out why that is and how you can work it to something that you can deliver.

How long did your apprenticeship last with Mason Daring?

It was just a few years. It was a couple of years on and off. And then for the next few years, he would hire me on and off for projects that were very specific.

Do you think a composer coming out of school today will have a hard time finding someone to apprentice with or mentor them? What do you think the next step would be once you've gotten a degree in film scoring?

I think it's changed drastically since I got out of school. There are a couple of ways to go. There are definitely composers who need help; the thing is, they're not going to advertise for a film composer to help write. They need somebody to get their system up and running, they need engineers, they need music editors. I think that those positions are really valuable for the same reason I really enjoyed working with Mason—to just get in the door and watch. I would suggest though, that if you get in that position, set a time frame so you're only doing that for so long. The other possibility is really you can set up shop and have a sign that says "I am a film composer" on your door and really start going after the independent films that are happening around the country. Go out there and do your best. One of the things about being a film composer is you have to build up a clientele. A great thing for me is I have directors who do projects every few years but they always call me.

I'm working on a film right now with Roland Tec, which is the third project we've done. I won't pass up a score from one of the filmmakers I've had a long-term relationship with.

You have to build up this group of people who love what you do. Start out with the indie films. Don't promise them a fifty-piece orchestra. Promise them two or three key players that you know will work hard for you.

It seems as if we're getting more visual media, and more ways to distribute visual media. Do you think long term there will be good career opportunities for people who want to work in the visual arts, or do you think there will be a glut with way more people trying to get into the industry than there are actual jobs out there?

I think that in the creative fields, there has always been a glut of people trying to get in. You have to be persistent and willing to stay in there for the long haul. The assumption is that you have the talent, but the question is whether you can hang around long enough to make it. So if you have a long-term goal, maybe you won't be a full-time film composer right away, but that long-term goal is that in ten years you will be, so you can work toward that. I think there's always been a glut. But if you are persistent and believe in your music, people will start to believe with you.

But if you are persistent and believe in your music, people will start to believe with you.

Looking back at your career to date, is there anything you wish you knew from the outset that you know today?

Wow . . . I think that the thing I didn't know was I was going to be a business person. I assumed I would just be writing music, and I wouldn't have to worry about money and worry about contracts and all that sort of stuff. You have to have a business sense. You have to be willing to think about your contracts and think about your bank account and think about all of that stuff.

. . . the thing I didn't know was I was going to be a business person. I assumed I would just be writing music, and I wouldn't have to worry about money . . .

Is there a Yoda-like last thought to share with someone who's going to start on a quest to become a composer?

> *The thing that I've realized—and it's happened to me many times in my career—these moments are going to happen when you really need to make a leap of faith.*

The thing that I've realized—and it's happened to me many times in my career—these moments are going to happen when you really need to make a leap of faith. You really have to believe in yourself. You have to just go for it. If you don't go for it, then you're gonna wonder for the next ten years if you should have just gone for it. You also have to realize that when the work comes, be prepared to do it. Don't pass on a job with a previous client unless you absolutely have to.

The other thing that I've been very fortunate to grasp is that your life is actually happening at every moment. As much as you need to be dedicated to your craft, you can't let your life slip by unattended. You need a community around you. Don't alienate yourself in your own world.

Chuck Taylor

Managing Editor, Top 40/AC, *Billboard* Magazine

One of the most influential publications covering music on an international basis is the venerable magazine Billboard, *which has been covering entertainment for more than 100 years and is headquartered in New York City. And one of the most influential voices at* Billboard *belongs to Top 40 Managing Editor, Chuck Taylor. His rise to prominence as a music journalist is chronicled in this interview, where he discusses his clear path of turning an early obsession into a fulfilling career in music.*

What drew you to a career in music?

By the time I was ten years old, I was already obsessed with listening to the radio and—in particular—hearing Casey Kasem count down the top 40 every Saturday. I would sit with pen and paper and copy down the hits, then mark the songs that I owned on 45, keeping a running tally of how my tastes aligned with the national charts.

The passion only mounted as I got older, and by the time I was a freshman in college, I had started my own weekly countdown, based on my personal passion for the songs I heard on the radio. Yep, pure geek. At year-end, I would mathematically configure my top 100 and record my own annual top 40 countdown as a Christmas card for friends. To this day, it sure has made it easy to categorize music on my iPod. I can simply upload each year's top 100 songs and listen to the soundtrack of my life. Maybe not so geeky, after all.

Can you recall your first paying gig or job in music?

When I was sixteen, my mom told me that a local radio station was offering free tours of the studio. I called up, barely able to speak I was so nervous, and added myself to the list.

On the day of the tour, it snowed hard, but I was determined, and since the station was only a couple miles from my home, my mother was cool enough to let me go. It turns out that I was the only one that showed up, so I got a personal tour of the facility, seeing live DJs for the first time in my life, looking through the record library, and meeting the general manager.

He asked if I was interested in working in radio and pulled some news copy off of the AP newswire, which he had me read in front of him. In high school, I was on the public speaking team, so as terrified as I was, it was a task I could handle.

Now this is back in the day—1980—right before FM became king, and this was a country AM station, which at 16, was the epitome of uncool. But when the GM offered me a job on the spot—Wayne Campbell was his name—I hardly had to think twice. He offered me minimum wage to do fill-ins and weekend graveyard shifts. We're talking around $3.35 an hour, but of course, I would have done it for free.

I mainly worked Fridays, midnight to 6 A.M., and Sundays 6 A.M. to noon, and during the summer I commandeered vacation shifts, but the experience was magic. There was no one else at the station, so I would look through the stacks of albums and search through all the new records on the program director's desk. I learned to appreciate country music at a time when George Jones, the Statler Brothers, and Barbara Mandrell were still logging hit after hit.

I remember one late night, I was fishing through records on the music director's desk and found one from Olivia Newton-John that I had never heard of. In those days, she was just transitioning from country to pop, so I suppose country radio was still being serviced. It was a song from a new movie and I decided that it couldn't hurt to give it a spin on the air. The song was "Magic" from *Xanadu*—of course which had nothing to do with country—and as I came out of the record, I made the mistake of trying to pronounce the movie name... "That's Olivia Newton-John from the movie... X-a-nuda." Ah, the memories.

...if there was ever anything that cemented my desire to work in the business, two years at WWOD-AM were my elixir.

This was small-town radio. I grew up in Lynchburg, VA, and there was little in the way of music scheduling and no computerized playlists, so the freedom we had was astonishing by modern-day terms. But looking back, if there was ever anything that cemented my desire to work in the business, two years at WWOD-AM were my elixir.

What particular skills, training, or education has been helpful in your career?

I went to James Madison University in Harrisonburg, VA, majoring in communication arts with concentrations in speech and journalism and a minor in English. I thought about focusing on radio, but figured that being a great DJ is more about personality than a particular skill, and I knew that journalists not only had to have talent, but to know the rules as well. So I went that route.

But aside from education and formal training, there is nothing better than pure personal obsession to hone your talent. For me, that meant keeping a journal from the time I was in the seventh

Whatever it is you love, find ways to live it before someone pays you to do it.

grade. Practicing words. Finding ways to express experience and to make it as visual as possible. I also used to make tapes for friends, playing songs, and pretending to be a DJ. "WMOO, your station of sound." I made up my own top 40 chart for twenty years. Whatever it is you love, find ways to live it before someone pays you to do it. Then when you eventually get that dream job, you'll have the confidence that you at least can fake it really well until you're convinced that you really know what you're doing.

Who were some of the early mentors who influenced you?

Casey Kasem, absolutely. Every Saturday, he counted down the top 40 hits of the week, and I felt like he was talking to me alone. He had the rare talent to be simultaneously universal and intimate. I learned at an early age that no matter what you're doing, it's as important to be entertaining as it is informative. It's my number 1 mantra whenever I write. Even if I'm saddled with the driest, seemingly most boring topic on earth, you can never assume that a reader is obligated to plow through what you write. A truly talented journalist never forgets that style is as important as substance.

A truly talented journalist never forgets that style is as important as substance.

Can you share your career path from your first job in the industry to your current position?

When I was a college freshman, I discovered *Billboard* magazine. One of my dorm-mates saw me writing down Casey Kasem's "American Top 40," sitting beside a radio on a Saturday night and informed me that the student union subscribed to *Billboard*, which, of course, then contained the very chart that Casey used for his countdown. Pretty much a life-changing event.

At the time, I was obsessed with the pop singer Sheena Easton (1981), which gave me impetus to obsess over the music charts every time she released a single. I would Xerox the Hot 100 and sit in class studying every song's move, peak, and fall. To this day, you give me an 80s' hit and I can pretty much tell you where it peaked on the charts.

So from that moment on, *Billboard* was the holy grail, and as I worked my way through various jobs, I held that as the standard.

My first job in journalism was for the *Washington Business Journal* (1985), where I oversaw special sections that showcased the region's top industries, from real estate and telecommunications to finance—and media. That gave me the opportunity to report on and learn more about radio.

I moved to a publication called *Radio World* (1988) in the Washington area, which was primarily focused on engineering and regulation. I put in my time reporting on those topics, and worked my way up the ladder to become managing editor for its international edition, where I got to write a column called "USAirwaves." I reported on music trends, radio programming, and pretty much anything I thought was relevant. It was my chance to be Casey Kasem in print.

Eventually, *Radio World* launched a programming and sales magazine (*Radio World Magazine*) and I was named editor. I decided to put *Billboard's* radio editor Phyllis Stark on my comp list—more to satisfy an ego-driven whim than anything else—and I'll be damned, when I attended a radio conference one year, I met her and she knew who I was. I was stupefied.

I was at *Radio World* for almost eight years, when I got a call from *Billboard's* managing editor. Phyllis was moving to Nashville to become bureau chief for the magazine, and they were looking for a new radio editor. Would I be interested?

I remember trembling on the phone when I called Ken Schlager back. The idea of actually working for *Billboard* was surreal to me. I FedExed him clips and a cover letter that I probably poured about a gallon of sweat over—and waited.

Ken called me for an interview, but he was going on vacation, giving me a two-week window to prepare. I remember playing tennis with friends and having them quiz me with every potential question he might lob at me—what is your greatest weakness, why should we hire you, what if you were presented with such-and-such situation, how would you report it. I knew I had a single shot to make or break my lifelong dream, and there is no better way to defeat anxiety than preparation, so by the time I finally took the train from D.C. to New York, I was practically scripted. This was the big time and there was no room for error.

I knew I had a single shot to make or break my life-long dream, and there is no better way to defeat anxiety than preparation…

I aced the interview and though it took six agonizing weeks to finally hear back from Ken, I got the job and moved to New York three weeks later (1995).

And by the way, when I arrived, Sheena Easton was on Broadway in *Grease*. I made it my business to meet her and ended up writing a ridiculously long three-page career retrospective, given the nod by then-editor Timothy White. Life was complete.

I've been at *Billboard* for ten years. Started as radio editor for three years, added the position of single reviews editor in the third year. Launched a new radio column called "AirWaves," which profiled a hit single at radio every week, including artist, radio, and record label interviews. It became the third most-read column in the magazine at its peak. Moved up to senior writer, focusing on artist profiles and page 1 exposés. Wrote about trends in the industry and major new releases from the likes of Celine Dion, Elton John, Bette Midler, Mariah Carey, Tony Bennett, Jewel, and the like. Pretty much became the mag's pop expert. I was then promoted to senior editor, where I helped approve assignments and all feature content, did a lot of editing (my specialty became adding color to dull news stories). I was simultaneously music editor, deciding on, assigning, and occasionally writing artist stories on new album releases. After Timothy White died, there was a brutal shake-up, and I was moved to *Billboard Radio Monitor* as top 40 managing editor, writing about radio again. Currently, I am a senior correspondent for both *Monitor* and *Billboard*, and am still single-reviews editor. Phew!

What is your day-to-day role today in your organization?

As with most publications in the Internet age, *Billboard* is no longer just about print. We have three Web sites, which require feeding on a constant basis: BillboardRadioMonitor.com (radio), Billboard.biz (industry) and Billboard.com (consumer). The mornings usually start with writing stories for the Web sites. I have a two-hour news meeting every Monday for *Billboard*, where the staff—New York City, L.A., Miami, Washington, D.C., and London—all propose story ideas and we exchange ideas about how to fatten them up with sources and ideas from our specific beats. On Wednesday, I have a news meeting for *Billboard Radio Monitor*, where we discuss stories we're planning for the weekly print edition.

All told, we work about three weeks in advance for print stories, whenever possible. Stories range from 1,200 words to as much as 3,000 words, depending on the depth of the assignment. At *Billboard*, every beat is expected to generate ideas, though it's not unusual to be handed an assignment or to be asked to assist a reporter with a major piece.

As single-reviews editor, I assign and edit or write eight reviews a week for *Billboard*, due on Monday at 5. I choose what we review based on merit, radio action, and chart performance.

I get to the office at 9:00 and work until around 5:30. Typically, I have music events two or three nights a week (of course, the coolest part of the job), oftentimes with open bar and food and appreciative conversations with artists. It truly is the glamorous life. Concerts are free, CDs are free, and life is a fine time.

But then there's the payback. Because the workday is filled with phone calls, meetings, interviews, and general hubbub, I do the majority of my story writing when I get home from an event. Fortunately, I'm a night bird. I'm considered a fast writer, so it takes me four to six hours to write a major piece for the magazine, which I then polish on the subway in the morning.

So there really is no typical workday. Writing from midnight to 2 A.M. is a mainstay two to four nights a week.

What part of your job gives you the greatest satisfaction?

Even after ten years, there's a major buzz that comes every Friday when the magazine comes out in print and you see the fruits of labor. Writing is such a personal, often isolating profession. When your words at last reach the public eye, it's terrifically gratifying. Then, when you meet an artist and they quote something you wrote or thank you, it's the cherry on top.

Being a journalist is sometimes an insecure business, because it is so personal. If you're good at what you're doing, a little bit of heart and soul goes into every story. To read it over when it's in print, on paper, and to know that you've told the story effectively, is still a high.

Describe an entry-level position in your organization.

Because of its history and reputation, *Billboard* requires some experience to come on board. But that doesn't mean that you have to have a mile-long track record. The most important variable is to develop a specialty and become connected within it. If r&b is your thing, write for Web sites and get to know record label contacts and publicists. If you're a tech-guru, navigate your way through the various providers. Skillful writing is, of course, a requirement, but a fat Rolodex is a close second. Access is everything. If you're the finest writer in the business but you can't get X, Y, or Z on the phone, you're essentially a nonstarter.

Access is everything. If you're the finest writer in the business but you can't get X, Y, or Z on the phone, you're essentially a non-starter.

Could you share three skills, attributes or qualifications that you would look for in an entry-level hire?

I have to go back to my thoughts at the top: whatever it is you love, obsess on it early. The fact that I can talk about radio from the '80s and recite chart figures from long before I had an actual job in the industry has not only made my job easier, it's earned me respect and a reputation as someone that knows what the hell they're talking about, both internally and in the trenches.

But to answer your question: the talent to entertain with words as well as to inform, ability to quickly develop sources, and a willingness to work for whomever will print or post their writing.

Does *Billboard* offer internships?

Yes, we do. *Billboard* consistently has at least one editorial intern. And the edit staff is mighty appreciative, so they are seldom invisible—unless they make no effort to make a little noise. As single-reviews editor, I am happy to provide opportunities for interns to write about new music. Not only do they get a byline in an international pub, but I enjoy editing as a team and coaching them to glory… after all, I came from little Lynchburg, VA and made it all the way to the big city. In addition, there may come a day where they're my boss. So they are treated with respect. One never knows, right?

At the completion of a successful internship, would that person be considered a candidate if there were a job opening at *Billboard*?

That's a tough call. Not out of the question, but openings at *Billboard* are few and far between. We're a pretty tight staff with fairly low turnover. To be honest, I cannot think of an instance where we have hired an intern out of college to join the editorial staff… There have been some, however, that freelance for us after they've left.

Long-term, what's your sense of the career opportunities offered in your field?

Print will never die, but it's certainly in the midst of a radical transition. The smart money is on talented writers who are also savvy in the ways of the Web. *Billboard* and *Billboard Radio Monitor* have endured what I think are the most painful in terms of growing pains—to put hard news online and make the print brands more feature oriented, but this is clearly continuing to evolve. College students have a wealth of indie Web sites to freelance for, and they should gobble up such opportunities, because more and more, that kind of experience makes its mark on old dames like *Billboard*.

> *The smart money is on talented writers who are also savvy in the ways of the Web.*

Looking back on your own career journey, what do you wish you knew at the outset that you know today?

Practical experience always wins out over textbook training. How you use what you have learned is more important than anything you can recite from a journalism course. Also, in the music business, building relationships is the consummate skill. Being able to call or e-mail a source or a publicist and say, "I really need to grab X for a quick comment on Y" and get the reaction you need is more important than any clever adjective or verb you might have in your parcel.

...I don't think anybody ever feels quite ready when the "big" opportunity is in front of them. God knows, in my first six months at Billboard, *I felt like I was faking it; when I wasn't fired, I finally realized that, hey, maybe I really do know what I'm doing.*

Any parting thoughts for those considering a job in the music industry?

Persistence. I got pretty lucky in landing my dream job. But I've had plenty of people bug the hell out of me to the point that I respond just to get them off my back. And then they get results. It might be no, but there's always the chance that it's going to be yes, so isn't it always worth the full-on effort? Sure, you have to pay some dues, but I don't think anybody ever feels quite ready when the "big" opportunity is in front of them. God knows, in my first six months at *Billboard*, I felt like I was faking it; when I wasn't fired, I finally realized that, hey, maybe I really do know what I'm doing. Point is, you have to be your biggest advocate. Know your strong points and sell hard.

Alan Stoker

Recorded Sound and Moving Image Curator, Country Music Hall of Fame

Growing up surrounded by music, Alan Stoker knew from an early age that his career path would head straight into the music industry, but as a performing and recording musician. As a young man, he took on a day gig working with the Country Music Hall of Fame, and over time, his passion for music and recording technology led him to a dream job that he could never have conceived: a Grammy-winning Recorded Sound and Moving Image Curator for the unique collection held at the museum. Throughout his career, he's maintained his love for performing and manages to find time to drum for three bands.

How would you describe what you do at the Country Music Hall of Fame?

What I do is sort of a mix: some of it's music industry, some of it's tourist industry, some of it's museum exhibit work, some of it's the archiving and collections industry. So it's interesting work.

What drew you to work in music?

A complete obsession with music. I come from a musical family. My father was a piano player that came to Nashville in the early '40s to play in a group on WSM radio, a gospel group. He played with a couple groups—his name is Gordon Stoker. He later started playing piano with a vocal quartet called the Jordanaires. In 1951, he turned over the piano duties and started singing with them. He is still singing with the Jordanaires.

So from a young age, we always had a piano in our house—sometimes two, as a matter of fact—so I've been around music all my life. When I was growing up, my father was on the Opry, he was on TV, and he was on records. He listened to all types of music. I specifically remember hearing a lot of Little Richard; he loved Little Richard. I remember hearing Ray Charles singing "What'd I Say." Records like that. And then country things like "Big Bad John" by Jimmy Dean and "Crazy" by Patsy Cline—recordings that my Dad sang on. And of course, Elvis records because the Jordanaires did all the early Elvis hits. I've been around music and around records all my life.

Can you recall your first paying music gig or job in music?

I got a drum set around 1967 when I was 15 or 16. Somewhere around 1970, I started playing with a rock 'n' roll band and played at my local swim club for 75 cents admission. I think we each probably made about a dollar.

What skills or training have helped you in your career?

Well, a couple of things. I was a music major in college: a percussion major and a voice minor. Being a music major, I was in orchestra and college band, so I had a really good idea of what instruments really sounded like in both an ensemble setting and solo setting. I didn't realize at the time that it was going to be helpful, but I've realized since that having that experience of knowing what instruments really sound like—not coming through a microphone and speaker, but actually being in the room with them—how valuable that is. I would encourage anybody who's thinking about a career in music to go hear any live music they can. Go hear a symphony, a jazz band, a country band, or a piano recital. Hear everything, because it'll help you understand how musicians play and how their playing styles affect the sounds. It's very important.

Many young people haven't heard much live music. They've heard a lot of recorded music, and they don't know what an instrument really sounds like. Just listening to music—being a music geek—listening to all kinds of music is very important. I've always been interested in the recording side of music. When my dad would take me to sessions, I loved being in the studio, sitting on the organ bench where nobody was playing, and just listening to them—seeing how they looked at each other to know who was playing what. I still love doing that today. I'd rather sit in the studio than in the control room. I did that throughout high school. When I graduated, my parents built a new home. We put a 4-track studio in that basement. That's where I got my first hands-on recording-studio experience, recording and doing mic placement and things like that. I had a rock band all through college, and I'm still in three bands today.

Does actively playing music help inform your work?

Yes, it does. I just have to be careful of protecting my hearing. I have two different kinds of earplugs I use, depending on what group I'm playing with.

What came next?

I started to get a little experience in the studio. I also started working part-time at the Country Music Hall of Fame at their gift shop and at the front desk when I was in college, as a summer job. In 1976, after I had been in college for two years, I was working on what they call a commercial music degree, which taught you a little bit about the music industry and a little bit about teaching. I wasn't sure what I wanted to do. They didn't have the recording-industry management programs then. There were only two or three of us on that particular program. I went to George Peabody here in Nashville, now part of Vanderbilt, but it was a separate college then. After about two years, they dropped that degree program because there were only three of us in it. I could only apply about two to three hours of credit to another degree, so I decided I would take a break for a while until I decided what I wanted to do.

Later that year, the Hall of Fame doubled the size of their building and hired me full time. I've been working full time here since 1976. I was really just in operations at that point—front-desk supervising, hiring, firing, scheduling and all that stuff. I got to know all the people and I loved the mission at that time. A couple years after that, '78 or '79, the Hall of Fame acquired [historic] RCA Studio B. Everybody knew that I had recording experience, and they said, "We're not going to mess it up if you're down there, so why don't you go down there." So I was manager for RCA Studio B for about two years. Then, in 1980, the Hall of Fame decided to install a radio transcription and transfer facility. They hired a guy named Art Shifrin out of New York. I met him and interviewed with him and said this sounds like something I'd like to do; it's music and it's technology, I love all that. They hired me to do that in 1980, and I've been doing it ever since. I love it and I realize I'm very fortunate because I couldn't have even visualized a job like this at that time. I wanted to be a touring/studio musician because that's what my dad had done. I love coming in and doing this job, and I love still playing music. The job here has expanded a lot since I've been here. Now I'm doing work with a moving-image collection—films and videotapes—a lot of exhibit prep work, and a lot of special projects.

Could you identify a few early mentors?

I would say certainly Art Shifrin. He did a lot of early transfer work from disc sources. He trained me. I helped him install the transfer facility and learned a lot from him in the process. A guy named Bob Pinson was on staff when I started working here at the archive. This collection is now named after him, as he passed away in 2003. Bob was a great record man. He knew a lot about 78s and transcription recordings. He taught me a lot about how to transfer 78s, how to make them play properly, how to de-warp them if they were warped, and how to fix a cracked record. He taught me a lot of the things that I'm trying to pass on now.

Obviously, my father was a big influence. He's still living and still performing. Not only in his career, but also in the way he treats people. I'm always meeting people here who tell me how much they like my dad. That makes me feel great. He never really pushed me into music, but I think he knew I loved it.

So the opportunity for your life's work appeared when you were still in college! That's different than most students' experiences.

Yeah, it definitely is. Like I said, I really went to college to play music. I was thinking I wanted to be a famous drummer in a big rock band. Really, when I started working here at the Hall of Fame, it was always with the caveat that I have these gigs I play on the weekends and I was going to have to take a couple weeks off here and there to play these shows—and it's funny because I still do that. I didn't even know a job like this existed.

I've often thought, "How did this happen?" I think I was in the right place at the right time, and went through the right doors and expressed an interest. I've never refused to do any type of work. I think that's a big thing. You can't think "I'm gonna be a big engineer so I'm not going to be the guy who gets coffee." You've got to do anything you can, if you love music. I was thrilled just to be around music, listen to music, and do transfers all day. I got *paid* to do that!

Could you give us a snapshot of what you do day-to-day, and who you work with?

My official title is Recorded Sound and Moving Image Curator. I work in the department where all the recorded sound and moving-image assets are that we have in our collection. We have around 300,000 audio recordings—that would be transcription discs, home recordings, 78's, test pressings, radio shows on both disc and tape, LPs, 45 rpms. We have some cylinder recordings, but not many. My job is to help take care of those and to identify which ones are in need of further preservation work. We have a couple of grant projects going on now. One of them is an acetate disc to digital archive that was funded by the NEA, National Endowment of the Arts, in their *Save America's Treasures* program. It's a three-year project. It allowed us to purchase the equipment and hire an engineer for three years to start the transfer of our unique acetate collection. We started doing that a little over a year ago. We have around 15,000 discs and we had tentatively hoped to do around 4,000 to 5,000 of them in the first three years, but I don't think we'll quite get there. So I'm overseeing that project. We also have a film grant, to fund the film inspection and evaluation program that we're doing. We have around 4,000 films in that collection, and that grant is funded by the IMLS, Institute of Museum and Library Sciences group. That one's just started, so I'm also overseeing it.

Day-to-day, I'm currently working on an audio CD to accompany a book that the Hall of Fame is putting out called *A Shot in the Dark*. It's about Nashville's independent record labels. Martin Hawkins wrote the book. There will be an accompanying CD with it.

I prepare all the audio and video exhibit work using Adobe Premier Pro. I collaborate with people all over the world if they're doing documentaries on country music. It's a very interesting job. Nothing's the same, day to day. There's just a tremendous variety to what I do that keeps my job fresh.

As far as all the different things you've enumerated, what gives you the greatest satisfaction?

Well, I still love performing music. And I love working on exhibits in the museum. We created a memorable exhibit last year, "Night Train to Nashville," which honored the connections between country music and r&b here in Nashville. There were two accompanying volumes of two CDs each. Volume 1 won a Grammy in 2005.

I got to accept a Grammy on that one, which was a great honor. I also love doing the exhibit work in the museum. I love seeing stuff that we've worked on for five or six months actually have the grand opening and see that people really appreciate it—either the clips that we've chosen for them or the sound bytes that we have for them to listen to.

In a sense, you're keeping the stories alive.

Yes, we are. We're walking a line between entertainment and education. In a museum, that's what you're trying to do. You want people to know they're being educated. You can combine these two elements successfully, and I think we're pretty successful at it. That way, you educate people and entertain them at the same time.

How many people work in the archives?

An archive is a very secure area. We have to do background checks and such, which knocks a lot of people out. You'd be surprised, we only have six or seven full-time people, so it's not a very large staff for a collection of this size. There are also currently two grant-funded positions here. We do take some interns from both the local high schools and universities.

What skills or attributes do you see with others you collaborate with that make you think, "This person is going to go somewhere."

Curiosity is one. There was one guy who worked here for about a year and a half. He came here, and it was clear he loved the music. He was like a sponge, and he didn't act like he knew all there was to know. He reminded me of myself at that age. Anything he could learn he would learn, anything he could read he would read, anything he could listen to, he would listen to—you know, that type of passion. I think that's very important. You have to be open to anything anybody wants to talk to you about.

You mentioned earlier there is an active internship program.

We have a big volunteer and internship program here at the Hall. You can work at events, you can work in publicity, public programming; there's a lot of openings. We have a full-time volunteer and internship coordinator.

Five or ten years down the road, what's your sense of career opportunities in the whole world of preservation and archiving?

Well, five years ago, I wasn't too excited about it. I think now there's finally a realization that if we don't transfer things from the analog into the digital realm, things are going to be lost. I do think there is a need for people to know about analog recording—to know how to operate and align a tape machine for playback. Going from analog to digital is where your initial expense, time, and labor are involved. Obviously, if you don't do it right at that time, you've blown it. So I think record labels and other institutions are starting to realize that they've got to transfer this material to a digital format.

Five years ago, I thought that people at the record labels didn't even think of that. Their concern is to get the latest hit out, not realizing some of their catalog is extremely valuable. A few of the labels and institutions are realizing they need to get these transfers of their catalogues done fairly quickly. I don't know if schools are even teaching analog playback. I think it's invaluable. To know where to go, you have to know where you've been. If I was the owner of a studio and I had two guys who had basically the same skill set but one of them had a lot of experience working both digital and analog recording, I would say that guy is more to my advantage. He has a wider scope of what things sound like and how a signal is routed, rather than relying on plug-ins and letting the computer do it all.

Looking back on your own career journey, is there anything you wish you might have known earlier or from the outset that might have been helpful for you to know?

Not for me personally. I think that for anybody coming up now, it would be to their advantage to take some basic business courses. It's also very valuable to learn how to budget your own time—time management skills. I don't know, my job is so unique! I don't know that I would have done anything differently.

As far as someone considering a job in the music industry, any final thoughts or guiding principles you would want to share with them?

Learn as much as you can. Try not to get involved with anyone or anything that distracts you from your goals. Really devote yourself to doing the best you can, and that means treating people right, and not taking advantage of them. Plus, I think you have to respect your health and save your hearing.

David Jahnke

Hal Leonard Corporation

Quite a few of the music industry leaders interviewed for this book started with an overriding passion for making music. David Jahnke, Vice President of National Sales for Hal Leonard Corporation—one of the world's premier print music publishers—started out wanting to play the trumpet but ended up with a pair of drumsticks in his hands and the ambition and drive to play his way through high school and college, where he prepared himself for success in life and in the music industry. As some of the other interviews have suggested, skills and training are key building blocks to having a successful career in the music industry, but the so-called soft skills, such as attitude, conversational ability, and willingness to go the extra mile for a customer, are equally important according to this interviewee.

What drew you to a life in music?

I would say that my mom and dad were the biggest influencing factors in getting me into music. My dad played saxophone in high school, but by the time I was born, he was no longer a practicing musician. Both my parents sang (and still sing) in the church choir. I remember going on family vacations and having sing-alongs in the car instead of listening to the radio. My first memory of singing a solo was at a Christmas Eve service when I was five. My musical endeavors took a turn in third grade when I started guitar lessons. When fifth grade rolled around I wanted to play trumpet. Unfortunately, by the time they called my name for the audition, they already had twenty trumpet players. The instructor said she needed drummers so I took the rhythm test. I passed and I've never looked back.

Can you recall your first paying gig?

My first paying gig was when I was in eighth grade. There was a group of high school freshmen that had a band and for some reason their drummer couldn't make a gig. They heard about this kid who was a year younger and asked me if I wanted to sub. They were playing at the Knights of Columbus Hall for a private party, so I went in with one or two rehearsals and we played. They liked it so much that they kicked out their regular drummer, and we ended up playing together throughout high school. They became my best friends, and we had a blast together.

How much did you guys make for the gig?

I think I came home with around $20. They paid the whole band about $100.

In addition to your parents, were there other early mentors who influenced you?

One man in particular, Dennis Glocke, my seventh-grade band instructor. I remember him because he had the ability to connect to kids of that age—very demanding but patient and inspirational. What I remember most is that he made playing in the band fun. My next major influence was my high-school band director, A.J. Hoefer, who was extremely demanding—in fact, downright intimidating! I kept practicing and made it into the Wind Ensemble, which was the top band, which you had to audition for. I then progressed up to section leader in eleventh grade. As the section leader, he demanded that you show up to rehearsals ten to fifteen minutes early every day to set up and tune all the percussion instruments. I had to strobe tune the tympani three times a week to make sure they were in tune with themselves. He was very strict, but...

He was treating you guys like professionals.

Exactly, and that started me down a different path. I learned that music can be fun—but it can also be made into a career, if you push yourself. So I started taking more private lessons, and I had many teachers who helped guide me. But these two helped to get me focused and in the right frame of mind for a career in music. In retrospect, they taught me that anything worthwhile takes practice and discipline. Talent will only get you so far.

What kinds of training or skills have been helpful to you as your career has developed?

College was a big factor in getting me to where I am today. I believe college teaches one main skill: time management. I didn't know it at the time but college forces you to prioritize between the stuff that needs to get done and the stuff you want to do, like socializing. I only wish someone would have communicated this to me during my freshman year! I feel I did okay, but no one really teaches time management, and that is vital to any career.

...no one really teaches time management, and that is vital to any career.

As I was about to graduate with a degree in Music Merchandising and Audio Engineering, I visited my academic advisor. He said; "Yep, you have enough credits to graduate. Congratulations. I've got absolutely nothing for you job-wise. Good luck with your music degree."

So I started looking around on my own. I still needed to do an "internship," so I looked at three options. At that point, there was Universal Recording Studios in Chicago. I had an option to work there as an unpaid gofer, from midnight through 8 A.M. I looked at moving to Grand Rapids, MI to work in the Yamaha warehouse. My job would have been putting heads on tympanis as they were coming in from overseas. The last option was based on a really good relationship I had with a local music store in Appleton: Tony's Drum Shop. Tony Wagner, the owner, knew me pretty well because I bought a lot of gear from him. He was a sole proprietor, with two locations: Appleton and Green Bay. He knew I was going through the music-merchandising program, so I showed up on the day of graduation and said, "Tony, I need a job." He said "Perfect timing. My manager is moving to Minneapolis in a week, and I'm going on a USO tour to Germany. I need someone to take over store management. So what do you think?"

As it turned out, that retail music store experience was the best thing I could have done. I cannot stress how important it is for music business students—regardless of where they want to go or what they want to do or what organization they want to get a job in—a retail experience is the best thing they could ever do. If you are in college and looking for a part-time job, go work in a music store. It's so vital. It's the only way you can really understand what's going on in the industry.

> *There are many opportunities within the music industry, but the only way to* get *a job is to sell yourself.*

Communication is the key to success in any organization. I know there are musicians out there who don't want to go into sales as a career, and that's fine. There are many opportunities within the music industry, but the only way to *get* a job is to sell yourself. Competition in the job market is fierce, and if you can't communicate and sell your abilities, you'll be passed over regardless of your talent.

Can you take us from starting at the drum shop, up through today, at Hal Leonard? There were some stops along the way, I'm guessing.

Working at Tony's was a great experience. I was also playing in three different bands and teaching private lessons. I had the ideal life of a bachelor and then that one fateful day happened: I got married. My wife was in her last year of college and money was really tight. I started thinking that there has to be something more I could do.

I loved the drum shop, but because it was a smaller location my only career path there would have been to buy it. If I knew then what I know now, I may have taken that chance but at the time, I didn't think I had the skill set to take on a business of my own.

So I started looking at different career paths. I applied at pretty much every drum company I dealt with. Companies like Pure-cussion, Tama, Zildjian, Yamaha.... I started researching the "who's who of the music industry" and came across Hal Leonard, a company I knew about because we stocked their books. I didn't know who to contact there, so I ended up sending my application and letter of introduction to a man by the name of Keith Mardak. I had no idea who Keith was at the time—ignorance is bliss. [Author's Note: Keith Mardak was Hal Leonard's Chairman, CEO, and President. He still holds the position of Chairman and CEO.] Two weeks after I sent my résumés, I started an active phone campaign. That is the one thing that college grads just don't seem to do today. I called everybody that I sent a résumé to, just to see if they received it. I think Hal Leonard was third on my list of people to call, so I called and asked for Keith. His assistant answered and said Keith was busy. I left a message and to my surprise, ten minutes later Keith called me back. He said, "David, I heard you called." I said, "Hi, Mr. Mardak, my name is David Jahnke and I work at Tony's Drum Shop. I sent a résumé and I just wanted to make sure you received it." He replied with "Oh yeah, I remember it. Tell you what, I'm going to have our National Sales Manager, Larry Morton, give you a phone call." Twenty minutes later, Larry called me! I was blown away. Sure enough, two days later I was down in Milwaukee for my first interview. That was the day I cut my hair and bought my first suit. I didn't know if Hal Leonard was a suit and tie company, but I was going to show up in a suit and tie anyway.

You decided to err on the side of caution.

Right. It's always better to be overdressed than underdressed. As it ended up, Hal Leonard was a suit and tie company. I had my interview with Larry, and to this day he says—and I find it true—you know within the first few minutes of the interview whether or not someone is a candidate for your organization. I passed the interview and started one week later.

Even with my college degree and three years of music retail management under my belt, I started out at the lowest position on the Hal Leonard sales team: Telesales. An entry-level position handling incoming sales calls. Now, if you would have talked to me when I was working at Tony's and said, "Hey David, I'm looking at my crystal ball and I see you working for a print-music publisher, spending 90 percent of your day talking on the phone," I would have answered, "No way! Give me drums or give me death!"

Well, I found that I actually *like* talking on the phone and helping people solve their problems. I also came to realize that Hal Leonard was an exceptionally well-run organization. From the people I worked with to the products they offered, it was beyond expectation. I subscribed to their way of thinking and within three months, moved from Telesales to District Sales Manager responsible for a territory. Hal Leonard helped me to realize that I had a passion for helping customers and that I had a natural ability of turning negative situations into positive. For me, I just had fun getting to know people from all over North America. That's what Larry saw within those first three months that I had worked here. I had fun and made it a point to have fun doing whatever I was doing. I'll tell you, it was a blast having my own territory. I love connecting with dealers at that level. You get to see what's working for them and give them ideas on ways that they can improve. While Hal Leonard is a good-sized, successful corporation, we are still very much a people-oriented, friendly, person-to-person music business.

The music products business is very much one-on-one, there's no question about it.

That is what makes the music industry so much fun. We are all frustrated musicians happy to have day jobs! From District Sales Manager, I stepped up to Senior District Sales Manager. In the mid '90s, Hal Leonard launched a new joint venture company called Hal Leonard Europe. Larry needed someone to be the liaison with our international counterparts, so I volunteered. In '98, I was promoted to National Sales Manager and instead of having my own territory, I now helped other District Sales Managers with their responsibilities. A year later, I was promoted to Vice President, National Sales, which is my current position. I oversee North America sales, our call center, and our distribution partners. I've been with Hal Leonard for fifteen years, and my job changes every day. It's exciting, fast-paced, fun, and I love it! But my favorite part is still visiting dealers—in fact, this week I was out in New Jersey, going out on the road with one of our reps visiting stores. Last week, I was out in North Carolina doing more of the same.

So, now you're the mentor, passing on ideas, techniques, and strategies for success.

Our reps are all very knowledgeable, but yes, we share what we can about what works in retailing. Print music is the unwanted stepchild of the music industry because most stores, unless they're hugely dedicated to print, are really into the combo gear. They understand the importance of print but they don't like to deal with products that have an average retail price of $14.95. It's just not as exciting to sell something that's $14.95 as compared to selling a piece of gear at $300–$800. What they're finding with print and accessories however, is that the margins, just like a grocery store, are best on the staples. At the local grocer, a customer puts his purchase on the counter, but they don't ask, "Hey, can I buy this loaf of bread you've marked at $2.49 for $1?" Think about it. That is what happens with combo gear. Everything is price negotiable. With print, if the product is listed at $14.95, the customer will gladly give you $14.95.

So that's a new tactic a retailer can look at and think, "Although it's going to take me a little longer to sell $1000 worth of print than a guitar and amp, that $1000 in print is going to have a better margin on it, one I don't have to haggle over or match an Internet price point.

Right, and for some of the stores that do commission-based sales, the sales reps are starting to realize that as well. In commission-based retail sales, the employee gets paid based on profit margins. A sales person can improve their weekly commissions by selling 5, 6, 7 books a day, whereas they may only sell a $300 guitar once a week.

The "stepchild" mentality is starting to turn around. Print is all about profit per square inch and GMROI (Gross Margin Return on Investment). Really, if I had paid more attention in my accounting class in college and learned about GMROI, I would have probably purchased Tony's Drum Shop. Most store owners are musicians that simply need a good accounting lesson.

Could you describe your day-to-day work?

My job changes every day. As a VP, I have a business plan that I need to execute but as a manager, I have thirty-eight people who come first. One of the best pieces of advice I've ever received was from Keith when I accepted the National Sales Manager role. He told me: "If you let the administrative side of your job take priority over the people you manage, you will fail." I repeat this phrase daily, and it helps me to keep things in perspective. People are our greatest asset. We have great people, and my biggest responsibility is to help them grow. It's not easy, but it's very rewarding. The last part of my job is to handle difficult situations or customers. Every company will stumble from time to time, but I love being able to solve problems and flip situations around to everyone's benefit.

Let's talk about an entry-level position at Hal Leonard. First of all, how many employees are at Hal Leonard?

We have about 350 employees. The majority, about 230 people, are in our Winona (MN) facility. Winona houses our printing, distribution, accounts payable, and warehouse operations. The rest are here in Milwaukee where we have the pre-press, business affairs, sales, and marketing operations. By pre-press, I mean editorial, transcribing, engraving, and graphic design.

There are many entry-level positions in both facilities. In Milwaukee, the largest division is the sales team, so we have the greatest need for entry-level people. Our sales lines are open Monday through Friday, 8:00 A.M. until 9:00 P.M., as well as Saturdays and Sundays 9 to 5. Telesales/Customer Service is a perfect entry-level position.

To work in editorial, you need to have (musical) chops. You need to have the ability to put on headphones, listen to a song, and edit what the transcribers give you to make sure it's accurate. Our editors need to have a higher level of musical ability than our sales team. Each area—business-affairs department, sales, graphic design—requires specialized skills. But in sales, I can generally bring in people who are looking for a career in the music industry and set them on a career path.

As far as hiring telesales staff, what do you look for?

You've heard the phrase that there are three things that will sell your house: location, location, location. There are three things that will sell me on a potential telesales candidate: attitude, attitude, attitude. During the first interview, I'll look at the candidate's body language, how they greet me when I go down to meet them, and the elevator conversation. My office is on the second floor, so we take the elevator and I purposely stop talking as the elevator door closes. My goal is to see how long the candidate will let the silence go on. If they let it go on the whole elevator ride, I know this person is not good for sales. I'm looking to see if they can draw a conversation out of me. If they can do that, I know I have somebody who can have a career in sales.

I'm looking to see if they can draw a conversation out of me. If they can do that, I know I have somebody who can have a career in sales.

So does Hal Leonard offer internships?

At this point, we don't, but it's something we are investigating. I have a lot of friends that teach music business and music merchandising classes. I've told them to let us know when they have a prospective student that is interested in what we do. I'll usually do an informal phone interview to find out if they might fit. If they have the right skills and attitude, I'll set up a regular interview, which can lead to full-time employment.

Down the line, five to ten years, where do you see career opportunities?

There are great career opportunities in music, in publishing, and in sales. There will always be a need for people who are energetic

...having the need for people who can communicate will never change. As long as there are products to sell, we'll need outgoing people to spread the word.

If you think you have the ability, then you need to go out and let other people know that you are something special.

and can be the voice and the face of Hal Leonard. Print music may change and the delivery of music will change. But having the need for people who can communicate will never change. As long as there are products to sell, we'll need outgoing people to spread the word.

Any Yoda-like final thoughts for the readers?

If you think you have the ability, then you need to go out and let other people know that you are something special. You cannot let a résumé speak for you. Find out who the decision maker is in the business and call them, even if it's just for an informational interview. If someone is looking for a career in sales, that's huge. Doing this will pretty much guarantee you an interview at most music companies. If you can turn the informational interview into a conversation where the decision maker is talking more about themselves than the job, you've hit a home run.

Gary Miller

Vice President, Motion Pictures and TV Clearance and Licensing, Universal Music Publishing Group, Los Angeles

Gary Miller is Vice President, Motion Picture and Television Music, Clearance and Licensing at Universal Music Publishing Group ("UMPG") in Los Angeles. He is a 1990 graduate of University of the Pacific's Entertainment Management program.

Gary supervises a department of twelve people and regularly negotiates deals with a client roster including clients Walt Disney Pictures, 20th Century Fox Film Corp., Warner Brothers Television, and Universal Pictures; all the major advertising agencies throughout the U.S.; and scores of music supervisors within the film and television community. Universal Music Publishing's roster includes chart-topping songwriters such as Prince, Elton John, 50 Cent, Foo Fighters, and many others. He is also involved in the design and implementation of UMPG's future Web-based licensing system that will have a significant impact on the process in which deals are done through the Film & TV department.

Prior to joining Universal, he worked in various management roles at such firms as PolyGram Film & TV Music, MCA Music Publishing, and The Clearing House, Ltd. During his tenure as Clearance Manager at The Clearing House, his clients included some of the most successful television series such as The Cosby Show, Roseanne, Grace Under Pressure, *and* America's Most Wanted. *CBS and NBC-TV were among Gary's regular licensing clients.*

He has played guitar for more than thirty years and continues to play the occasional date around L.A. with his band. He has a hard-disk-based recording studio at home and is the proud father of two future musicians.

What got you into the music business?

Well, I'm a musician at heart. I moved down here [L.A.] for a year from Santa Rosa, CA, where I grew up to attend a music school. While I was there, I decided that it was best for me to finish up my degree and that's when I went back to University of the Pacific. The reason why I chose UOP was that it was really one of the only programs on the West Coast offering a degree in Music Management at the time.

After graduation, I moved back, and it was natural that I try to get a job in the music business, but I kept playing my guitar, too.

Do you recall your first paying gig and/or job in the music industry?

My first gig was a Top 40 band in a local club in Santa Rosa. We lied about my age to play so I think I was nineteen at the time, out playing at the bars. Let's just say I did whatever I needed to do to be able to play out at clubs and live performances. As a guitar player and kind of a rock and pop guy at heart, those were the venues: clubs. That's when I got out and first got paid to play.

My first music business job was an internship with Warner-Chappell Music, in their tape production room. They also had all their song files in there, sheet music. It was the backbone of the creative department. So that was what I lined up for myself upon graduation.

I had some friends who were graduating at the same time and they both had internships with [jazz pianist] Chick Corea. We all happened to be out looking for a place to live, and they needed to stop in at their soon-to-be internship office. We started talking and then Boom! I landed a second internship with Chick Corea Productions. This woman, Shirley, handled internal publishing for Chick, and that turned out to be the internship that actually led to something.

My last day there, a music supervisor happened to be in the studio. Shirley introduced me to her, and we just started talking. The music supervisor was considering hiring somebody part-time, and I landed that job. So that was my first paying music business gig. She was working out of her home. Basically, she had a few different composers that she represented and one record label, GNP/Crescendo. What she hired me to do was get in touch with the various music supervisors on television shows and make some contacts.

And pitch the music you repped?

Yeah, and pitch. Actually I made my next connection through them. It's funny because after I had met her, I went over to meet with her and her partner for an interview. We were talking, and they told me about a place called The Clearing House, which was an independent clearance company that worked on behalf of various TV producers for studios basically acquiring rights for the shows. They had mentioned this friend of theirs, George, who had gone to work for them and pretty much met everybody through there and was now working at EMI. So I wrote the name of the place down and immediately came home and put a résumé in the mail to them.

About a month later, as luck would have it, their HR person called me and said, "I came in today and your résumé just happened to be sitting faceup open in the pile. We've been talking about hiring an entry-level person." They ended up making me an offer, and so that was the path to my first full-time music business job.

So it was not exactly a straight path! As you joined the workforce in Hollywood, what skills or training did you find to be the most helpful?

The music industry has become so multifaceted today. It's no longer just trying to get a job at one of the major labels or a big publishing company. There are so many different things to do in the music business with the various mobile media, Internet, and other new companies. But I think what serves me best, and what I would emphasize to people considering getting into it, is to understand that there are the separate business and creative tracks. On the creative side, it's street smarts and it's being able to get into clubs and check out bands year-round and just having a good taste for music. It's a matter of being there.

Whereas if you want to get into the business side, having a clear understanding of copyright law, and a basic understanding of entertainment deals—these fundamentals are essential. The concepts involved in negotiating and intellectual property are central. So for me, it was being able to walk into that first interview with the president of The Clearing House and impress her with my knowledge and confidence. In our interview, she recommended a couple of books, such as *This Business of Music,* as useful reads. It turned out these actually had been my textbooks in school, and I knew them quite well. Discussing them with her made all the difference. Today, she is one of my clients and she also proudly takes full responsibility for my success in the business!

I would say that whatever situation you walk into, being prepared, being ready to deliver, not making the empty promises, and having some good business background will go a long way.

I think it's so important...there's nothing wrong with pursuing a creative dream but the reality is that you can have a really good job if you understand the fundamentals of the business side of it and still have plenty of opportunities to be creative.

I agree. And if by being creative, you mean pursuing a career as an artist, you need to know the business side, because otherwise, people will try to take advantage of you every turn along the way. That's the reason I went back to school: to be sure if somebody wanted to handle things for me (as an artist) that I could read between the lines and see who would be the best representative for me.

Any early mentors?

Yeah, with that first as a gofer at the Clearing House there were a couple people there: my immediate supervisors and then a couple other people above them. I just made it known to them that I was interested in the position that had the most contact with clients. That was my goal: to just be out there and get my name out in the mix. So there was a guy there named Randy Parker, and Randy gave me most of my solid advice. There are things he told me back then that I still rely on—right down to instances where I was made the scapegoat and Randy knew it wasn't me and he supported me. I remember him saying, "In this business, you have to just put on a Teflon skin and just let it roll off." He heard me and saw where I wanted to go. The mentor thing only goes so far in the music business because it's a very competitive business. Everyone's looking out for their own job.

I was at the Clearing House for three years and had reached my peak there. I saw that I had moved along as far as I was going to go right then, so it was time to start looking at other possibilities. It really got driven home when the (1994) earthquake hit L.A., and we had to move out of our Hollywood office and relocate downtown. I was really over California and ready for a change. A friend of mine in Arizona had a company that he was doing some work for and they needed help with licensing, so I moved out to Arizona for three months—it was the worst three months ever. I couldn't get out of there fast enough!

What happened was I was at work in Arizona one day, and my current boss, Scott James, called along with the person who I had previously done deals with at what was then called MCA Music Publishing. The receptionist said it's Scott James and Don Kennedy. (MCA Music became a part of Universal Music Publishing, where I now work.) Of course, the first thing that popped into my head was, "Okay, there's no other reason Scott would be on the phone with Don than maybe they have an opening." Sure enough, they were calling me because they had worked with me at the Clearing House, and I had developed a good reputation around town. People always had a pleasant experience with me, and I always got the job done so my name had been tossed around. It's funny because looking back now, I realize I haven't really updated my résumé in sixteen years.

You've just done good work and established strong connections across the industry.

Yeah, I just got that first opportunity, did well, and then it became my calling card. So they called me based on a referral. I didn't even send out a résumé. So I was at MCA Music Publishing from October of 1994 until April of 1997. At that time, I had gotten to be friends with a woman I had dealt with on the record side at PolyGram. She told me that if she ever had the budget she would hire me, and two years later she got the budget and called me. So Boom! There's another job where I didn't even send a résumé. I moved to PolyGram, on the record side. All of my experiences were in the Film and TV synchronization licensing area, so when I went over to PolyGram, instead of representing songwriters as you would at a publisher, I was representing the label for the masters and there were about forty labels under the PolyGram umbrella, including Motown, Mercury, Casablanca, Polydor, and A&M to name a few. When the merger happened, I found myself at another crossroads where I felt like if I wasn't going to be put in charge of something, I was kind of at the end of my rope as far as just plugging along in the music business.

As chance would have it, that's when I got the call. It was during the process of the merger: Don Kennedy was leaving, so Scott James called me, asking, "How's it going over there…any interest in coming back?" Scott gave me the opportunity to take over the department, even though I was lacking any real managerial experience. At that time, it was five people, including myself. Since then, revenues have increased 500 percent, and I'm overseeing twelve staffers.

Talk a little bit about your day-to-day role within the department and then within the larger entity of Universal Music Publishing.

Day-to-day, I think my role here is to lay out the guidelines, making sure I have trustworthy people who have the right experience in the right positions, so that I don't have to micromanage, in addition to being responsible for everything that happens in this thirteen-person department. I have my own clients that I deal with, as well. I am the ring-tone department, I am the videogame department, I work with various motion-picture studios, and I am the guy for commercials for North America. I also field incoming requests from about ten of the forty foreign offices we work with.

Who are some of the songwriters that your office represents?

U2, Prince, 50 Cent, Foo Fighters, Jack Johnson, and some back catalog, like the older songs by Elton John and Bernie Taupin. We own or represent more than one million songs. [For more complete catalog information, visit www.umusicpub.com.]

What gives you the greatest satisfaction at work?

I'd say it's the opportunity to deal on behalf of these amazing songwriters and at the same time have the opportunity to have ongoing relationships and be in contact with a lot of different people out there in the community. That's what makes it interesting to me. If I was just sitting somewhere, closed off from the rest of the world pushing papers, it probably wouldn't be too exciting for me.

What do you look for in an entry-level job candidate?

I look for job experience that would have given them skill in the organizational end of things, as well as time on the phones. It doesn't have to necessarily be an internship in the music business for me. Obviously, you look at past work experience even at the entry-level position. If they held a handful of jobs for two to three months, you question that. I guess what I look for is consistency. I even think that for what we do, having the right educational background, experience in the customer service area—like waiting tables, where you have to be very organized, and on your toes—goes a long way. Ultimately, it is customer service.

Does one's paycheck rely on customer happiness at the end of the transaction?

Yeah, and understanding that the customer is *always* right. I've had to deal with that when a staffer comes into my office looking a little green and gets flustered when the heat gets turned up. No matter how wrong the customer might be, it's my philosophy that they're always right. So, just try to finesse the situation. But just demonstrating solid organizational skills, using that organizational experience in previous jobs, and not showing any job hopping—the inability to hold on to a job.

Does Universal Music Publishing offer any kind of internships, and if so, is it possible that a successful intern would be considered if there was an open position?

Absolutely. One of our manager-level staff is a guy who interned here while he was at USC. He's been here for a few years now. There's another guy who interned, then earned his law degree, and we hired him.

Considering all the changes going on to the industry due to new technology, where do you see things headed in the long run, and as far as career opportunities for someone in music publishing?

As far as the impact that the digital distribution of music is going to have on the majors, that's a crystal-ball answer that I personally don't have. There's so much going on, so much rapid change that it's hard to say how much of an impact it will have. We know it's going to be significant. Will it break the machine or will it just force change? I think it will just force change. If there aren't these record companies, there is going to be some kind of company out there that's getting music out there, and in order for companies to survive there has to be some sort of a business model. Musicians won't be able to just sit there making music for free. There has to be a way for people to make money. If that's the effect that digital music has on making music, we'll have to get used to not hearing much new music. Whatever evolves will still require music business professionals to represent talent.

Any parting thoughts?

I'll share my own philosophy. I never woke up one day and said, "Gee, I want to be in the music business." I always wanted to be an artist; I wanted to be a musician. But you have to ask yourself certain quality-of-life questions, I guess. I come from a place of always wanting to do the best I can no matter what I'm doing; I pick up the guitar and want to do the best I can. At my job, I want to do the best I can. It just always has to do with presenting yourself professionally, knowing your business.

As far as networking goes, it's hard to network if you're not confident. It's hard to just go to a networking party and think you're going to make these big contacts and have it happen. You have to go there knowing your stuff and presenting yourself with some confidence. You have to be comfortable in your own skin. "This is who I am and this is what I have to offer." Keep your eyes and ears open to all sorts of opportunities. You might be focused on just one that is really quite hard to get, but try not to do that at the expense of other opportunities that may pop up and be equally as rewarding in the long run.

Leslie Ann Jones

Director of Music Recording and Scoring at Skywalker Sound

Leslie Ann Jones has been a recording and mixing engineer for over thirty years. Starting her career at ABC Recording Studios in Los Angeles in 1975, she moved to Northern California in 1978 to accept a staff position with David Rubinson and Fred Catero at the legendary Automatt Recording Studios. There she worked with such artists as Herbie Hancock, Bobby McFerrin, Holly Near, Angela Bofill, and Narada Michael Walden, and started her film-score mixing career with Apocalypse Now.

From 1987 to 1997, she was a staff engineer at Capitol Studios located in the historic Capitol Records Tower in Hollywood. She recorded projects with Rosemary Clooney, Michael Feinstein, Michelle Shocked, BeBe & CeCe Winans, and Marcus Miller, as well as the scores for several feature films and television shows.

In February of 1997, she returned to Northern California to accept a position as Director of Music Recording and Scoring with Skywalker Sound, where she continues her engineering career mixing music for records, films, television, and commercials. In 2003, Leslie was nominated for a Grammy Award for Best Engineered Recording, Classical, and received a Grammy Award for the Kronos Quartet's recording of Berg: Lyric Suite, which won Best Chamber Music Album.

Leslie is a past chair of the Recording Academy's Board of Trustees and a member of the Oakland Cultural Affairs Commission. She also serves on the Grammy Foundation Board and the Recording Arts Advisory Board for the Ex'pression College for Digital Arts.

What drew you to music or recording initially?

I grew up in the music business, because my parents were performers and I was a guitar player. I just kind of progressed from that. I actually was drawn to music first, then the recording business later.

What can you share about your first paying gig in the business?

Well, as a recording engineer, I was working for ABC Records, which was owned by the ABC Television Network. They had a recording studio.

I'd already done a lot of live sound and had taken a couple of recording engineer courses, which were the first offered in L.A. I actually wanted to be a record producer and manager; I wanted to emulate Peter Asher. I didn't really plan on being an engineer. But I thought I should learn something about engineering, to make me a better producer/manager.

So I just went and asked. I knew the studio manager, Phil Kaye. I told him I wanted the job, and he said, "Well there aren't any other women doing what you want to do. I don't know how it will work, so we'll just see how the clients react to you. We'll just have to play it by ear."

What background, training, or education has proven helpful for you during your career?

Let's see, I think reading a lot proved really helpful. Most people that go into this line of work have at least some sort of natural inclination for either the music or the technology.

As I said, the two recording classes that I took were the first offered in L.A., and mostly for me, it was because I was so self-taught that I really needed to double-check what I thought I knew.

But I started out reading magazines like *Stereo Review* and *Hi-Fidelity* because there was no *Mix* magazine when I started out.

Many people came to it from kind of a broadcast or Heath Kit home-electronic background. (Heath Kit was a catalog company in the 1950s–1970s that provided home-electronics kits for ham radio and hi-fi enthusiasts to build their own equipment.)

Those classes helped me a lot because by the time I got the job at ABC, which was essentially making tape copies on an eight-hour shift, I had already learned quite a bit about sound.

I was familiar enough with tape machines so that no one had to point and say, "That's a 7-inch reel. That's a 10-inch reel." I wasn't terribly nervous and I understood the basic process of recording.

> *I sometimes think now what happens is students learn too much, and when they go into their first job, they're not able to keep an open mind.*

I sometimes think now what happens is students learn too much, and when they go into their first job, they're not able to keep an open mind. I feel that some of the schools forget or don't spend enough time on the fundamentals. Instead they emphasize learning how to run Pro Tools or an SSL (Solid State Logic) board. And then, of course, they get to their first job and the place doesn't use either one. So don't overlook the importance of really mastering the basics.

I was the person who raised my hand whenever there was an opportunity to take on something new. When you do that, people naturally start to feed you more information.

Were there any early mentors who influenced you?

There were many. I kept a really open mind and I asked a lot of questions. I was very eager to learn and jump right in and do new things. I was the person who raised my hand whenever there was an opportunity to take on something new. When you do that, people naturally start to feed you more information.

But I would say my first main mentor was [engineer and producer] Roy Halee. And then after that, it would be [engineer] Fred Catero and [producer] David Rubinson.

When I met Roy, he was head of A&R for ABC Records. Roy had engineered and produced Simon & Garfunkel, among many other great artists such as Blood Sweat & Tears, Bob Dylan, Journey, Laura Nyro, Boz Scaggs, and Paul Simon. When I worked with Roy, he was working with Rufus and other artists signed to ABC.

And Fred, of course, recorded Janis Joplin, Santana, Herbie Hancock, the Pointer Sisters—every kind of major artist that was representative of the San Francisco sound—as well as Barbra Streisand, Bob Dylan, Chicago, and other CBS artists.

David Rubinson was the producer who developed many of those acts, and he and Fred were a team working together out of the Automatt [now a parking lot at Fourth and Folsom in San Francisco].

Let's talk a little bit about your role in the day-to-day workings of Skywalker, because I understand you wear a couple of different hats in your job.

Well, I not only run the studio, but I'm responsible for every aspect of the recording operations: booking the studio, the administration, the budget, the personnel, hiring/firing, buying equipment—all of that.

I help to steer it and market the scoring facility. Really, the scoring stage operates like any small business.

Plus, I'm still a recording engineer. So although I don't record every session, I do record about 30 percent of what goes on here.

What part of your job gives you the most satisfaction?

Obviously, the studio work is always very satisfying. But it's easy to get burned out when you do too much of it, which is why I chose to pursue a job that is a bit different, but one that is still rewarding and a lot of fun. Whether I'm the engineer or not, I really enjoy when people have a great time here.

...being in the room when a great performance is happening is still the main thing that inspires me.

However, I would say that being in the room when a great performance is happening is still the main thing that inspires me.

Could you describe an entry-level position at Skywalker?

On the scoring stage, that gig is as a runner, which we have now, although it's not a full-time position. The runner is just called in on an as-needed basis, because we only have the one music studio.

For the rest of the Skywalker facilities [home to the post-production and mixing stages for hundreds of hit movies, as well as the special-effects division, Industrial Light and Magic], most people come in as central machine room operators (MRO) for the mix stage. Sometimes they might come in as transfer people, as well. But that requires quite a bit more experience and education.

A transfer op may have been somebody who worked at a smaller facility for a year or two, got their feet wet, and knows the difference between a single stripe and dual-stripe mag, drop-frame and non-drop-frame timecode, and so forth.

Could you identify three attributes or skills—it could be either—that you would look for in an entry-level person?

I think we tend to gravitate towards people that have the right amount of enthusiasm.

We don't have a lot of people working here, and there isn't any formal time period that you're going to stay in each job. It just seems that those people that tend to excel at what they do, who grow and progress through the organization—start as a mix tech and progress to a mixer—are the ones that have the most self-motivation. They can think for themselves, they are smart, and they invest the time to educate themselves.

I really think not knowing too much and not knowing too little is key. I mean, even for a runner, the guy we have now studied for a number of years at Berklee College of Music in Boston. I don't have to worry about him knowing the etiquette in the room or being unfamiliar with equipment. He has a really strong music background. Yet he doesn't know so much that he expects to walk in and be an assistant engineer right away. He's willing to make food runs and do whatever it takes to keep the session running, just so he can be here.

But there are only so many jobs, so you have to be flexible and be willing to fit in wherever you can. You need to stay attuned to the opportunities that might present themselves and be willing to jump in and take a chance.

That's what I've done in the last twenty-five years—let's see, I've had five jobs. This is my fifth job. And one of those jobs is counting the three years I spent as an independent engineer. I am pleased to say that, in each of my jobs, I have gone past what I thought I knew or tried something kind of different, with an element of risk, realizing that the next career move wasn't necessarily safe. That's the only way you can really grow.

And that risk/growth relationship is a preview of what you're going to have to do when you finally sit in the chair as an engineer anyway. You are going to have to get past whatever knowledge you have to when the client says, "That's too orange." You have to figure out what that means and how to make the track sound more "green."

You should know enough about what you're doing and the tools that you have available to you to creatively get the job done.

What is the salary range for an entry-level position?

Interns get paid less than staff positions, although they do get paid. It is anywhere from $10 to $18 per hour depending on what the person will be doing.

When a person is getting started in the business, they are there to primarily learn—not so much to earn. Try to get into a good learning situation, because the money comes later.

Yeah. Actually, that's why I really recommend that a person get a job in the biggest studio they can find and not take a job in a one-room place. Chances are, they're not going to really learn in a one-room studio.

Skywalker has an internship program. Could you talk about it?

It is handled through our human resources department. First, a department like ours must decide each year whether or not to request an intern because the salary to pay the intern comes out of each department's budget. And then if anyone applied for an internship with the scoring stage as his or her preference, we would probably get one.

But every company is different. Some do it like Capitol Records, where they would hire six interns from local music business programs throughout L.A., and they would spend a week in each department.

You mentioned you have a runner/intern now on the scoring stage. Can you estimate what percentage of new hires are current or former interns?

Around 20 percent.

Do you have any tips you can offer to somebody who is thinking about getting into the business? When you started, you walked in and approached Phil Kaye at ABC and said, "I'd like to engineer here." Things are quite a bit different now, obviously.

Yes, I think they are different. A lot of people that we consider tend to come recommended from other people in the business. We also have a relationship with certain schools. I might e-mail the head of the recording department asking if they have any outstanding students, which is exactly what I did the last time we were looking for somebody.

I contacted Los Medanos, San Francisco State, and Berklee College of Music and just asked if anyone had a couple of bright young kids. A referral like that is one way to get a start.

The other way is just to call around, and if somebody says they're not hiring, send them a résumé and follow it up with another call. Or, you can ask if you can come by, drop off your résumé, and see the studio. That way, the person who is in charge of hiring gets a chance to meet you, even though they might not be thinking about it at the time.

That approach may not work at some facilities that just do not have time or availability to accommodate drop-in visitors, but for many studios, it will work, so it's worth a try.

You should ask, "May I stop by and drop off my résumé and meet you, and spend about five minutes speaking with you?" Studio managers are generally very busy people, but at least you've had the opportunity to meet a person in the music community and hopefully make a favorable impression.

As far as resources, is there anything you think someone coming into the business should be looking at?

Well, I think for somebody just starting out, *Mix* might be a little too much. I guess *Recording* or *EQ* magazine might be a better place to start.

We haven't yet talked about knowing computers, either. You really should know the fundamentals of either a Mac or a PC, and having some knowledge of hard-disk editing is quite an advantage.

I would also suggest joining the Recording Academy as an associate or as an affiliate member, because you still have access to any of the workshops that are offered once you're on the mailing list. A lot of those events are free. So the networking and educational opportunities available in that organization are available whether you're a voting member or not.

A lot of schools have student AES (Audio Engineering Society) chapters; I know San Francisco State does.

As far as conventions, I would think now, NAMM would be a good place to go to learn a little bit about who the players are in the technology side of recording.

Long-term, what's your sense of the career opportunity represented by becoming a recording engineer?

It can still be a [good] career opportunity, but I know that even well-respected veteran engineers are learning Pro Tools or some other hard-disk editing system, because clients are kind of expecting that and they want that available to them. Colleagues of mine have said, "Why should they pay someone else [to do hard-disk editing], when they can pay me?"

So that's certainly job security. I'm still pretty bullish on that, but I think there are many opportunities out there with distribution changing with the Internet, uploading, and new technologies.

Do you have any parting thoughts?

Master the basics and the fundamentals.

I think that's the big advantage of working in a big place and not in a small place. You're exposed to a lot more. In my nine years at Capitol, I was pushed to do so many things, not only the level of clientele that we had, but just kind of the things we were asked to do. All the Frank Sinatra Ednet ISDN sessions for the two *Duets* albums happened at Capitol. Then we shifted gears to record a film score with a large orchestra at the next session. You wouldn't really get that kind of experience in a one-room studio. It makes you much more valuable as an employee because eventually, you are going to have to look for another job. It always happens.

Do you have any Yoda-like pearls of wisdom to share in closing?

Use your ears, Luke—use your ears.

Murray Allen

Vice President of Postproduction
Electronic Arts, Inc.

Murray Allen's career spanned more than fifty years in the music industry. He was a musician, producer, session player, studio owner, and studio designer, and at the time of this interview, served as Vice President of Postproduction for one of the world's most successful electronic-gaming companies, Electronic Arts, based in Redwood City, CA.

During the golden era of big bands, he played sax and clarinet with the Glenn Miller, Sauter Finegan, Bobby Sherwood, and Skitch Henderson bands. Murray backed up artists including Frank Sinatra, Tony Bennett, Frankie Laine, and Perry Como. His session work includes dates with Stevie Wonder, the Platters, and Andy Williams.

When the guitar began to rule pop music, Murray started to engineer recording sessions, rapidly becoming one of the most in-demand engineers in Chicago, recording the likes of Ramsey Lewis, Duke Ellington, Steve Allen, Stan Kenton, and Sammy Davis, Jr. In the early '70s, he became president of Universal Recording, where he would stay for the next seventeen years. During that time, the studio won numerous Emmy and Grammy nominations and compiled a substantial number of Clio awards (the Oscar-equivalent of the advertising industry).

Murray's insatiable quest for knowledge and love of technology led Universal to many "firsts" in the recording industry: pioneering the use of digital-audio workstations in commercial production, offering video sweetening (in 1971) before SMPTE time code was developed, and mentoring other studio owners and managers in recording-studio management.

During Murray's watch at Universal, more than 250 feature film and television soundtracks were recorded by the studio staff including: Steel Magnolias, Home Alone, Flatliners, The Witches of Eastwick, Brighton Beach Memoirs, Sea of Love, Midnight Run, *and many more. In its heyday, Universal employed more than 400 employees.*

While at Electronic Arts, he headed up audio and video postproduction, quality assurance, testing, and customer service. He was sound designer of the Grammy awards telecast for twenty years, and an active member of the Recording Academy and SPARS.

Murray was a man with a boundless supply of energy, an uncanny ability to identify and develop new talent, and a passion for excellence in everything he undertook. One quote from Murray sums up his apparent ability to do just about anything to which he set his mind: "I'm not concerned with problems. I'm only concerned with solutions."

What drew you to the music and recording business?

Well, it's a funny story. I started playing an instrument when I was about six years old. I started on piano, and then I migrated over to clarinet when I was eight years old. But my first love was physics. I really loved being an engineer and doing all kinds of stuff that related to physics.

I became a musician because I had a fear of water.

When I was in high school, however, everybody had to take swimming, and I've always been afraid of the water. So the only way you could get out of swimming was to be in the military band. Now because I already played clarinet pretty well, I joined the military band. So I became a musician because I had a fear of water.

Later on, when I got out of high school, I went to Illinois Institute of Technology (IIT) because I wanted to be a physicist. That was my goal. But I already was a working musician. I'd been working as a musician since I was about thirteen years old. I had my own Society Band at the Morraine Hotel on Chicago's North Shore when I was sixteen years old.

When I was enrolled at IIT in the 1940s, an engineer with a masters degree working on the Manhattan Project was earning about $7,500 a year. As a musician I was already making $8,000 a year. So I thought, why do I want to spend all this time getting an advanced degree in physics, even though I love it, to earn less money? Coming up through the Depression, money has been a very important motivation for me.

So, I then became a professional musician. I went to New York. I wanted to study from Joe Allard, who was considered the best clarinet/saxophone teacher in the country at that time. And when I was there I got to play a little bit on the Calvacade of Bands, WOR radio, and I worked full-time at Roseland Ballroom as a lead saxophone player. And then I was going to be drafted for the Korean War.

I came back, and I went to college to stay out of the draft. And I finally got tired of that. So I enlisted in the army. I figured I should get it out of the way. But because I enlisted in the army, I was able to choose my duty station, and I joined the Fifth Army

Band. Next, I got myself a radio show that we did five days a week. We did it with my own five-piece band. And my piano player for three years was the incomparable Bill Evans.

I was stationed near Chicago, and during that time, I started moonlighting, playing record dates. It was highly illegal and definitely against the regulations. But I did it and I never got caught.

When I got out of the army, I went on the road with a band to work at the Hilton chain for about a year, after which I took my own band into the Conrad Hilton Hotel in Chicago. I was there for two years, and I was working record dates and everything else. Then finally, I had so many record dates, that's all I did. I became a full-time studio musician. I did that from about 1956–57, all the way through to the mid-1960s. I recorded hundreds of albums and singles.

Anyway, around 1965 I could see that rock 'n' roll was starting to come in. Where I used to work about twenty-seven sessions per week, it was getting down to maybe twenty. I've always kept charts and graphs on whatever I was doing. Got down to about twenty sessions a week, and then about fifteen. We used to have about five saxophone players in every session—Henry Mancini-type arrangements. We were getting down to three or four saxes.

Well, I was the number-two call, so I always worked. But I thought I needed to make a decision. I've either got to learn to engineer again, or I have to learn to play the guitar. One of the two.

Backtracking a bit to my time in New York in the early 1950s, I worked the Roseland Ballroom. We had air shots every night where we broadcast over CBS and ABC, and then NBC. The next day I'd go over to the station and listen to a playback of what we did. They used to record it. I sounded terrible.

So I went over to Manny's Music store one day, and I bought an Ampex tape recorder and speakers, amplifiers, and microphones. It took me three years to pay for it, but I learned how to use it and how to make a decent recording. Having a science background, it was no big deal. I learned how to mix, record, and take the machine apart and put it back together again. I knew how to repair it and keep it running just right.

Consequently, going back to the mid-1960s, I decided to get back into recording. I knew what makes an Ampex recorder work. I knew about mixing. I started mixing a few dates, and all of a sudden, clients wanted me to start mixing for them.

Because I was making so much money in residuals playing on commercials, I said, "The only way I'll work for you as a mixer is if you also hire me as a musician." So they started doing that.

What happened then is that I became extremely busy. The other mixer in Chicago at that time was a man named Bruce Swedien. Now Bruce was going to work for another company in Chicago, but he had a one-year no-compete clause. So for one year, I became the number-1 mixer.

I was mixing sessions at RCA, CBS, and at Universal in the morning, and recording music. But in the afternoon, they were taking the 8-track tapes back over to Universal or some other place to finish. They put the announcers on and did the final mix.

I didn't get a piece of that action. I was only getting the music part. So two other engineers and myself opened up a studio called "Audio Finishers," a real hole-in-the-wall. But, then we added some experimental acoustic treatment to it, and we called it the Audio Finishers so that we could do that finishing work in the afternoon.

But then RCA in Chicago closed down for a year because they wanted to move, and Curtis Mayfield and all these Chicago acts needed a place to record. Well, it turns out that at this time we got the first 16-track recorder in Chicago.

Acoustically, the place was great for stacking [overdubbing], since it had great separation. So all of a sudden we started getting all the Curtis Mayfield work, Donnie Hathaway, Roberta Flack, and we started "stealing" business from CBS and from Universal, because the sound of our little room was so good. Plus, we had the only 16-track in town. And because we were good mixers, we got great sounds.

Universal came to us and said that we were killing them. They asked if we could enter into some type of agreement. We knew that our studio was limited in what it could do, because it was so small. Universal had such large, great-sounding rooms.

So we made a deal with Universal. One thing led to another, and eventually we took over management in 1970, then bought the studio in 1975. I still was working sessions, by the way, and engineering. I was going back and forth between the two studios.

The rest is history. We quickly became a gigantic operation—a major studio. We were nominated three times for TEC awards. We did over 250 feature films. We did every note of music in the original *Blues Brothers* film, which I'm very proud of. We had a cassette manufacturing plant working under contract for CBS and Motown. At that time, we had more than 400 employees.

But a funny thing happened. After twelve years running Universal, around 1985, I started getting very tired of running a recording studio. I hate to admit this, but we started getting to where everything was stacked one track at a time. We didn't use big orchestras anymore. Producers who were getting into the business now were not musicians. Computer programming was the coming wave for pop-music production.

And although we were the first studio to do so many things, I was getting very bored. We had to spend so much money just to keep up with the competition, it was terrible. So I decided to get out of the studio business. I sold the company in 1989 and I stayed on for about another year. And then I was a consultant for about a year. I worked with Editel [one of the leading postproduction houses] in Chicago.

I also worked with Tom Kobayashi who left Lucas Arts at that time and founded Ednet. I helped him work with Crescent Moon Studios down in Florida, and put in a T1 line between them and Capitol Studios in Los Angeles—so that Gloria Estefan could do her Christmas album from her home in Florida and the band could play live in California.

Phil Ramone was the producer. Phil and I have worked together for so many years. That technology is what kicked off the Sinatra *Duets* album, which was the first chart topper that proved that artists could collaborate over T1 or ISDN lines from anywhere in the world. The artist, producer, and musicians no longer had to be in the same studio.

How did you make the move to Electronic Arts?

Silicon Valley in 1993 closely resembled the record business back in the early 1950s.

One day, the phone rang and it was a headhunter asking me, "Murray, would you like to go out and live in California?" He said there's a job opening at Electronic Arts, and I came out here and I interviewed. Silicon Valley in 1993 closely resembled the record business back in the early 1950s. So I said, "Yes, this is going to be fun."

Do you remember your first paying gig?

When I was thirteen, we used to go out and play at the local park districts. Whatever they collected at the door, we split amongst the band. So we would get $2 or $3 each, or something like that.

Actually, when I was about twelve years old, I was on a radio show in Chicago called *The Joe Kelly Quiz Kids Band*. We did a couple of shows. We didn't get paid for it because in those days, the musician's union was extremely strong.

Sure. You couldn't be paid without membership in the union.

That's right. And we couldn't join the union until we were sixteen. So they gave us a waiver. They had to have a bunch of musicians stand by and get paid while we did the actual playing. But the first actual payment I got was these little park-concert type things.

You mentioned earlier that you had loved science and had studied it avidly both in high school and afterwards at the Illinois Institute of Technology. That obviously came in handy when you bought your first Ampex tape recorder.

Well, I understood about electronics and signal flow, because I had a scientific type of mind. I still do to this day. In other words, I do not want anybody telling me, "This does not work." Instead, let's see why it doesn't work, and let's figure out how we make it work. I'm not concerned with problems; I am only concerned with solutions.

You mentioned a couple of people early on who were influences on you. Is there anyone in particular?

Well, Bill Putnam was a big influence, actually because he built Universal.

There were about fifteen guys that were the original owners of Universal Recording. One of them was a guy named Jerry Bradley. He owned a club in Chicago, a nightclub called the 5100 Club. He was the one that introduced me to Danny Thomas, who was the comedian at his club. Our high-school band did a session at Universal, and that's how I met Bill Putnam. He engineered the session.

And I remember the tune we recorded was "A Starry Night." Da da da da da da [Murray hums the melody]... by Tchaikovsky. Those were fun days, in 1946.

Bill was an influence on me, from an engineering point of view, early on.

A lot of guys influenced me early in my life when I was on the road. Like Morrie Feld, who was the drummer with the Benny Goodman Sextet for many years.

When I was on the road, I was in the backup band for Frankie Laine, and the drummer and my roommate was Morrie. He taught me about the importance of rhythm and time in jazz. Another one was Joe Daly, a Chicago saxophone player. He and I were roommates in a lot of bands. He was a great jazz player. Mel Lewis, Louis Bellson, and Peter Erskine all had a musical impact on me.

And, of course, Bill Evans was a tremendous influence. I enjoyed working with him every night for three years.

Now fast-forward to today. Tell me a bit about what you do at Electronic Arts.

From an audio and video [production] point of view, I try and keep people [moving] back towards the center. There's a natural tendency for younger people to try to experiment. They all have tastes, but many don't realize what makes a production really work. So try to keep things aimed towards the center, knowing that if it doesn't have that magic, it doesn't mean a damn thing.

In any sort of audio or visual production, you have to have a vision for what the project will come out like, and go with it. I hate committees.

In any sort of audio or visual production, you have to have a vision for what the project will come out like, and go with it. I hate committees.

Pick the right people to get the job done. You know, not everybody may agree that this is the best way of doing it, but as long as you are in what I call that "window of acceptability," you're cool.

Is some of your time spent as a coach, mentoring to some degree?

I do a lot of mentoring. That's probably the biggest thing I do at Electronic Arts. But I have 300 people working for me, so a lot of it is just making decisions like, "How do we handle this? What do we do about this?"

The most important lesson I try to impress on my staff is to never use the word "no." I do not want anybody to say, "We can't do this." I want them to say, "Well, let's think about this. Let's see what it will take to get the job done right."

The most important lesson I try to impress on my staff is to never use the word "no." I do not want anybody to say, "We can't do this." I want them to say, "Well, let's think about this. Let's see what it will take to get the job done right." Whether it is about money, people, or whatever is required. Then you can make the decision; if it's too costly, you don't do it.

What aspect of your role at Electronic Arts do you enjoy the most?

Building teams. I've built a number of teams in the time I've been here. I was given the assignment of starting a customer-support team. This was three and a half years ago. We are now considered to be the best technical-support group in the whole business.

Management asked me to develop a product-testing team. When I started the testing team, I had two people. I now have 150 people on the testing team, and we did 62 titles this year. Today's games have a great deal of depth, so testing is a complex process.

I believe that to be a leader, you have to first have been a follower.

Building these teams is obviously something you enjoy greatly.

Well, that's what I did at Universal. I like to build teams, build loyalty. I believe that to be a leader, you have to first have been a follower. In other words, before you can play first saxophone, you have got to spend a lot of years playing second saxophone. So you know what it takes to be part of a team and make it work. Once you do that, the most important thing is being honest, being fair, and being consistent.

I stress that you must be honest, you must be fair, you must be consistent, and you must have a passion for what you do. If you don't have a passion, you should get out of the business right now.

I stress that you must be honest, you must be fair, you must be consistent, and you must have a passion for what you do. If you don't have a passion, you should get out of the business right now.

What's an entry-level position like at Electronic Arts? What would somebody be doing there when they started out?

In my groups, most people start off in technical support. First, they have to pass a test, and then go through a rigorous three-week training program, and we send them back to school to learn about what we do. Next, they go through a two-week, hands-on mentoring and polishing process.

At that point, they're ready to get on the phone, solving problems for our customers—which is the toughest job in the world.

But through that, they learn what our customer needs. It's very important that you always listen to your customer. If you don't listen to your customer, you are in deep trouble.

In other words, they develop a dialog with the customers and they develop a skill for understanding what our customers need—how the games work. Of course all these persons are avid gamers, so that's another requirement.

I guess there's no shortage of gamers!

No. And then from there they move on to testing. And from testing they may move into production, marketing, or the online division. However, it all starts at the beginning, the customer equation. Essentially, it is all about the product and the customer.

How about people working in audio or video production?

We bring experienced people in. My mixer, I hired from Universal Studios in L.A. I recruited my video staff from a post-production company. People have got to get their experience from somewhere else and come to us as a journeyman, not an apprentice. We haven't got time for training with our production schedules.

On the audio side, they're going to know the basics of Pro Tools. They're going to know the basics of samplers or sequencers...

A lot more than basics. I mean they have to have experience—credits where they've been successful in the studio. The same goes for video.

Can you tell me the salary range for an entry-level person?

When someone starts out in technical support, they get started at anywhere between $10 to $12 an hour.

Do you have any type of program where students who are in their final year of school or college can be exposed to what goes on?

We have a full-time staff that does this. And we actually go to the universities. We have recruiters that go out. We bring in interns. We have co-op programs. Sure. We do all of that. And the interns we recruit are paid positions.

We go to Stanford, MIT, and various other schools. We look for programmers and artists, but mainly programmers.

We give them a project during the summer, and if they do well with it, we try and get them back the next summer. When they graduate, we try to hire them.

Are there any tips that you could share for someone wanting to enter the recording or interactive-music business, to help them get their foot in the door?

First of all, you've got to decide what you want to do. In other words, if you want to make money, then you should go into the banking business or to Wall Street or Montgomery Street here in San Francisco. If you want to sell jewelry, then work on 47th Street in New York City.

However, if you want to be in music, either go to L.A., New York, or Nashville. I prefer New York or Los Angeles. Wherever there's more competition, you'll have more opportunity. Never go to a place where there's no competition because there's no opportunity for you there.

When I interview people here, I always ask the question, "What do you do better than anybody else in the world?" Pick one thing. I don't care what it is, but what do you do better than anybody else in the world?

Whatever you end up doing, you've got to learn to do better, at least in your own mind. You have to do it better than anybody else in the world does.

When I interview people here, I always ask the question, "What do you do better than anybody else in the world?" Pick one thing. I don't care what it is, but what do you do better than anybody else in the world?

The person must have enough self-esteem to really feel that they indeed do something better than somebody else. Now maybe they really do, which is even better. I also ask them to make up a "balance sheet" on their strong points and their weak points. Are you honest? Honesty is absolutely critical. It is important that a person doesn't lie, doesn't cheat, or isn't devious.

And you hang out. You have to hang out with the people that you ultimately want to work with. So if you want to be a songwriter and work with rock bands, get a copy of *Billboard*. Find out all about rock bands and who their publishers are. Start calling them. Get to know their names. Learn their secretaries' names. You should learn the people's names that are in the flow of that business.

When you go talk to them the first time, say, "That last record you did was the greatest thing. I love those lyrics." So that they know you are interested in them and what they do. If you're lucky, they'll do the rest of the talking and you'll be hired!

Let them do the talking and they're more likely to hire you.

Are there any magazines, books, articles, or organizations that people who want to get into the business should keep their eye on?

It's all on the Web now—just start surfing. You've also got to start looking for job sites on the Web; there's so many of them.

But basically you should focus yourself. Decide what you want to do and how you want to do it. Just aim in that direction and work at it.

It may take you a month, it may take you two years, or it might take you five years. But when you get there, you've got what you want.

However, don't put a timetable on your career. You may not hit the heights right away... but Richard Strauss didn't start writing good music until he was fifty years old.

My goal is to hit the peak of my career about a day before I die. [Laughter]

What's your glimpse into the future? Will entertainment media continue evolving?

Oh yeah, sure. Yeah, it has to. To just be competitive, sure. Television is going to change with 2,000 channels. There's a lot of opportunity there. I hope the quality improves. With most of the music on TV, it's gotten so bad. It's because people get out of college and they have Pro Tools or some kind of a sampler. They start creating music without any experience. And the producers that hire them have no experience either.

> *One thing I preach is that [good] music has to be entertaining music. It's got to hit you in the nerves. It's got to make you want to get up and dance. It's got to make your whole body want to shake.*

One thing I preach is that [good] music has to be entertaining music. It's got to hit you in the nerves. It's got to make you want to get up and dance. It's got to make your whole body want to shake. And if it doesn't do that, then there's always an opportunity for somebody who truly has the intuitive talent to create good music and good audio. And boy if you have it, then we need you!

Gary Gand

President of Gand Music & Sound
Northfield, Illinois

Gary and Joan Gand own and operate Gand Music & Sound in Northfield, IL, a suburb of Chicago. They have been a husband-and-wife team for more than thirty years, first playing in the same band and eventually opening a small guitar shop that has grown into one of the premiere music and recording retail stores in North America.

My interview with Gary clearly demonstrates the passion, commitment, and drive a person must have to get to the top of the music business. Gary's multifaceted career includes stints as a performer, session musician, guitar-repair whiz, engineer, and now president of a retail store that is known not only for the quality of its sales and service, but also for the savvy advice that Gand employees share with their customers. He talks about a career path that not many artists or musicians consider when they are starting off: music retailing. As you'll see, it can provide a stable financial base that still allows you to follow your musical dreams while managing to pay the rent.

Joan has been a pianist since the age of five and studied electronic music at Northwestern University. She manages the operations of the store as well as advertising, catalog production, purchasing, and the Gand Web site. Gary has served as a Director of NAMM, and is a Syn-Aud-Con graduate. Gary still finds time to go out to do live sound—not just to keep current on the latest technologies, but because he genuinely enjoys helping entertain a coliseum full of people. Joan and Gary's enthusiasm and passion for the music business is infectious to all who have the good fortune to work with them.

When did you and Joan start the business?

I started in 1971, with the keyboardist in my band at the time, who is my wife, Joan. We met in high school, and we've been together ever since.

Unlike the trend towards chain music stores, you operate one retail location.

Right, one location, one store. We call ourselves the last of the independents. Our strategy has always been to have one super-store rather than a bunch of less-than-super stores. Rather than spreading yourself too thin, we decided to take the approach that we were going to keep the one location that we've grown in and put all our eggs in one basket.

How many employees do you have?

Right now we've got about twenty-five. Plus a lot of independent engineers and technicians, fix-it guys, consultants—whomever it takes to keep things rolling.

What drew you to music, the recording side of things initially?

Like a lot of kids, I saw the Beatles on *Ed Sullivan* when I was about ten years old. I wanted to play music. The whole folk boom was happening at the time in the early 1960s. My dad was a musician in college, a trumpet player. He bought my mother a guitar during the folk days. When she hung it on the wall, he immediately took it down to the basement and started to figure out how to play it.

And literally within hours, I was down there asking, so what's going on down here? And my dad showed me how to play it. Then my sister came down to see what we were doing, and within a few months we had a group, the Gand Family Singers. We started playing local coffee houses and Boy Scout meetings, that kind of stuff.

It sounds as if the influence of music around your home played a big role.

My dad had a big-band in college. My mom was a fan. So there was always music in our house. The radio was always on. I mean, I used to fall asleep every night listening to classical music.

We saw a lot of music when I was a kid. My parents took me to see everybody: Segovia, Ravi Shankar, Jimi Hendrix, the Beatles, Frank Zappa, Cream, to name just a few.

And then eventually, we got into the family station wagon and headed out on the road. We played all the folk festivals. Played the University of Chicago and Berkeley, all the fiddle festivals down south, Disneyland, and television appearances.

When I got to be a teenager, I started playing rock 'n' roll. I was a banjo player, playing bluegrass. So I switched over to electric guitar. And that got me in front of a different audience. At the same time, we did some tape recordings with our folk trio. And you know, you go into a studio, which at that time was literally two microphones and a tape machine in somebody's closet.

But later, by the time I was really playing electric guitar, things had developed beyond the Beatles' *Sgt. Pepper's* and *Tommy* [by the Who]. You know, the real recording revolution had started. So by the time I got into the studio with my own bands when I was a teenager, we were already recording to eight tracks.

I grew up being a technical person; the kid that was always building model planes and taking the family record player apart and putting it back together. I couldn't help but want to be on the other side of the glass [in the control room] while things were going on. I took a really active role in recording sessions. You know, we'd run through a take and then I'd run on the other side of the glass and I would watch the engineer cue it up. I was fascinated by exactly what he was doing and why.

> *...I'd run on the other side of the glass and I would watch the engineer cue it up. I was fascinated by exactly what he was doing and why.*

I would ask, "How are you getting that sound on the snare drum?" I learned most of it firsthand. And then I did studio work [as a session musician] for a long time, to supplement my music income. I played on commercials—a lot of beer commercials.

When I got to be eighteen, I was playing at night and doing session work in the daytime. And that's when I decided to open the store. I was doing a lot of repair work and buying guitars at pawnshops and fixing them up and reselling them for a profit. I needed somewhere to do it. So I opened a small office above a shoe store, which over the years grew into this 10,000-square-foot business.

And you met Joan somewhere along the way—was she in the band?

Right. About this time, Joan started playing in the band. She was a keyboard player and she also played mandolin. She was playing mandolin a little bit with the folk group, and then she was playing keyboards in our fusion band. She was doing some session work, too, at the same time.

I asked her to do some bookkeeping for the store, and she was studying electronic music at Northwestern University. That was the year they opened an electronic-music lab, so although I wasn't enrolled there—I went to college there. [Laughs.] I used to sit in on her classes, and I worked in their electronic-music studio there, kind of on the "QT," at night. You know, to learn all about synthesis, and multitrack recording firsthand.

So you and Joan really started early.

Yeah, we started early, and I've got to say, for a lot of people, to be successful in the music industry, you have to get into it early. I think it's something you have to be into firmly by the time you're a teenager. It's really not something that you get out of college and say: "You know, I think I'd like to be in the music industry." It's got to be in your blood. I think that's a trait of anybody who is successful in anything.

If you look at kids who are good at sports, you find out that they started playing when they were five years old. They've always been into hockey or riding horses or whatever it is.

Can you describe your first paying gig?

My first paying job in the music business was actually a duo; it was me and my dad playing a Cub Scout meeting. I think we probably made somewhere in the two-figure range. [Laughs.] Maybe $10.

Have you had any formal training or education that's proven helpful during the years you've been toiling away?

Well, I took a DeVry electronics course in high school. I was a little bit of an outcast because I was a vegetarian and had really long hair, which at the time wasn't allowed.

So I took a lot of shop classes and tried to avoid the mainstream. But I did take this DeVry course, which was real early in the morning. That was a really good class for me. I learned all about tubes and transistors.

Basics. Stuff that sticks with you all along.

Yeah, and I took mechanical drawing, which was a great course because later on when I was working in the studio environment, it was all about block diagrams. Signal flow and learning to read schematics. Understanding patch bays and wiring. Mechanical drawing and the electronics course helped me put it together in my mind.

I would say, any kind of science and math courses you can take... do it.

The other thing is, studying electronic music in the early 1970s, at that time it was all done with patch cords. It was all monophonic. And that was an incredible learning experience because that really prepared me for everything that came along later on in the studio world. Understanding equalizers and filters...

This is all pre-DSP [digital signal processing], so everything was right in front of you. Now, when you look at a synth, it's all buried menus. And you really don't know what's going on inside there.

Until you dig down and do some analysis.

Which most people don't do anymore, because it just takes too much time.

They get a few cool sounds and they stick with them.

But I actually had to build these sounds from scratch, so I had a very intimate understanding of the signal flow, and how the filters worked, and how you modify a sound with an envelope generator and voltage control.

Let's talk a little bit about what happens in a typical day at Gand Music & Sound.

One of the things that we did when we started the store is we chose our hours around musicians' hours. So we open at noon. And we're open until 8 P.M.—seven days a week.

There's no point in this being a 9-to-5 kind of situation because musicians don't work from 9 to 5. So we really tailored ourselves to ourselves. I mean we were musicians, we were players, and all of our original customers—a lot of whom are still shopping here—were working musicians.

So, whatever business you're in, you should tailor it to your customer.

But a typical day here is we get in about 11:30, pick up our voicemail, and get the store in shape. We clean up whatever is left over from the night before, vacuum. We check all the displays and make sure everything is still programmed from yesterday. At noon, the pandemonium starts. We open the door and it just flows in.

We've got twenty phone lines and they all light up. People come pouring in the front door. We bat balls all day long.

You know, it's exciting. There's never a dull moment here. We've got a constant stream of new gear coming in all the time, because we basically built our reputation on being the high-tech guys.

Every day we're getting some kind of new product in here. Most of which doesn't work. [Laughs.]

So your staff has to figure out how to make some of the gear work.

Yeah, they figure out how to make it work and where the bugs are. And what the workarounds are. We then advise our customers accordingly.

You probably sometimes advise the manufacturers, too, I would guess.

A lot of times, yeah. As many times as that happens, and as used to it as you try to get, it's still frustrating. You know, gear is frustrating. But at the same time, if you can master it, the results are incredible.

As far as day-to-day job responsibilities, are you involved in just about every aspect of the business?

Yes, I'm constantly searching for new products. I talk to manufacturers about things that I would like to see happen. Things that need to happen with products that they already have on the market.

I also handle a lot of the publicity, perfecting the image that Gand has. I make sure our name is out there. I write releases for the magazines and our Web site. I enjoy writing. It's like another aspect of performing. If you are a musician, you can communicate in so many ways. You can write lyrics, you can play music, you can do things journalistically, you can do album cover layout, you can do album notes, and you can write product reviews.

...there's nothing better for me than somebody coming in to the store and saying, "You know, I just built this rack and I'm having all these problems." I'm rarin' to go at it, so I'll say, "Let's see what it will take to get it working right."

What's your favorite aspect of your job?

Simple: the gear.

I'm a gearhead. I just love gear, equipment, and technology. Gear is cool.

I'm still a very hands-on guy. I mean there's nothing better for me than somebody coming in to the store and saying, "You know, I just built this rack and I'm having all these problems." I'm rarin' to go at it, so I'll say, "Let's see what it will take to get it working right." Get rid of ground loops. Figure out why only one channel works. Rip the top off of a piece of gear and see what's going on inside of it.

So if a musician walks in and he says, "I can't figure this thing out," you're not up in an ivory tower somewhere, looking at spreadsheets all day?

No, definitely not.

You're actually down on the floor where the action is?

Well, I do spend part of my time analyzing our business and our performance, so I do a good deal of looking at spreadsheets, but if I get a whiff of what is happening on the floor and I can get involved, I will.

If I have information I can share, I will. Because there's a lot of people in this industry that have shared their knowledge with me. There is so much of it that it's a lot easier now. So much of it is available in magazines and online. But when I started, there was none of that.

There were no vintage-guitar books, recording handbooks, or schools—none of that stuff. I had to talk to the guys in person and learned a lot that way. One of the most important things you can do if you have knowledge is share it with others.

Let's talk about somebody who starts off at your store. It's his or her first day. Who are they? What kind of a background do they have? Are they a musician?

Well, a lot of the kids that we have that start here are Columbia grads, from Columbia College [in Chicago], which is the big broadcasting and recording college. Many of them intern here. We're part of Columbia's intern program. And then after they've interned here for a while and they learn the ropes and learn our computer system and everything, I just tell them point blank: when you graduate come and see me. And many do.

I'd say probably a quarter, maybe as much as 33 percent of the people we have here are Columbia grads.

If you want to get into the business, aligning yourself with a good school that has an intern program with a local studio or local store or whatever is a great way to get in. Test it out and see which part of it you like.

I think the music industry offers good opportunities for women.

Some of the guys work for our sound company, and they go on the road. Some of the guys are sales people here. Some of the guys work for our install division. There are all different outlets. And also, we have a lot of women working here in management positions, not secretarial positions. It's a good place for women to get a job, too. I think the music industry offers good opportunities for women.

Generally we start people here at the front counter, just so they can learn people's faces and learn how to meet and greet, and get familiar with our regular customers.

And then depending on where their talents may lie, that's kind of the incubation period. Then we like to get them into a department. We're departmentalized here, like a department store. We have a guitar department, we have a keyboard and synth department, we have a software department, we have a recording department, and we have a PA department. Each one is specialized, so that the people in that department are extremely knowledgeable, instead of one guy who knows a little bit about a bunch of things in a store.

And having done all of those jobs myself, I know how hard it is to do them all well. It's better for the customer if they can speak with a specialist. That's how we do it.

Whatever inclination you show being at the front counter, that is generally where we'll put you. What is interesting is our store manager came in as a keyboard salesman. At the time, we didn't need a keyboard salesman. We needed a recording salesman. And we told him that. He says okay, so I'll be a recording salesman. He was able to adapt. So many times a guy will come in with one thing in mind, but there will be a job opening somewhere else. You have to remain flexible.

Could you name a few key attributes or skills for an entry-level person?

The number one thing we're looking for is a good personality. When we say a good personality, we like someone who is friendly and outgoing, because you can't teach somebody that. We can teach you the technical side of the equipment, but we can't teach you how to be friendly.

> *The number one thing we're looking for is a good personality. When we say a good personality, we like someone who is friendly and outgoing, because you can't teach somebody that.*

Then the next thing is, you need to have some kind of knowledge of the audio world. That may be as limited as having a huge record collection, or it may be as extensive as being a software programmer. It may be having worked in a studio, or being on the concert committee in college. If you don't have a clue about music and you just like music, that's not enough.

Now, interestingly enough, our keyboard salesman right now is a classically trained clarinetist, and we don't sell clarinets or band instruments. Everything that is sold here is electric, with the exception of acoustic guitars. He's an incredible musician, a smart guy, and he likes people. It doesn't matter that the keyboard isn't his favorite instrument.

In fact, for about ten years, we've had a woman who was our lead guitar salesperson, and she doesn't play a lick of guitar. But she knows everything there is to know about a guitar and knows how to make the customer comfortable when she's showing them. If you want to talk shop, she's your person. If you want to jam, then hey, you're on your own.

The other thing about the music business that I find helpful is that appearance is basically meaningless. If you are concerned with your appearance, or if you have the kind of appearance that makes it difficult to get a job in the mall...

Come and see us. [Laughs.] We've got people here with green hair, pierced everything, and lots of tattoos. And they're waiting on customers who may be rappers with baggy clothes, or a woman in diamonds and an evening gown. Individuality is a natural part of the music world.

How about the salary range for an entry-level position?

We start people out in the $400-a-week range, about $10 an hour. Plus, health insurance kicks in after six months' employment—once we know you are here for a while, we put you on. We also offer bonuses and incentives based on performance. So sales people here that have a few years of experience, are good on the phone, keep in touch with their customers, and do a lot of follow-up work can make some serious money.

Is your internship program paid or unpaid?

It's unpaid. Most schools won't let you pay their students, but they do receive college credit.

How long does it normally last?

It usually goes for a quarter. Sometimes it will go for two quarters, depending on what they have got going and what the school has going. Usually what I find is students will come and work here for a quarter or two. They'll work at a studio for a quarter or two and then they are working somewhere else music- or broadcast-related. Maybe they will work at an entertainment agency, radio station, record store, or something like that.

Do you review them at the conclusion of their internship with Gand?

Yes, we do give them evaluations, and I think it's important that they get credit for it. Because what's the point? I mean the experience is wonderful, but...

They should get the college credit, too.

The other thing that comes from that for us, an internship gives us a peek into what these people are all about. If and when they come back and apply for a job, we've already got a pretty good idea what they are good at and if they'll be able to contribute.

Are there any tips you can share for somebody wanting to get into the business?

Well, you need experience. Jimi [Hendrix] said it best, "Are you experienced?" And when people come in to work in any of the divisions of our company, that's one of the first things I want to know, once they pass the rest of the tests. I want to know if they are friendly and if they have a car. You have got to have a car to be able to get to work. And you've got to be punctual. People that show up late or drag their feet, forget it.

> *One of my sayings is, it's impossible to be on time—you are either early or you are late. If you could get to the rest of your life about ten or fifteen minutes early, good things will happen to you.*

You know, something that I learned being in concert audio for all that time is, you have to be on time. It is probably something that doesn't get stressed enough. One of my sayings is, it's impossible to be on time—you are either early or you are late. If you could get to the rest of your life about ten or fifteen minutes early, good things will happen to you.

There's a lot of other basic stuff. One is to tell the truth. If you need some time off work to go play a gig, don't call in sick. Just say, "I have this audition," or "These guys are coming to see my band," or whatever it is. Be upfront about it, because it is more important to be honest than anything else. Trust is such a huge thing. And once you break that, there's no way to repair it. Once you lose somebody's trust, you can't get it back.

Another thing that's important in the music industry, on any side of it, is you have to be able to shift gears quickly. This is something that they can't teach in school. You have to be able to just sit there and wait with absolutely nothing happening. And then "Boom!" The bell rings, the band shows up, and you've got to go full speed. Zero to one-hundred in three seconds.

Are there any resources that you would recommend?

Well, if you can't get experience firsthand, get it by reading about it. There are so many great resources now with all of the magazines. I mean they are all good. Even if you only read one or two of them regularly.

But the best thing to do is to go to gigs. Go to the studio and hang around. Go down to the local club and hang around. Befriend somebody at one of the local concert halls, like one of the stagehands or somebody that can get you in. So you can come in the afternoon and watch the band set up.

When I was a kid, my dad said to me Saturday, "The circus is in town. We can do one of two things. We can go see the circus show tonight. Or we can go over there right now and watch them set up. Which would you like to do?"

I said, "Let's go watch them set up." I'd much rather watch them set up, build the tent, put the stand together, meet the animals, and see the clowns. All of that stuff.

To actually watch these guys put it together just fascinated me. So I think, whatever aspect of the business you want to be in, go hang out and watch somebody else do it.

If somebody wants to earn a decent living, what's your take? Is retail a good choice?

Retail is a great choice. It's a great place to be because...year after year after year, there are more retail music sales. The growth is very consistent. There are more people into music, and they are buying more stuff. There is more stuff on the market that they want. When I started out in 1971, I was just selling vintage guitars. They stopped making old equipment a long time ago, and I'm still in business. [Laughs.] How about that?

> *...year after year after year, there are more retail music sales. The growth is very consistent.*

So we branched out and started selling new equipment. And then we started selling PA equipment. And then they invented the synthesizer. And then everybody wanted to record themselves. Then there was the drum machine. And then there was the sampler. And then we started selling computers. We were the first Apple Macintosh music dealer back in the 1980s. There's always new stuff.

Now there are MP3s, iPods, and Podcasting. Everybody is burning their own CDs. It's fantastic. And it is not going to stop. The fact is, everybody wants to be entertained. They always did. I mean, they used to feed people to the lions and call it entertainment.

So we're still going to see the same thing. They call it the World Wrestling Federation now. People love to experience "the big gig."

For me, I still have a client that I go out and do concert sound gigs for six times a year. It's a complete briefcase gig. No schlepping gear. It keeps me current, but at the same time, it's the same thrill that I had going to the circus with my dad. I mean, you go into a huge ice arena with nothing in it. Eight hours later, you're throwing a big party for 20,000 people.

The audience comes in and the show starts, and they get that look on their face—you know, they're awestruck.

And then eight hours later, you are gone, like a gypsy. You disappear into the night. It was just a magical dream.

> *Do the absolute best job you can at what you're doing now, because it shows.*

Are there any parting words of wisdom if you want to have a fulfilling career?

I think the most important thing is whatever you do, in the music industry—any industry, whatever job you're in: always do the best job you can, whether you are making doughnuts at Krispy Kreme or setting up mic stands at the local studio.

Do the absolute best job you can at what you're doing now, because it shows. And you should derive satisfaction with that, even if the job is menial. And that trains you for "the big gig." Whatever it turns out to be.

And it takes discipline and practice to make it in the music business. Remember, you need to be pushed in order to grow. And the only way to grow is to continuously challenge yourself.

Gregg Hildebrandt

Northern California Sales Representative for TASCAM Division of TEAC of America

If you want to learn about the latest developments in recording technology, there's no better source than Gregg Hildebrandt. In his more than twenty-five years in the industry, he's been involved in a number of revolutions, such as the move from tube to solid-state electronics, from analog to digital, and many others. During his sixteen-year tenure at TASCAM, a name synonymous with the evolution of recording in America, he has been a product manager, clinician, division manager, and regional sales rep.

Although he modestly admits to little or no musical ability, his interpersonal skills and knowledge of recording technology have made him a respected industry resource. At the time of this interview, Gregg had recently left TASCAM's U.S. headquarters, where he had been division manager, to get back to his first love: working directly one-on-one with dealers and customers, listening to their needs, and helping them develop solutions with TASCAM technology.

Initially, Gregg, what drew you to music?

Actually, it was kind of by accident. I was going to college at Fresno State at the time, and working on a major in electronic engineering and a minor in computer science.

I got a job working in a music store in Fresno fixing guitar amplifiers, because at that time solid-state amplifiers had just hit the scene. So a lot of companies were coming out with solid-state guitar amplifiers. That's how I ended up in the music business.

You knew which type of transistor did what, in other words?

Yeah, because it was a unique time, right at the end of the tube-technology era and the beginning of solid state. Kustom had just come out with a line of guitar amplifiers and so the music store that I worked for in Fresno was the Kustom dealer. And of course, they had a lifetime guarantee. So since solid state was not as stable as it is now, you could say it kept me pretty busy. [Laughs.]

You mentioned you were studying electronics and computers at Fresno State. Did that help your career?

To be perfectly blunt, neither the electronics background nor the computer-science background has really helped that much, long

> *The formal training that's been the most helpful to me, believe it or not, is various sales training and sales seminars.*

term. Those technologies were developing so rapidly. Frankly, they evolved way past what I had learned within a matter of two or three years.

The formal training that's been the most helpful to me, believe it or not, is various sales training and sales seminars. I have always been fascinated with just the theory of selling because it requires convincing people to your way of thinking.

Did you have any early mentors?

Absolutely. My first job was at a music store called Sound Stage in Fresno. That store still exists. The Spitzer family owns it now, but at the time Bob and Camille Wilson owned it. Bob Wilson was really my biggest early mentor. Because again, I had no music background whatsoever—just a technical background.

Bob came to me one day and said, "You know, you are pretty good talking with customers. Why don't you become a salesman and sell things for me?" And I said, "Gee Bob, I could never be a salesman." Because at that time, my impression of what a salesman was—what most people's impression is—a used-car type of salesman. You know, with white shoes and a white belt. [Laughs.]

And Bob said, "No, all you really need to do is just explain the products to people. And if it's the right product, they will buy it."

And I answered, "But I'm not a musician. I don't know anything about this type of equipment."

Then he asked me, "Well, I tell you what, what are you really interested in?" I told him that I liked hi-fi and stereo equipment. So he said, "Well, that's great. Why don't we open up a little stereo section here, and why don't you pick a few lines and get started selling hi-fi equipment? Okay?"

So we did that, and of course it was about six months later that I kind of evolved into learning more and more about musical instruments and started selling musical instruments.

He saw something in me and really got me started in the business and was very much of a guiding hand the first several years. He actually made me a store manager and then a branch manager as well.

For people to excel, they have to work on something that they are enthusiastic about. Bob knew that and put it to good use to get me into selling. He likely knew that long term, he wasn't going to be a hi-fi dealer.

Often the toughest part of selling, especially for people who are new to sales, is demolishing their mental image of the pushy used-car salesman. The myth is that all sales people have to be high-pressure types. To this day, I find that really, it is just explaining the concept clearly and concisely, and then listening to what the customer has to say.

Bob Wilson actually taught me to be a pretty decent guitar salesman, even though I couldn't even tune a guitar at the time. Other stores would hire hot guitar players to sell guitars, and of course when somebody comes in, and the salesman pulls a guitar down and starts wailing on it—there's a real intimidation...

The customer promptly walks out the door.

Yes. And with me, I didn't have that option. I would put the guitar in their hands [laughs]...and beg them, "Do something with it... please."

You mentioned earlier, you represent TASCAM products throughout northern California. So that means you are calling on...

Music stores...everything from small music stores to pro-audio accounts, to film facilities like Skywalker, Saul Zaentz, and Zoetrope film centers. Because TASCAM has such a broad line of recording products, I also call on sound contractors and a few broadcast accounts as well.

Before that, I was division manager of TASCAM for eight years, and I lived in Los Angeles. Frankly, that's life in the fast lane. After a certain amount of time, it became pretty obvious that I was ready for a change; I needed to kind of slow down a little bit.

I was fortunate because my boss knew that I had always wanted to move back home to northern California, where I was born and raised. He suggested, "Why don't you open up a sales office for us up there?" So I did. I'm back out with customers, and I love it.

I work with a wide variety of different users, with different applications and different levels of experiences and expertise—everything from a guitar player who is trying to buy his first mini-studio, up through Skywalker Sound, which is trying to figure out how to cram as much audio information over a high-speed network as possible while they build the next blockbuster movie soundtrack.

What's the ratio of time you spend out in the field versus your home office?

Well, I typically try and spend one day a week in my home office, and that's generally on Monday. And then I spend the rest of the week out in the field, because that's the part of the job that I enjoy the most—getting a chance to work with people, and doing sales training and product training. I also like talking to some of the higher-end users that are trying to figure out how to push that envelope a little bit.

So you're helping people get the most out of the latest products and technologies, and training retailers to understand and educate their end users about how TASCAM products work.

Yes, but the part of the job that is still the most fun, believe it or not, is when you are talking to somebody who has never done any recording before. I like to go through the basics of how multitrack works and what that can do to expand their fun. You will see their eyes light up when they realize the possibilities, and that newfound sense of discovery. It's really something.

. . . the part of the job that is still the most fun, believe it or not, is when you are talking to somebody who has never done any recording before. . . . You will see their eyes light up when they realize the possibilities, and that newfound sense of discovery.

Could you describe an entry-level position at TASCAM?

TASCAM is a manufacturer and a distributor of recording products in the U.S. What most people would probably think of as entry-level would probably be at our headquarters in Los Angeles for order entry and things like that. But what I would consider more of an entry-level position from a sales standpoint would be a sales rep position. Essentially, that would be going out and calling on end users and dealers on a regular basis.

Could you identify some of the key skills for someone getting started in the sales end of the business?

Absolutely. I think number 1, a salesperson needs to be a "people" person, somebody who enjoys talking and listening to people. Because far and away the easiest way to sell something is to get the customer talking, and then listen. Which is just so much easier if you have a genuine interest in people.

Number 2, a person has got to be very self-motivated. It isn't a 9-to-5 job when you are out in the field doing sales. There isn't a supervisor looking over your shoulder every step of the way. So you must be self-motivated and understand that your time is your most valuable asset.

. . . understand that your time is your most valuable asset.

And then 3, I think it helps to be pretty well organized. When you are a sales rep, you run an independent branch office. You are doing everything from paperwork to dealer mailings, and putting together material for trade shows, clinics, and presentations.

Organizational skills ensure that every effort you put out pays off in the greatest number of ways. That's critically important.

What would be the salary range for a rookie sales rep?

It again depends entirely on the territories, but probably in the $36,000- to $48,000-a-year range, including both base salary and commission.

Is there any type of internship program at TASCAM's home office in Los Angeles?

We have just started hiring interns within the TASCAM division. The corporate office has done some internship programs, more from a business-administration standpoint.

One of the things we recently discovered is that a great deal of the schools require an internship in order to earn a degree. So one of the things that we have started doing within the last year is to bring on some interns, as an experiment. And as a matter of fact, I am going to be getting one soon here in northern California.

How has the experiment gone so far?

We have had one in Phoenix, working with our regional sales manager now for about six months. And the experience has been very, very good because it allows people to get out, work with some of the dealers, and find out if they really do want to do this type of work as a career. In fact, the person that was working with our regional in Phoenix was just hired by one of our dealers upon graduation.

Is the internship a paid or unpaid position?

It's unpaid, because the schools require it to be an unpaid position. However, we do cover an intern's expenses for gas, phones, copies, and what have you.

How long does the internship run?

They are typically positions that are designed to be six months to a year in duration. Just enough time to expose them to the realities of a sales position, while also getting exposure to some potential employers.

Do you have any tips for someone starting out to get their foot in the door?

The biggest tip that I would offer would be to take your time and pay your dues. Upon graduation, an awful lot of people expect to start off with a high-paying, high-visibility job. Very few people actually do. So I think to be successful with a company, you need to work your way up. You need to have a very broad background. I would suggest someone get a position in a fairly small music-retail environment, where you have the opportunity to wear a lot of different hats.

Upon graduation, an awful lot of people expect to start off with a high-paying, high-visibility job. Very few people actually do. So I think to be successful with a company, you need to work your way up.

They should learn about many different products, because in that environment, you need to. That doesn't mean that getting a sales position in a bigger retail establishment isn't good. But you don't quite have the opportunity to experience some of the things like going to the bank in the morning or dealing with the UPS driver. Those types of things seem real basic, but until you have an opportunity to make some mistakes, you don't realize how important the little details are.

You should get an entry-level position where you're going to get the broadest exposure to the realities of what you've got to do. In our industry in particular, very seldom do you end up in a position where you have a large staff to do all the different functions. Even when I was division manager of TASCAM, everyone in management wore a whole bunch of different hats.

Are there any magazines, books, or trade associations that you would recommend as resources?

Trade magazines such as *Mix*, *EQ*, and *Pro Sound News* are very good. There's an awful lot of information on the Internet. Just start searching for things that interest you. You will be amazed at how much information you can find. But subscribing to two or three of the industry magazines makes the most sense, because that will really give you a good feel for what's going on.

The other thing that I would recommend for anyone going out on an interview would be to take the time to learn a little bit about the company you're interviewing at. You'd be amazed at how many people show up for a job interview, and don't have any idea whatsoever of what the company that they're trying to get a job with actually does!

It's impressive when somebody does come in for an interview and obviously has taken the time to read a couple of catalogs or brochures. It really sets that person apart from the great unwashed that are just trying to get a job.

What's your long-term view as far as careers in the music, recording, or entertainment business?

I think they are excellent. They are evolving quite a bit, but I think they're particularly good from a sales and a product standpoint.

> *...in the best or worst of times, entertainment and music have always tended to thrive, because it's something that everybody enjoys in one form or another...*

Let's face it, in the best or worst of times, entertainment and music have always tended to thrive, because it's something that everybody enjoys in one form or another, whether it's performing or listening to...or participating in, in some form or another.

For instance, if someone is buying an instrument, there needs to be a nice fit between the type of instrument, its cost, and the customer's level of playing. Is the customer a beginner or a player with lots of experience? And so that's where the expertise of a salesperson really pays off.

Just like in the clothing business. I can't imagine buying a suit over the Internet. It's the same thing with musical instruments and recording equipment. People still want to have them in their hands and feel them and touch them and listen to them. That keeps our long-term prospects very, very good for the industry.

Do you have any tips on market segments you think that will be particularly hot in the future?

Yes, absolutely. I think that it's going to be the nontraditional users. In the past, when I got started in this business, pretty much whether you were selling musical instruments or recording equipment, we had a very limited potential audience. I mean, the only reason somebody would want to record multitrack music would be if he or she was a professional musician.

Now, with a lot of the computer-based software packages and sequencers, and a whole range of affordable instruments and recording tools, we've broadened the potential user base significantly. Plus the pricing of technology keeps coming down, so that people can do everything from taking home movies and putting them into the computer, then adding soundtracks to them, and things like that.

I think it's going to be these types of nontraditional users, who represent a huge market. This group will be absolutely booming in the future.

Do you have any parting words of wisdom?

You will be as successful as the relationships you build over the years.

The music business is totally a people-oriented business. It's not something that can be easily faked. You will be as successful as the relationships you build over the years. Care about what you do, how you do it, and the people you work with. The rest will come to you.

Appendices

Appendix A. Author's Career Path

Keith Hatschek

Author

I've taken the liberty of providing a capsule of my own music-industry career path because I believe it clearly illustrates that few, if any, careers in our field follow a predictable, straight-line path. I hope you find my story useful as a reminder to always listen for the sounds of doors opening with new opportunities for you.

In 1965, as a teenager, I came to California from North Carolina. I grabbed onto the first thing that interested me in my new environment: music.

My family arrived in the Golden State just before school adjourned for the summer. It was just kismet that people up the street had a band. The boy who had been playing bass moved away and there was no one to fill in. After the guys checked me out for a few days they said, "Well, if he has a skateboard, he can't be too weird." They came to my house and said, "Look, anyone can play the bass, it's only got four strings. Why don't you come on over here, and we'll try to show you how to play it."

As a teenager, I had scored—social interaction! It helped that I grew up listening to music. My parents listened to the radio and records and my dad played the piano when he was young.

So I started to play the bass, and of course the cool thing was that when we practiced, girls stood outside of the garage. So right away, I knew there was definitely an opportunity here for something beyond just blisters on my teenage fingers.

I took to playing music. I loved it. The two things I liked the most were the interaction with other musicians and the mathematical nature of music. If you've ever arranged or composed music, you know there's a very close relationship between mathematics and music, in terms of how the elements fit together—a symmetry.

Although I'm no longer involved in playing or writing music, my kids recently made me get my guitar out, re-string it, and buy an amp. I strum on it a little bit these days while they play the piano.

I loved music. I loved sound. I continued playing in bands. By the time I was in eleventh grade, we were getting paid $300 a night to play at dances. It was big money in the 1960s. Wow, $300. My share seemed like gas money for the rest of my life!

So from there, I went to college at the University of California, Riverside, and for one year I was in the music program and I was doing great. The dean of the music department, "Doctor Don," encouraged every student with an interest in music to pursue his or her musical dreams. Doctor Don used in play in Paul Whiteman's orchestra during the heyday of the big bands.

His belief was, as long as people are listening to music and their toes are tapping, then they're learning. So I was playing in a jazz ensemble, learning how to write four-part harmony, and studying theory. However, I wanted to be close to my friends, so I transferred to the University of California campus at Berkeley, with enough credits to be a junior. I immediately flunked out of every aptitude test you take to make sure that you are really a junior in the music program.

When I went to do my interview, my instrument was the jazz guitar, leading the teacher to ask, where was my "real" guitar? I said, "Well, this is a real guitar, it has six strings—there's my music and here is my audition tape."

He replied, "I'm sorry, you'll have to go down to the basement at the student union where the pep band plays, and that's not for credit. You will have to start over as a freshman with a recognized instrument."

So ended my collegiate music-performance education. I switched gears and earned a degree in history, just to basically escape college with a degree. And I kept playing in rock bands. I had a band in the Bay Area in the 1970s. We eventually secured a development deal with Capitol Records. Unfortunately, they found out after we recorded three songs that no one wanted to play us on the radio. That introduced me painfully to the harsh reality of the record business. In the 1970s, if your song wasn't on the radio, you (and your record label) didn't make any money.

I was playing a jingle one night in San Mateo, California, at a now defunct studio. The engineer fell asleep at the mixing board during a take. We were done playing and we said, "Play it back." Musicians are in one room, the studio, and the engineer is in another room, the control room. We couldn't see the engineer. We were standing up, and we finally went in the control room and the engineer was dead asleep on the mixing board.

That experience changed my perspective. I went home and thought, "If that guy can have a job running a recording studio and he falls asleep on the job, I can do better." Famous last words!

After this experience I visited two legendary studios, Wally Heider's and the Automatt, in San Francisco. I said I want to work in the studio and the managers all said, "Don't do it. Don't do it. Do anything but that."

Undeterred, I thought, "I'll show you guys. I'll build my own recording studio." I was in my twenties—and I knew I could conquer the world. So I built a studio in 1979 in San Carlos, California. Bayshore Studios was born as a rehearsal room for bands, and acquired a TASCAM 3340 4-track, then evolved to an 8-track recorder. I picked up two partners along the way. We bought some more gear, and some more gear, and yes, a bit more gear.

After a few years I got married, and my wife and I started a family. One day I came to the realization that "Wow, I am working twenty hours a day, seven days a week, and I have a family. Hmm, what am I going to do?"

I decided to close my business and go to work for another studio. A tough decision to make, but in hindsight, it was absolutely the best thing to do. I had done my own apprenticeship to learn the basics of recording and business. Then I had a successful twelve-year run at a studio called the Music Annex, which is still in operation in the Bay Area today. I started as a tape copyroom person and engineer for my previous clients.

After a year and a half at Music Annex, I was answering the phones while the regular phone person was out to lunch. While I subbed on the phone, there were more sessions booked. The owner of the studio thought, "Hmm, maybe there's an opportunity here. Every time Hatschek is on the phone, our bookings increase. So if I put him on the phone all day, think how much time we could book!"

So he made me an offer. "I'm paying you this much as an engineer, and you're not working all the time. (Beginning engineers seldom are in session all day.) I'll pay you a bit more to work in studio management selling studio time and to come up with ideas so that we can hustle some more business." And I said, "Okay, I'll try it."

I still did a few sessions with bands I really liked and for projects I was well suited for. I got more involved in planning and studio management. Business increased. Music Annex opened two new divisions to develop a market for audio postproduction in 1984 and for cassette and CD duplication in 1986. Business increased some more. The company was profitable, and my earnings rode the crest of the company's growth. I got promoted. I got promoted again. By now, not engineering sessions didn't faze me because I was stimulated and challenged by helping to grow a successful multimillion-dollar studio business.

One of the prime products was the duplication of audiocassettes with music and spoken-word programming. It was a great business. The company did very well through the 1980s and early 1990s, and then pretty soon people started saying, "Yeah, I think I'll just put my record out on a CD. I don't need a cassette."

I went to the owner and suggested that we should consider the sale of that division of the company. That was the division I spent most of my time managing. The owners agreed and after about a year, we located a buyer. And once the sale was formalized, it hit me, "Wow, the company is selling this division! It's really happening. All those people are going to report to another person, not to me anymore."

It became clear then, in 1995, that I needed to find something else to do. That's when I came up with the idea of starting my own consulting practice. And pretty quickly, it grew into a full-service, music-technology marketing and public relations agency. We specialized in working for companies in broadcasting, recording technology, and the media industries. We helped our clients tell their story through press relations, advertisements, direct-mail campaigns, and all types of marketing programs to increase their profile and sales.

Although I had begun teaching part-time at San Francisco State University in their successful Music and Recording Industry program in 1994, I hadn't contemplated teaching full-time until I began speaking at various colleges and universities in support of this book's first edition in 2001. Shortly thereafter, I was visiting with a friend and colleague who had graduated from the University of the Pacific's Music Management program, and he mentioned that the program's founder had retired and the search was underway for a new Program Director. The idea took root and the next day, I called him for a referral to Pacific. After a series of interviews, I accepted the position and wound down my agency business so that by 2002, I spent the majority of my time teaching some of tomorrow's music-industry leaders what I have learned in 35 years in the music business.

I've come a long way since sitting in that garage in 1965 learning how to play the bass line to "Gloria." I have developed a broad range of skills, first as a musician, then as a recording engineer, then as a studio manager. Making the jump to the business side of the recording-studio game was a break that soon showed me how much I could grow in that area. Then I pursued a tighter focus on marketing, promotion, and advertising for a range of clients around the world, before shifting to higher education. Every move has built on the skills developed in the previous jobs.

I believe my own career is typical of many careers in the entertainment industry. Most people come to it with a set of skills and perceptions of what they see themselves doing, but the fact is that at the end of many successful careers, people have jumped tracks a number of times to take advantage of new opportunities. You find a lot of the people in the A&R departments of labels that were once members of bands. You find a leading entertainment attorney or personal manager who once worked in a music store. You find label presidents that started out as gofers at a booking agency. You'll meet personal managers that started as theater ushers, and many company presidents or music-business teachers who on occasion still strum their guitar or blow their horn to stay connected to their core passion: music.

Appendix B. Selected Resources

CAREER AND INDUSTRY RESEARCH TOOLS

Books and Directories

A library that has a reference or business reference department is a perfect place to initiate your career research. The reference books listed below may be found at most public and school libraries. Reference librarians are also a wonderful resource to assist you in locating information about companies that you may be researching. If you ask for assistance in researching a specific company or career path, you will be surprised at the resources that the librarian will be able to help you locate and use.

Hoover's Handbook of American Business. 16th Ed. Austin, TX. 2005.
A two-volume directory of U.S. corporations. Provides basic data on company size, locations, and types of business activities. (Quick company snapshots may be found at Hoover's Online for many publicly held companies; however, the printed directories have much more information available than the free portion of the Hoover's Web site.)

Hoover's Handbook of Private Companies. 11th Ed. Austin, TX. 2006.
Useful for researching privately owned companies.

Ward's Business Directories. 48th Ed. Thomson Gale Publishing, Farmington Hill, MI. 2006.
Similar to the Hoover's Directories but also provides data on the firm's market share. A special volume in the set allows for geographic-based search.

National Directory of Arts Internships. 10th Ed. Barton, William and Christensen, Warren, editors, National Network for Artist Placement, Los Angeles. 2006.
A comprehensive guide to locating internships in the performing arts fields. Updated annually.

Plunkett's Entertainment and Media Almanac. Houston, TX. 2006.
In-depth profiles of 400 of the leading companies in the music, media, and entertainment industries. Excellent and up-to-date set of articles describing the latest trends, as well as a host of industry statistics that highlight which market segments are expanding most quickly.

Directory of Corporate Affiliations. LexisNexis, New Providence, NJ. 2006.
An essential guide to who owns whom in corporate America, especially helpful in the current era of entertainment-company consolidation.

Musical America: International Directory of the Performing Arts. Commonwealth Business Media, East Windsor, NJ. 2006.
A reference work that lists information for jazz and classical artists, agents, promoters, arts organizations, and much more useful data.

Opera America: Career Guide for Singers. 6th Ed. Opera America, New York. 2003.
A comprehensive guide for vocalists considering careers in the world of opera.

The Musician's Atlas. Musician's Resource Group, Montclair, NJ. 2006.
An annual directory that has lots of do-it-yourself information, as well as many helpful lists of resources for the independent musician or band.

The Indie Bible. 6th Ed. Music Sales Corp., New York. 2004.
Similar to *The Musician's Atlas*, it also has an extensive section on radio stations that will play new music, and magazines, journals, and Web reviewers that will accept submissions of independent music.

General Internet Resources

The following Internet databases and search tools may be accessed at most public and college libraries. They are all subscription-based services, but provide an extensive array of articles that may be searched to investigate companies and careers. Search engines such as Google and Yahoo! can be helpful, but they often do not include full-text articles from many leading magazines, newspapers, and business journals. Accessing in-depth articles such as these may be done via these resources.

Factiva. Formerly the Dow Jones information service, Factiva is a comprehensive search tool that provides access to a nearly limitless range of contemporary news articles and reports from all of the major sources of information. It might be helpful to ask a reference librarian to assist you in your first few searches to learn how to best access the information it can locate.

Lexis/Nexis. Another search service that provides a rich library of contemporary news and business data. Publicly held companies will have the annual reports available here, as well as often posted on the firm's own Web site.

Academic Search Premiere and *Business Source Premiere.* These two databases are available at many public and school libraries and aggregate many useful resources for investigating specific companies, trends in the music industry, and leading personalities in the business.

Billboard. [www.billboard.biz/bb/biz/index.jsp] This is the home page for *Billboard* magazine's online business magazine, BillboardBiz.com. It's full of breaking news of the music industry and a good means to keep up with business developments in the U.S. and abroad. Billboard.com, the online edition of the weekly print magazine, has slightly different content slanted more toward artists, releases, charts, and consumers, so both sites are worth bookmarking. The free versions offer plenty of information to keep you up-to-date, although you have to navigate through quite a few pop-up ads on the Billboard.com site.

Job-Related Web Sites

RileyGuide.com. Although it is not a job search engine, this site provides a tremendous range of useful advice and tips on everything from job interviewing to salary negotiations. It has a handy A–Z listing of career fields and industries including Acting & Entertainment, which has some useful links.

Vault.com. This site has free and pay portions to its site. Within the free section, there are articles, how-to tips, excellent information on internships, and especially helpful, company snapshots for some of the larger entertainment firms. Check to see if your school or college may have a subscription to this service that you can use to access the full range of information.

Berklee College of Music (www.berklee.edu/careers/resources.html#business"). This portion of Berklee's Web site has an extensive list of books, short job descriptions, and a list of industry associations that supplements the list found in this book's appendix.

University of Hartford (www.library.hartford.edu/allen/allen_musicresources.asp). University of Hartford's Allen Library has this useful site that allows you to do subject-specific searches for resources, book titles, and Web sites. Click on the lower drop-down menu, which reveals a list of subject areas, and click on "Management." You'll see a list of helpful resources.

Job Directories and Search Engines

We'll start with some of the larger search engines and work our way down to industry-specific job-listing boards.

Yahoo! Hot Jobs. Many of my students have found this the most useful job-search site, even though it is not limited to the music industry. One of the reasons is that it allows you to narrow your search criteria in a number of ways such as: date the job listing was last updated, job location, job category, whether a job is posted by an employer directly or by a staffing firm, and by number of years experience required. For someone just starting out in the industry, this last feature can quickly eliminate mid- and senior-level jobs from any search, allowing you to focus more closely on the job opportunities for which you are most qualified to compete.

Monster.com. Similar to the previous site, it allows you to refine your searches by zip code and location (especially helpful with respect to New York City and Los Angeles, where the proximity between your job site and your home may be crucial).

CareerBuilder.com. The third of the large, general-purpose job-search engines, it has many of the same features of the two previous sites, along with an easy way to sort jobs that are defined by the listing firm as "entry level."

Craigslist.org. This site has one great advantage over many of the other sites: each version of Craig's List is localized for a specific market. In addition to a variety of job listings searchable by category, on the same site you have information on housing and other categories that may be useful to research especially if you are planning to relocate for your job. A recent search in the San Francisco region under the categories Art/Media/Design and TV/Film/Video turned up a few jobs for Lucas Arts Video Games and Meyer Sound Labs. Another way to search is to use the Jobs header, then type in a key word such as "music" or "videogame" and see what results are generated. You might also check under the "Gigs" section at the bottom of the page, as a recent look here for NYC turned up a number of Indie record label internships.

Entertainmentcareers.net. A well-organized site that offers many categories to view job and internship listings. A recent search under the "Music" category brought up 32 jobs, all of which were in the greater L.A. or NYC metro regions. It also has regional job banks for Chicago, NYC, and northern California. One of the best sources for internship listings, a recent look revealed 701 internships posted here.

Berkleemusic.com. First, a brief disclaimer: this site is not mentioned only because Berklee Press is the publisher of this book. The site is not only the gateway to the online music school, but it offers a very useful "Jobs & Gigs" portion of the site including an industry-specific job-listing service. Anyone may view job titles and locations for free on the site. There is currently a free "test drive" allowing you to use the site's search agent to sort and view the listings that best fit your career interest. Annual membership is $49, which at the time of writing, is deferred if you enroll in any online course offering. A recent glance showed nearly 1,000 music jobs in five categories. Members also may sign up for a gig- or job-posting notification service that alerts you when a job matching your personal criteria is added to the site. They are planning to have some materials up there that support the workshops in this book. Be sure to also review the Free Career Resource pages that are available on the site.

VarietyCareers.com. Part of the *Variety* magazine family, this portion of their Web site is a good resource for looking at various types of entertainment industry job descriptions. The majority of positions listed are for L.A. and NYC. It focuses more on broadcasting, marketing, and cable TV-related positions, but a number of music-related jobs were listed when I last visited the site. It has a very useful job alert feature that notifies you when a job is listed, similar to the one above.

Music-jobs.com. This site also offers UK and German versions of its site for those considering an international career or internship. The site works best if you register and become a member, which is free. You can then upload your résumé to the site, where it is viewed by employers. It also has gig and message boards to share information with other job seekers. A current look revealed more than 130 music-industry jobs and internships posted. A handy feature is that members can view a weekly summary of which firms have looked at their résumé.

Showbizjobs.com. Another very well-organized site, it allows sorts by region, job category, salary range, full-time vs. part-time or contract positions, and more. The basic search services are free; however, for $35, you can register and post your résumé and job interests. The many testimonials by registered members who landed industry jobs indicate that for those who don't or can't make the time to search daily for new job listings, this might be a good strategy. A few other nice features of this site are that you can view short company profiles, and also search by industry and how recently the job has been listed. This is especially handy as you can set the search feature to only show jobs listed in the most recent twenty-four hours or week, for example.

Mymusicjob.com. This site also has a wide range of international job postings and offers search criteria including country, region, job category, and full time vs. part time, internship, summer job, etc. Although there are many free job listings, the most recent postings—those uploaded by employers in the last three days—are only available to members. The cost is $14.99 for a two-month membership. Members can also upload their résumés, which the site claims are regularly viewed by its 600 employer-company members.

OTHER BOOKS

Avalon, Moses. *Confessions of a Record Producer*, 3rd edition. San Francisco: Backbeat Books, 2006.

Dannen, Frederic. *Hit Men*. New York Times Books, 1990.

Field, Shelly. *Career Opportunities in the Music Industry*, 5th edition. New York: Checkmark Books, 2004.

Gordon, Steve. *The Future of the Music Business: How to Succeed with the New Digital Technologies*. San Francisco: Backbeat Books, 2005.

Half, Robert. *How to Get a Better Job in This Crazy World*. New York: Signet, 1994.

Hatschek, Keith. *The Golden Moment: Recording Secrets of the Pros*. San Francisco: Backbeat Books, 2006.

Howard, George. *Getting Signed: An Insider's Guide to the Record Industry*. Boston: Berklee Press, 2005.

Kimpel, Dan. *Networking in the Music Business*. Benicia, CA: Artist Pro, 2001.

Kusek, Dave and Leonhard, Gerd. *The Future of Music: A Manifesto for the Digital Age*. Boston: Berklee Press, 2005.

Olsen, Eric, Paul Verna, and Carla Wolff. *The Encyclopedia of Record Producers*. New York: Watson-Guptill Publishers, 1999.

Passman, Don. *All You Need to Know About the Music Business*, Fifth edition. New York: Simon & Schuster, 2003.

Payne, Richard A. *How to Get a Better Job Quicker*. New York: New American Library, 1982.

Stone, Chris. *Audio Recording for Profit*. Woburn, MA: Focal Press, 2000.

INDUSTRY BIOGRAPHIES

Branson, Richard. *Losing My Virginity*. New York: Three Rivers Press, 1999.

Buskin, Richard. *Inside Tracks: History of Pop Music from the World's Greatest Record Producers*. New York: Spike, 1999.

Copeland, Ian. *Wild Thing: Memoirs of Ian Copeland*. New York: Simon and Schuster, 1995.

Dickerson, James. *Women on Top.* New York: Watson-Guptill Publishers, 1998.

Holzman, Jac and Gavan Daws. *Follow the Music.* Santa Monica: First Media Books, 2000.

Jones, Quincy. *Q: The Autobiography of Quincy Jones.* New York: Harlem Moon, 2002.

King, Tom. *The Operator: David Geffen Builds the New Hollywood.* New York: Random House, 2000.

Kooper, Al. *Backstage Passes and Backstabbing Bastards.* New York: Watson-Guptill Publishers, 1998.

Martin, Sir George and Jeremy Hornsby. *All You Need is Ears.* New York: St. Martin's Press, 1995.

Slichter, Jacob. *So You Wanna Be A Rock and Roll Star.* New York: Broadway Books, 2004.

Small, Mark and A. Taylor. *Masters of Music.* Boston: Berklee Press, 1999.

Swedien, Bruce. *Make Mine Music.* Milwaukee, WI: MIA Press/Hal Leonard, 2004.

A last note on finding books that may be out of print or not readily available.

If you are searching for a book that is out of print, try searching at www.alibris.com, www.abebooks.com, or the used listings on Amazon.com. These Web sites have useful search engines to help you locate out-of-print and hard-to-find books. At the time of writing, every one of the out-of-print works referenced in this book was available on one or more of these sites.

PERIODICALS (many have online editions)

Billboard
Mix
Pro Sound News
Electronic Musician
EQ
Keyboard
Recording
Radio & Records
Music Connection
Tape Op
Sound-on-Sound (UK)
Spin
Hollywood Reporter
Variety

Appendix C. Trade Associations

Academy of Country Music
4100 W. Alameda Ave.
Burbank, CA 91505
(818) 842-8400
www.acmcountry.com

American Choral Directors Association (ACDA)
545 Couch Drive
Oklahoma City, OK 73102
(405) 232-8161
www.acdaonline.org

American Composers Alliance
684 Broadway, Room 803
New York, NY 10012
(212) 362-8900
www.composers.com

American Federation of Musicians (AFM)
1501 Broadway, Suite 600
New York, NY 10036
(212) 869-1330
www.afm.org

American Federation of Television and Radio Artists (AFTRA)
260 Madison Avenue
New York, NY 10016
(212) 532-0800
www.aftra.org

American Music Therapy Association (AMTA)
8455 Colesville Rd., Suite 1000
Silver Spring, MD 20910
(301) 589-3300
www.musictherapy.org

American Society of Composers and Publishers (ASCAP)
1 Lincoln Plaza
New York, NY 10023
(212) 621-6000
www.ascap.com

American Society of Music Arrangers & Composers (ASMA)
P.O. Box 17840
Encino, CA 91416
(818) 994-4661
www.asmac.org

American Society of Music Copyists (ASMC)
Box 2557
Times Square Station
New York, NY 10108
(212) 586-2140

Broadcast Music, Inc. (BMI)
320 West 57th Street
New York, NY 10019
(212) 586-2000
www.bmi.com

Consumer Electronics Association (CEA)
2500 Wilson Avenue
Arlington, VA 22201
(703) 907-7600
www.ce.org

Country Music Association (CMA)
CMA Headquarters
One Music Circle South
Nashville, TN 37203
(615) 244-2840
www.countrymusic.org

Electronic Industry Alliance (EIA)
2500 Wilson Blvd.
Arlington, VA 22201
(703) 907-7500
www.eia.org

Gospel Music Association (GMA)
1205 Division Street
Nashville, TN 37203
(615) 242-0303
www.gospelmusic.org

International Music Products Association (aka NAMM)
5790 Armada Drive
Carlsbad, CA 92008
(760) 438-8001
www.namm.com

Music Educators National Conference (MENC)
1806 Robert Fulton Drive
Reston, VA 20191
(703) 860-4000
www.menc.org

Music Publishers Association
243 5th Avenue, Suite 236
New York, NY 10016
(212) 327-4044
www.mpa.org

NAMM (see above, International Music Products Association)

Nashville Songwriters Association International
1710 Roy Acuff Place
Nashville, TN 37203
(615) 256-3354
www.Nashvillesongwriters.com

National Academy of Recording Arts and Sciences (NARAS)
3402 Pico Boulevard
Santa Monica, CA 90405
(310) 392-3777
www.grammy.com

National Association for Campus Activities (NACA)
13 Harbison Way
Columbia, SC 29212-3401
(803) 732-6222
www.naca.org

National Association of Broadcast Employees and Technicians (NABET)
501 3rd Street NW, #880
Washington, DC 20001
(202) 434-1254
www.nabetcwa.org

National Association of Broadcasters (NAB)
1771 N Street NW
Washington, DC 20036
(202) 429-5300
www.nab.org

National Association of Recording Merchandisers (NARM)
9 Eves Drive, Suite 120
Marlton, NJ 08053
(856) 596-2221
www.narm.com

National Association of Schools of Music (NASM)
11250 Roger Bacon Drive,
Suite 21
Reston, VA 20190
(703) 434-0700
http://nasm.arts-accredit.org

Public Relations Society of America (PRSA)
33 Maiden Lane, 11th Fl.
New York, NY 10038
(212) 460-1400
www.prsa.org

Recording Industry Association of America (RIAA)
1330 Connecticut Ave. NW, Ste. 300
Washington, DC 20036
(202) 775-0101
www.riaa.com

SESAC, Inc.
152 West 57th St., 57th Floor
New York, NY 10019
(212) 586-3450

55 Music Square East
Nashville, TN 37203
(615) 320-0050
www.sesac.com

Society of Professional Audio Recording Studios (SPARS)
9 Music Square S., Suite 222
Nashville, TN 37203
(800) 771-7727
www.spars.com

Songwriters Guild of America
200 W. 72nd Street, Suite 35
New York, NY 10036
(917) 309-7869

209 10th Ave. South, Suite 534
Nashville, TN 37203
(615) 742-9945

6430 Sunset Boulevard, Suite 705
Hollywood, CA 90028
(323) 462-1108
www.songwritersguild.com

SoundExchange
1121 14th Street NW, Suite 700
Washington, DC 20005
(202) 640-5858
www.soundexchange.com

West Coast Songwriters
1724 Laurel St., Suite 120
San Carlos, CA 94070
(650) 654-3966
www.westcoastsongwriters.org

Index